The Tragic Science

The Tragic Science

How Economists Cause Harm (Even as They Aspire to Do Good)

GEORGE F. DEMARTINO

The University of Chicago Press
Chicago and London

The University of Chicago Press, Chicago 60637
The University of Chicago Press, Ltd., London

Published 2022
Printed in the United States of America

31 30 29 28 27 26 25 24 23 22 1 2 3 4 5

ISBN-13: 978-0-226-82123-8 (cloth)
ISBN-13: 978-0-226-82124-5 (e-book)
DOI: https://doi.org/10.7208/chicago/9780226821245.001.0001

Library of Congress Cataloging-in-Publication Data

Names: DeMartino, George, author.
Title: The tragic science : how economists cause harm (even as they aspire to do good) / George F. DeMartino.
Description: Chicago : University of Chicago Press, 2022. | Includes bibliographical references and index.
Identifiers: LCCN 2021058918 | ISBN 9780226821238 (cloth) | ISBN 9780226821245 (ebook)
Subjects: LCSH: Economics—Moral and ethical aspects.
Classification: LCC HB72 .D37 2022 | DDC 174/.4—dc23/eng/20220105
LC record available at https://lccn.loc.gov/2021058918

♾ This paper meets the requirements of ANSI/NISO Z39.48-1992 (Permanence of Paper).

Contents

Preface

In 2011 I published *The Economist's Oath*, wherein I argued that economics needs a new field of inquiry: the field of professional economic ethics. My motivation was that economists cause harm in the world even as they do good. The harm can be widespread and deep, and yet economists are not trained to understand the full range of the harms they induce, or to think carefully enough about how to act responsibly when they risk harming others. In my PhD program, which is not an outlier in this regard, we had not one conversation about how we economists induce harm and what ethical obligations follow from that fact. Only after the book was published did I realize that I had fallen into the same intellectual trap that imprisons many in the profession: the trap of thinking that "harm" is a self-evident concept, and that even if economists don't think carefully enough about their obligations regarding harm, they at least understand what harm is.

That presumption is mistaken. Harm is a complex and contested idea. Not least, harm is at once a positive and normative concept. That is, one cannot do any positive work with the concept, such as determining whether harm has occurred or measuring its extent, without the careful moral reasoning that defining harm requires. Nor can one discern which harms are and are not legitimate to impose in pursuit of social betterment without first reckoning with difficult moral questions. So the common economic strategy of presuming a bright line separating positive economic science from normative judgments can't work here, if indeed it works anywhere (I think it doesn't). The problem of the normative nature of harm, requiring controversial value judgments, has been repressed by the economics profession. Economists too often act as if harm were a commonsensical and uncontroversial concept, such that when people spoke of harm they all meant the same thing. The presumption permits them to get on with the project of investigating which policies cause harm, to whom, and in what magnitudes without wasting time debating just what harm entails.

This book represents an attempt to come to terms with the problem of harm in economics. The complexity of harm introduces difficult problems for economic theory and application, and ethical challenges for the profession. The book attempts to probe some of these issues.

This book is critical of the economics profession for the ways in which it induces and dismisses serious harms. But the book is not a full-on attack on the economics profession. It is a request to the profession to take better care with its practice. I believe that the profession should always remember that its preferred policy interventions are apt to cause harm no matter what good they achieve; that the harms are far more extensive than we've been trained to appreciate; and that the harms should not be dismissed as easily as the profession has tended to do. I will also argue that the act of harming, especially in the context of the professional-layperson relationship, is ethically fraught, and that economists are not warranted in believing that they are and should be society's harm accountants who tally up benefits and harms and then pronounce on economic policy. When a profession can harm others—deeply, badly—those others ought to be recognized as having rights and agency which include having a good bit to say about which harms to risk in pursuit of which valued ends.

A primary objective of the book is to explain to noneconomists the presumptions about harm that underlie economists' practice, especially in the area of policy assessment and advocacy. Noneconomists are often befuddled and even offended by the way in which economists assess policy—comparing benefits to this group against harms to that group. I share many of their concerns. Here I attempt to highlight and clarify some of the most problematic assumptions and procedures that lead to objectionable economic practice.

Critics of the economics profession have argued, rightly, that over the past century the profession has tended to oversimplify and even trivialize harm. It has oversimplified by means of severe reductionism, in which all harms, no matter their nature, depth, duration, or causes, are reduced to the loss of "welfare"—a concept that we will investigate throughout the book. It has trivialized harm by treating all harms as if they were entirely reparable, through compensation. Assuming compensability allows the profession to design policies that stand to induce widespread and enduring harm provided the purported benefits are of a greater magnitude than the anticipated harms. This simplistic reasoning underlies compensation tests, expected utility calculations, cost-benefit analyses, social welfare accounting, and other techniques that economists apply to weigh policy impacts. But if the profession contributes to harms that are irreparable and noncompensable—*as it certainly does*—then all these strategies fail. It will become apparent that the economist's oversimplification and trivialization of harm matters concretely, affecting the lives of all of us and damaging the lives of far too many.

I will not argue that one can't theorize harm in the simplistic way that economists tend to do. I will argue that a profession that induces harm has no business doing so. Other professions, like medicine, engineering, and law, have learned that lesson. When a profession is in position to risk harming those it serves, it takes on an obligation to wrestle with the complexity of harm, the act of harming, the reparability of harm, the means to achieve repair, the claims of those who are harmed for repair, and the rights of those who face the risk of harm to decide whether to take the risk. Despite a long century of wrestling with the "moral geometry" of harm, I think an impartial observer would conclude that the economics profession has failed to give sufficient attention to these matters.

Based on the many presentations and countless discussions I've had with economists on these issues I've come to appreciate a deep professional anxiety. Serious engagement with the full complexity of harm, it is thought, would stymie economists in their pursuit of social betterment. Unless we subscribe to a simple, tractable, good-enough account of harm, the argument goes, we will descend into pointless debate over philosophical matters that will prevent readily available concrete interventions to promote social betterment.

That argument fails. Other professions that risk harming face many of the same challenges as does economics. Some of those professions grapple with the complex nature of harm, and yet the ongoing debates over harm don't prevent practitioners from doing good work. Every day patients are treated for their conditions even though no one believes that medical ethics today is a finished enterprise, codifying the uniquely right answers to harm-related questions. In law, tort litigation turns on conceptions of harm and harming. Courts routinely ascertain legal responsibility for harm even though litigators often question and occasionally disrupt accepted conventions on harm and harming. No reasonable medical or legal ethicist or practitioner believes that all harm-related matters must be resolved once and for all before one can in good conscience practice medicine or law.

I stake out a middle ground between indicting the economics profession for all harms its practice induces and absolving it of all responsibility. The indictment would make sense only if all economic harms were avoidable.

But that's not the case. In economic practice, acting induces harm. But so can failing to act. Absolution would make sense only if there were nothing the profession could do, better than it is already doing, to reduce the incidence of harm, prepare for harm, alter the nature of the harms its practice induces, engage as equals with those who stand to be harmed, and ameliorate the harms that arise despite best efforts to prevent them. But that's not the case, either. The profession can do much better in these regards. Here I seek to demonstrate just why this is so, and to map out what doing better might entail.

The book argues for harm's complexity, rejects the predominant conception of harm that informs the profession's standard approach to reckoning with harm, and explores how professional practice might be reoriented were harm to be given the priority it deserves. It draws liberally on the insights of others, including, most importantly, economic iconoclasts and noneconomists who have wrestled with the complexities of harm and who have demonstrated the limitations to the predominant economic approach. Those looking for a new theory of harm to ground economics may be disappointed. The book instead demonstrates the value of exploiting insights from existing accounts in economics and beyond. Not all of the difficult challenges associated with theorizing harm identified in the following pages are resolved. The book does not seek theoretical closure on these issues. In fact, the pursuit of theoretical closure underlies many of the problems with the profession's handling of harm. The goal of the book might be stated as probing how to act responsibly in the face of sustained theoretical aperture about harm. Other professions do it, or at least aspire to. Economics should, too.

The failure of the economics profession to engage ethically with economic and economist-induced harm matters. Reorienting economists' behavior is urgent. I share the view with other critics that the illiberal turn in US and world politics can be traced in part to the failures of the economics profession over the past fifty years or so to grapple adequately with harm. The economics profession is culpable in the contemporary backlash against democratic governance, civic obligation, and racial and other forms of equality. It is equally culpable in inducing the social conditions that promote the widespread rejection of expertise in policy making. The profession shares responsibility for the erosion of solidarity and empathy that marks contemporary politics in too many societies. Demonstrating this point adequately would require another book, one that others are by now no doubt writing. Here I ask readers to keep this hypothesis in mind as they consider the arguments at the heart of this book—arguments that concern the ways in which economists treat the harms associated with their practice.

This book unapologetically sacrifices technical precision for the sake of accessibility to noneconomists. I ask the forbearance of professional economists as I simplify complex material. Interested readers wanting to explore formal presentations of the issues should consult the economic and philosophical literature cited in the text and endnotes. Some chapters are necessarily more abstract than others, but in all cases I've attempted to convey the central insights with the bare minimum of technical jargon.

PART I

The Tragic Science

1

The Tragedy of Economics

> The economics profession . . . is the priesthood of a powerful secular religion. . . . Beneath the surface of their formal economic theorizing, economists are engaged in an act of delivering religious messages. Correctly understood, these messages are seen to be promises of the true path to a salvation in this world—to a new heaven on earth.
>
> —ROBERT NELSON (2001, xx)

Virtuous economists aspire to do God's work—to promote social betterment. Economists ranging from Karl Marx to John Maynard Keynes to the high priests of the Chicago School placed their science in the service of human salvation. Robert Nelson is right to identify economics as a secular religion led by those hoping to achieve heaven on earth. But economists' practice also contributes to harm. The harm can be severe, even devastating. Sometimes it destroys lives. Regrettably, the risk of harming is ineliminable from economic practice. This is the tragedy of economics. It is a statement of fact. *It is not an indictment of the profession.*

Economists seeking to do good but who are aware of the harms their practice induces have looked for ways to manage the resulting cognitive dissonance. That's understandable. It's disturbing to realize you're contributing to harm to so many you hope to help. Unfortunately, the predominant approach to resolving the moral dilemma is irresponsible. I'll refer to that approach as economic "moral geometry."[1] Moral geometry represses the complexity of harm and insulates the profession morally from the harms people suffer because of the policies it advocates. Moral geometry entails seductive, unambiguous decision rules that dictate policy choice when all the available options threaten harm. Methods like cost-benefit analysis attempt to resolve deep moral questions—such as what kinds of harm are appropriate to impose on some members of society for the well-being of others—by way of simple math problems. Having done the math, the economist can assess policy without giving much thought to those the policy will harm. Moral geometry allows economists to sleep well while others suffer the consequences of their practice. Approaching harm in that way is reckless. *That claim is an indictment.*

Causes of Economic Harm

UNEVENNESS

Competent, well-meaning economists cause harm for two principal reasons. The first is that the economic policy interventions they advocate induce uneven impacts across society, and sometimes across national borders. This problem is widely recognized in the profession, and is explored in the fields of welfare economics and social choice theory. Like technological innovations that emerge from the initiatives of private individuals in the economy, consciously designed public policy that is intended to improve the human condition can disturb social arrangements upon which many depend. Schumpeter (1942) argued famously that capitalist development induces a "perennial gale of creative destruction." So, too, can policy innovation. Typically, even the most promising economic policies have disparate effects on distinct groups of people. That insight led the "new welfare economists" of the 1930s to see harm in every policy intervention. Uneven impact is the rule in complex economies where individuals inhabit dense webs of economic, social, and political relations. The problem of uneven impact would arise even if all economic actors wanted and valued the same things. The problem is substantially exacerbated in societies where there is heterogeneity across individuals in their desires and values. In the context of COVID-19, for instance, we have been reminded that some individuals prioritize personal autonomy over public health while others do not. Even were COVID-19 containment policy to have the same objective impact on all people, the impact would be experienced as beneficial by some but deeply harmful by others.

IRREPARABLE IGNORANCE AND HARM

A second set of drivers of economist-induced harm has received far less attention than it deserves. It comprises the *epistemic* conditions under which economists operate. By "epistemic conditions" I refer to what economists do and don't know, and can and can't know.

Economists confront the problem of what I call "irreparable ignorance." They do not and cannot possibly know all they need to know to design interventions that avoid unanticipated consequences. The unforeseen consequences of economic interventions can be benign, and even beneficial. But they are often damaging. One important example involved Federal Reserve Chair Alan Greenspan in the years preceding the crisis of 2008. During his twenty-year tenure as chair, Greenspan used his immense influence to prevent tighter government regulation of financial markets at a time of substantial financial innovation involving new financial assets and trading strategies. He believed, right up until the financial implosion, that financial institutions could be counted on to regulate their own behavior. He was wrong. He acknowledged his error in testimony before the Government Oversight Committee of the US House of Representatives (Greenspan 2008):

> I made a mistake in presuming that the self-interest of organizations, specifically banks and others, was such that they were best capable of protecting their own shareholders. . . . Those of us who have looked to the self-interest of lending institutions to protect shareholders' equity, myself especially, are in a state of shocked disbelief.

Looking back now, it is easy to infer that Greenspan overlooked obvious risks from freewheeling financial activities prior to 2008. But his error reveals a more fundamental problem in economics. Economic practice entails wrestling with the unknown and the unknowable. Greenspan's error, widely shared by economists, was to believe he knew far more than he did. Greenspan failed to recognize that the larger the scale of an economic intervention—and keep in mind that decisions concerning financial regulation have global implications—the more severe is irreparable ignorance and the greater the chances for deep and extensive unintended harms. Economists often advocate very big interventions. "No other science," Charles Plott (2010, 7) correctly argues, "aspires to such difficult goals as influencing an entire economy or even controlling a single market."

Epistemic insufficiency connects with economist-induced harm in various ways. Economists can't know in advance how individuals and institutions will respond to economic policy interventions. Greenspan could not have known how financial institutions would exploit the freedom provided by light-touch government oversight, for instance. But the ultimate impact of policy interventions depends on those responses. Moreover, economists cannot know in advance how their work will be taken up by decision makers who formulate policy or applied by those empowered to administer policy. This gives economists an out that they regularly exploit when things go badly. "The science cannot be held accountable for how it is used or mistakes made when it is used" (Plott 2010, 7).

Is that the right inference to draw from the fact that noneconomists misuse economic theory? In fact, it isn't. The correct inference is that economists, just like other experts, at best enjoy *influence without control*. Unfortunately, influence without control can be very dangerous. Think of a ten-year-old child behind the wheel of a Humvee, careening down Main Street. Does the child influence what happens next? Of course. But does that child control the ensuing events? *Don't bet your life on it, or especially the lives of others.* I submit that this is exactly the right way to think about the situation facing an economist in the policy world who is trying to promote good economic outcomes. The greater the degree of influence without control, the greater the risk of inducing unintended harm. Let's call it the Alan Greenspan problem. It follows that as economists substantially extended their influence over the course of the twentieth century, they also increased their capacity to exert unintended and unforeseen harm. And with that capacity comes greater responsibility on the part of the economics profession to wrestle with its moral duties to those who may be harmed by its practice.

An Epistemic Paradox

Economics is marked by an epistemic paradox. Economists *know so much*, and yet *know so little*. Economists know more than laypeople about their field of expertise, which establishes their authority and influence. Laypeople might hope that economists are wizards who can steer the economy any way they like. And economists seeking influence are too often willing to exploit that misapprehension. But economists know far too little to do what is often asked of them. For instance, economists at best have imperfect knowledge about the values and desires of the inscrutable individuals their policies will affect or the full set of circumstances that constitute their lives (Hayek [1944] 2007). Unfortunately, knowing more than others is often misinterpreted as possessing adequate knowledge. While it is true that those with expertise in a field should have more authority over certain matters than those who do not, danger emerges when those in whom authority is entrusted come to believe they know more than they do, or even more than they possibly can.

Economists too often deceive themselves and their audiences into believing they know more than it is possible to know. As keepers of this Secret Knowledge, economists are rewarded in compensation, prestige, and influence for their expertise. At a 1991 speech at a World Bank–International Monetary Fund meeting, the famed Larry Summers told an audience, "The laws of economics, it's often forgotten, are like the laws of engineering. . . . There's only one set of laws and they work everywhere." He added, "One of the things I've learnt in my short time at the World Bank is that whenever anybody says, 'but economics works differently here,' they're about to say something dumb" (cited in Hardy 2019, 18).

The Larry Summers Problem arises when one assumes that being the smartest person in the room *by one's own estimation* implies being adequate to the task at hand—that *knowing more* means *knowing enough*. Economists too often lose sight of the wisdom attributed to Josh Billings (Keeler 1913): "It ain't so much men's ignorance that does the harm as their knowing so many things that ain't so." The arrogance has at least temporarily been dampened by a series of massive economic failures, such as the crisis of 2008, but only after millions have lost their livelihoods and many have lost their lives.

Causality and the Epistemic Problem of the Counterfactual

Economics explores causality. Economists want to know the causal connections between diverse events and variables of interest so that they can exploit those connections in designing beneficial interventions. Economists need to know whether raising the minimum wage increases unemployment, for instance. But as concerns causality in economics, the problem of irreparable ignorance is acute.

Causal claims in economics generally entail *counterfactual reasoning*. The truth of the claim that raising the minimum wage last year increased unemployment today depends on the veracity of the counterfactual claim that had the minimum wage not been raised, unemployment would be lower today than it is. The problem is that in economics we can't ever be certain about *what would have happened* in the absence of an event we take to be causal because that alternative historical path was permanently foreclosed as soon as the causal event occurred. So our competing explanations of what happened in the world and why are grounded in competing *fictions*—fictitious accounts of how the world would have been absent the causal event. In very simple cases that problem may appear manageable. We can be fairly certain that taxing soft drinks to improve public health will have the proximate effect of reducing soft drink consumption below what it otherwise would have been. Even in this simple case, however, we cannot know whether the measure will succeed in improving public health unless we know in advance whether consumers will substitute alcohol, ice cream, or cigarettes for soft drinks. In more complex cases, like the minimum wage, our knowledge of proximate and ultimate effects is much less secure.

The Elusive Nature of Economic Harm

In comparison with the harm that is caused by one individual acting directly on another, such as through fraud or a physical assault, economic harm is generally indirect, deferred, and diffuse. Tracing economic harm back to its origins in a single event, like a policy shift, is not just exceedingly difficult but often misguided. As is increasingly recognized in the social sciences today, the social world is irreducibly complex. Events result from the combined effect of innumerable forces and events, many of which are themselves complex. Economists try to skirt the problem by setting aside most variables when constructing causal models so that they can focus on just those few causal linkages that they take to be paramount. The strategy requires the assumption of ceteris paribus—that all else remains constant—while economists explore the isolated effect of a small number of variables on others. The strategy generates impressive blackboard demonstrations of causality. The problem, though, is that in the actual economy other things are changing constantly and unpredictably. These other changes can alter and overwhelm the power of the causal relationship captured in a model (Cartwright 1980). If in fact economic causality is complex, then we need to take some care in attributing *this* effect to *that* cause.

Economic harm is often structural, arising from the way economies work rather than from explicit wrongdoing. Even if everyone plays by the rules, many people may suffer economic harms, like unemployment and economic insecurity. Even if no one cheats, an economy may generate extraordinary levels of inequality that shred the social fabric while marginalizing those individuals who are disadvantaged, denying them economic and political efficacy. Structural harm is far too often accepted by economists as legitimate. Milton Friedman, one of the most influential economists of the twentieth century, dismissed racial economic disparities on grounds that the "negative" harms that result from normal market processes were to be taken as legitimate (even if regrettable), while government mandates to correct such problems were to be taken as unjustifiable "positive" harms (Friedman 1962, 112). In his view it was far better to live with racial injustice than to tolerate government coercion to address the problem.

The structural nature of economic harms can complicate the assignment of blame for harm, as is the goal in tort litigation, in which one party sues another over alleged harm. Fortunately, assigning blame is contrary to this book's purpose. My goal is to explore the responsibility of economists confronting uneven impact and epistemic insufficiency when their practice can induce deep direct, indirect, and structural harms.

Deweaponizing Harm

A hazardous profession should worry, a lot, about the harms its practice generates. But, in fact, the economics profession has instead pursued strategies that discount the salience of those harms.

That claim will strike many economists as absurd given the centrality of the practice of cost-benefit analysis to their work. But the standard approach to harm, including but not limited to cost-benefit analysis, trivializes economic harms. The standard approach takes a unidimensional view of harm. It defines harm in terms of the loss of welfare, where welfare is typically defined in terms of preference satisfaction. That is, individuals are harmed when they face diminished access to goods they prefer. Under the standard approach, all harms are assumed to be commensurable with one another and with benefits, and as fully reparable through compensation. The approach oversimplifies harm while allowing the profession to countenance even extensive harms in its pursuit of the greater good.

IATROGENIC HARM

Some professions that generate harm do much better. Medical practice is the imperfect exemplar in this respect, where the concept of *iatrogenic* (from the Greek, "physician-originating") harm is at the center of medical practice and medical ethics. Practitioners in clinical and public-health settings and medical ethicists understand that helping risks harming, most immediately to individual patients but also to people tied to patients through affection and financial and other forms of dependence. Physicians understand that the most virtuous and best-trained practitioners can and do induce harm. Much of the research on iatrogenic harm focuses on the failures of medical systems and institutions rather than on bad apples in the profession (Kohn et al. 2000). No standard of practice can eliminate all medical harms. A US government study estimates that 13% of hospital patients in 2012 suffered a potentially avoidable "hospital-acquired condition" (Department of Health and Human Services 2014). Medical practitioners and institutions cause harm for some of the same reasons that economists do. Physicians, too, run up against epistemic limits, while public-health interventions like pandemic containment strategies also generate uneven impact among society's members. Medical practice wrestles with the matter of iatrogenic harm by focusing on the nature of harm and by formulating protocols to avert avoidable harm and minimize unavoidable harm, as well as strategies to prepare for and mitigate the harms that befall those being served by medical care.

Iatrogenesis most immediately encompasses harms of a strictly medical nature, such as damage to patients' bodies. But the concept is also employed to capture harmful nonmedical effects of medical interventions. Examples include the impoverishment that accompanies "catastrophic health care expenditure" (Meessen et al. 2003, 581) and abridgments of individual rights that sometimes arise in the context of public-health interventions such as enforced quarantines (Giubilini et al. 2018).

In comparison, economics has given little serious attention to economist-induced harm. The predominant view in the profession is that while some harms are the price to be paid for social betterment, others are gratuitous. *Gratuitous harm is what other economists do.* The allegation of gratuitous harm is deployed in an ideologically charged fight between mobilized camps of antagonists formed around alternative theoretical perspectives. Each camp sees itself on the side of the angels protecting the gates of the cathedral from the infidels. John Maynard Keynes believed that those who peddled specious doctrines, like Marxists, were likely "to serve not God but the devil" (Nelson 2001, 34). More prosaically, Keynes criticized classical and neoclassical economists for inducing the gratuitous harms of unemployment and economic stagnation. By the 1970s monetarists were attacking Keynesians for crippling market economies and exacerbating business cycles. Successive decades featured new controversies of the same sort, with protagonists blaming gratuitous harms on others. Some of the critiques were warranted, some not. But the sad fact is that one is hard-pressed to find instances of economists exploring rigorously the harms *they themselves* generate.

Respectful debate across theoretical paradigms is essential to the vitality of any discipline. But a consequence of the fervent secular religiosity underlying economic debates is that economist-induced harm has been *weaponized* rather than acknowledged as a fundamental problem for which all economists share responsibility. Attacking opponents blocks introspection and self-critique, preventing the development of shared acknowledgment of economist-induced harm across schools of thought. The resulting misapprehension is that to diminish gratuitous economic harm, we just need to banish from the profession the charlatans and frauds who hold to incorrect doctrines. The predominant view holds that economic pluralism—the proliferation of contending economic theories backed by warring camps of economists—is the problem. That view is incorrect. In fact, the efforts of leading economists to establish one official economic church with one official economic gospel has sustained groupthink and left the profession woefully unprepared to deal with economic events that do not conform to its official version of how economies work. A case in point is the financial crisis of 2008. The collapse shocked a profession that had come to embrace sophisticated macroeconomic models that did not accept even the possibility of financial instability, and to discount the views of heretical economists who warned of crisis (DeMartino 2011b).

ECONOGENIC HARM

A weaponized approach to harm is not propitious for the development of deep insight into economist-induced harm. The profession lacks even the language to capture the phenomenon. The linguistic omission abets the profession in its collective repression of the tragedy of economics. Economists tend to hold to the view that what is not priced is not counted. The linguistic analogy is that what is not named is not seen, let alone properly theorized. To address this omission I have proposed the term "econogenic harm" to refer to the diverse harms that are induced by economic practice (DeMartino 2016). The study of econogenic harm would then be known as "econogenic zemiology," where zemiology refers to the study of social harm (Linklater 2011, 43; Hillyard et al. 2004).[2] The study of economic harm more broadly (including but not limited to econogenic harm) defines the scope of the field of economic zemiology. This book is intended as a contribution to economic zemiology that focuses in particular on econogenic harm. This is a field, unfortunately, that largely awaits inauguration.

A hope driving this book is that deweaponizing harm will allow the profession to pursue constructive conversations about these daunting issues. In principle, there is no good reason why economists of diverse schools of thought should not be able to productively engage questions concerning the harms their practice induces, in dialogue across ideological boundaries. Physicians manage to do it; so do engineers. Economists should be able to do it, too.

Repressing Econogenic Harm

The economics profession represses econogenic harm by appearing to give it careful attention. Economics does in fact wrestle with harm all the time, but in ways that don't begin to do justice to harm's conceptual and ethical complexities. Under the standard approach, economists rely on moral geometry to dispose of counfounding ethical problems concerning professional harming and the distribution of harms. In this approach, all economic harms appear to be fully reparable. Harm's victims can always be made whole through compensation. Unsafe working conditions that involve high risk of injury and even death can be compensated for with higher wages, for instance. No other profession gets away with treating harm in this way.

Do economists continue to repress harm, even today? The short answer is yes. One example will have to suffice. In 2010 John Siegfried, at the time the secretary-treasurer of the American Economic Association, edited *Better*

Living through Economics. The book presents what the contributors see as the unqualified accomplishments of standard economics. The list of contributors includes some of the most influential economists of the past generation. For instance, Anne Krueger, who had served both as the chief economist of the World Bank and as the first deputy managing director of the International Monetary Fund, supplied the chapter on the virtues of trade liberalization. Economists have known for well over a century that trade liberalization inevitably induces benefits and harms. It is therefore surprising that on the matter of harm Krueger has nothing at all to say. But objections about that oversight are preempted in the editor's introduction, where a stunning disclaimer appears. If a policy is consistent with the Kaldor-Hicks compensation test (Kaldor-Hicks justifies policy that will harm some people provided the gains to the winners are greater than the losses to the losers),

> then, at least in theory, the policy change could be constructed to make some people better off while making no one worse off. Absent such considerations as envy and other relative income issues, the policy change might then be declared "a good thing." Unfortunately, however, matters are not quite so simple. Whether, in fact, compensation actually must be paid, or whether it is sufficient that it could be paid, even though in fact it is not paid, remains controversial. *The chapters in this volume, by and large, ignore such distributional considerations. To do otherwise would drag the analysis into a morass it could hardly escape.* (Siegfried 2010, 2, emphasis added)

What is going on here? Siegfried is announcing, at the outset of a book that purportedly surveys economists' social impact, that the authors have been relieved of the duty to consider the complexities of harm in policy assessment. They did not have to concern themselves with the many ways that those who lose from policy are harmed, or whether measures must be taken to offset their losses. *Siegfried's strategy is not idiosyncratic; it reflects the dominant tradition in economics over the past century.* Economists are so acclimated to the idea that they can dispense with harm's complexity that they hardly take notice of what's happening here. We economists give ourselves a pass, repressing the complexities that attend our work so that we can get on with it, even when the harms entail serious, sustained disruption to the lives of others. It is a very good thing that other professionals don't do the same. From the doctors who attend to our bodies to the engineers who attend to our roads and bridges, other professionals operate according to strikingly different sensibilities that acknowledge and attempt to prepare for the risks that their practice induces.

ECONOMIC EXCEPTIONALISM?

Why do economists break with other professionals on the matter of harm and harming? The standard justification is suggested in the passage just cited and is ethical in nature. *Better Living* conveys a widespread sentiment in the profession that economists are doing sacred work, eliminating hardship and promoting social betterment in the aggregate even if their work unavoidably harms some individuals or groups. It argues that if economists were forced to wrestle carefully with the harm their work might induce before they acted, the profession would be stymied in its mission to promote social betterment. Society would suffer. Indeed, so the thinking goes—and this is one area where epistemic limitations in economics are explicitly recognized—since we can't ever know the full effects of our preferred policies in advance of their implementation, the demand that we comprehensively probe potential harms would paralyze the profession altogether. The effect would be to deny the world the enormous benefits of economists' interventions.

This kind of thinking is associated with a profound defensiveness that becomes visible in the face of criticism that economic practice induces harm. In her review of the *Oxford Handbook of Professional Economic Ethics* (DeMartino and McCloskey 2016), Krueger (2017) conveys her impatience with talk of harm:

> How would one "consider and identify" all the gainers and losers before taking action? . . . When I was Vice President for Economics and Research at the World Bank I found it ironic that many proposals were blocked by calls for further research. . . . A call for more knowledge was a call to retain existing policies. . . . If some [World Bank] funds are to be used for additional evaluations, a question arises as to whether more evaluations will yield a sufficient return to compensate for the foregone [*sic*] projects that might otherwise be funded.

The problem with the main thread of the argument is Krueger's mistaken inference from the request to think more carefully about econogenic harm. That request doesn't translate into having to know, prior to acting, the identities of all those harmed. The point, in an important sense, is the reverse. Given our epistemic limitations, we must presume that we can't ever know in advance who will be victims of the policies economists embrace, or the precise ways in which they will be harmed. The resulting obligation is to act responsibly, to learn what Wendell Berry (2005) calls "the way of ignorance" (cf. Welch 2000). Acting responsibly entails anticipating that some individuals will face predictable and unpredictable harms; preparing to ameliorate those harms; and, when deciding which harms are worth risking in pursuit of which social goods, acknowledging the claims of those who might suffer harm. Acting responsibly also requires incorporating those facing the risk of harm more directly into the policy-making enterprise. Is that asking a lot of the profession? Maybe it is. But it is the price to be paid for the enormous influence over the lives of others that economists have sought and now wield in the world. Simply put, influence entails responsibility. The greater the influence, the more extensive the responsibility.

WHERE NORMATIVE MEETS POSITIVE

Economists have attempted to sustain a bright line between what they call "positive" and "normative" analysis. Positive economic analysis seeks to investigate the way the economy works, not the way we might hope it works. It is thought to require objectivity, avoiding all value judgments. Normative analysis instead involves subjective judgments about the desirability of economic outcomes, such as full employment or sustainability. The claim that a particular policy is beneficial is, then, a normative claim. Under this way of thinking, positive economics comes first. We can't know what policies to propose, it is thought, until we know how the economy works.

The concept of harm, however, refuses to play by the rules. It is at once positive and normative. We can't begin positive analysis of harm, identifying and measuring it, without first reaching normative judgments concerning what it means to be harmed. And those judgments in turn hinge on value-laden conceptions about human needs and potential and about human relationships with others and with their natural and social environments. Harm judgments also depend on an adequate conception of human rights, freedoms, liberties, spirituality, and responsibilities. This implies that a comprehensive account of harm, which I barely sketch in this book, presumes a comprehensive account of these salient features of human existence. But all of these conceptions are contested. Distinct theoretical traditions reach distinct judgments about what effects register as harm, which harms are serious and which are de minimis, which forms of harm are ethically worrisome, which are and are not reparable. For instance, when a local government appropriates private property to build a highway while compensating the owners the full market value of their property, have the property owners been harmed? The standard approach in economics holds that no lasting harm has been done since the compensation makes the homeowners whole. But libertarians are apt to view the appropriation of private property, with or without compensation, as an egregious, irreparable violation of individual rights.

The implication is clear. Positive analyses of harm, such as assessing the presence and magnitude of harm, require normative judgments. Harm assessment requires difficult decisions about what counts as harm and which harms are and are not to be taken as ethically indictable. All of this implies that as regards harm, the positive and the normative are inescapably linked. Blurring the distinction between the two spheres of economics, harm violates the professional economic taboo that is thought to protect the objectivity of positive economics against incursions from the subjectivity of normative economics. We will take time to explore the proposed resolution to this problem. The standard approach to policy assessment, "welfarism," is often taken to be self-evidently adequate and in little need of elaboration or defense. In the view of Partha Dasgupta (2005, 226), for instance, "The ethical foundations of modern economics are . . . broad and strong." Unfortunately, and as the most careful welfare economists have demonstrated, that claim is entirely incorrect. Angus Deaton puts it concisely: "Economists have this sort of bastard idea of welfare economics, or of human well-being, which is not thought out at all" (Sen, Deaton, and Besley 2020, 16). In fact, most advanced economics students today do not study the normative foundations of the economics they practice. And so it is not surprising that Anthony Atkinson (2009, 793–94), a leader in the study of inequality, finds that there is a "yawning gulf" today between the normative criteria employed in economics and those in the policy world.

THE BLASÉ PRACTITIONER

Relatively few economists serve individual clients. Economic interventions, like public policy, affect many people over long periods. Moreover, interventions exert their effects through extraordinarily complex causal pathways under the influence of diverse contingent events. In part for these reasons, economists are never held accountable for their errors or the harmful impacts of their practice. These factors can lead to what Andrew Linklater (2011) calls the "blasé self," which blocks active sympathy even in the presence of severe suffering. The condition can arise from the fact that, unlike physicians who treat individual patients and are confronted directly with the effects of their interventions, economists confront those harmed by economic policy only at a distance, if at all. Moreover, economists may fall into the trap of *overidentifying* harm. Seeing harm everywhere, all the time, economists too often resign themselves to the inevitability of economic harm. Economists are inured to econogenic harm not by indifference but by a counterfactual premise, in full evidence in *Better Living*, that but for their expertise social harms would be so much worse.

Repression of the harms associated with their practice does not come easily, especially for those economists with self-awareness who seek to promote social betterment. One stratagem that has permitted caring economists to repress harms is to dismiss the claims of those who would be harmed to the goods they are to sacrifice for the public good. Economists deride workers who protest free trade and demand labor rights protections in trade agreements, claiming that the workers are hypocritical protectionists who pay lip service to international labor solidarity but in fact exploit fair trade to protect their own privileges. Environmentalists who resist ecological degradation in their neighborhoods are dismissed as NIMBY ("not in my backyard") free riders: even though environmentalists claim to protect the earth, *economists know* that their concerns are limited to their own little patch. Those who advocate for the protection of women's rights abroad are labeled cultural imperialists. Paul Krugman's stance on the fair traders utilizes this strategy. As he put it in one of his several dismissive critiques of those demanding fair trade during the 1990s (before he quietly switched sides of the debate in 2007), "In short, [fair traders] are not entitled to their self-righteousness. They have not thought the matter through. And when the hopes of hundreds of millions are at stake, thinking things through is not just good intellectual practice. It is a moral duty" (Krugman 1997).[3]

A fundamental conceptual distinction between *rights* and *privileges* underlies the economist's justification for imposing harms. Those who would be harmed by economists' preferred policies must be theorized as enjoying benefits to which they are not entitled, at the expense of others; as parasites who must be dispossessed of their ill-gotten gains. To the economist, the injustice is not in harming these people but in letting them continue to enjoy undeserved benefits that impair social betterment (Hayek [1944] 2007, chap. 9). In contrast, those who would benefit from economists' proposed policies are theorized as victims of the status quo who, in the absence of a proposed policy initiative, would continue to be denied their rightful rewards. This discursive strategy blinds the profession to what would otherwise be very troubling: that so many individuals and their communities, including many who are particularly vulnerable, are harmed deeply by economists' preferred policy interventions. The strategy easily bleeds into "moral exclusion" of certain groups, which justifies their harm as "appropriate, acceptable, or just" (Opotow 1990, 1).

Econogenic Harm and Illiberalism

One important feature of the recent illiberal turn in politics over the past several years is the widespread rejection of experts and even the idea of expertise. There is particularly strong antipathy toward economic expertise. As British Conservative Party leader Michael Gove put it famously during the Brexit campaign: "I think the people in this country have had enough of experts, from organizations with acronyms, saying that they know what is best and getting it consistently wrong." In a subsequent BBC interview (Gove 2017) he clarified by stating that he was referring primarily to economists. In the US and elsewhere the antipathy toward expertise spilled over onto public-health practitioners just when trust in those experts was vital to COVID-19 containment.

Could it be that economists' cavalier approach to harm over recent decades has contributed to the startling pushback against expertise in policy areas as diverse as trade, climate change, and even public health? The preceding discussion reveals my own suspicions, which are shared by other economists (DeMartino 2018; Rodrik 2018).[4] Economists are now facing a backlash from those whose claims they too readily discounted in their rush to pursue their preferred economic policies. Illiberal politicians have mobilized a latent anti-expert sentiment as a cornerstone of their wider populist programs.

If the critics are correct, then the illiberal turn represents in part a rebuke to the presumption of epistemic adequacy in the economics profession and the associated paternalistic ethos under which the economist is presented as knowing best. But this insight raises a difficult set of questions. What alternative ethos might temper or even replace economic paternalism? How might economists apply their expertise in ways that engage vulnerable laypeople as partners in knowledge formation and policy application, rather than as passive receivers of the benefits and harms of economic policy? Fortunately, we can learn from the practice of economists who are now rethinking how to wield economic expertise responsibly in a world they can't ever sufficiently know or control. Economic policy iconoclasts are taking seriously the claims of those who will be affected, for better or worse, by economists' practice.

First Do No Harm?

Since the publication of *The Economist's Oath* (DeMartino 2011a) I have had the opportunity to discuss economic harm with many economists. When I have spoken of the need for economists to take better care regarding econogenic harm, economists often infer that I am advocating the Hippocratic principle "First, do no harm." Krueger's response to the *Oxford Handbook* is again relevant. She asserts in her review (2017, 210) that "one of the policy prescriptions accepted through much of the book is 'first, do no harm.'" She takes this principle as an inviolable dictate and easily dismisses it on grounds that it would prevent all initiatives that risk any harm to anyone, even those initiatives that promise to reduce misery. She adds that even not-acting causes harm. The problem with her argument is that not one of the thirty-seven essays in the book endorses the Hippocratic principle. All contributors to the book who raise the principle problematize its relevance for economics. The editors of the *Handbook* ask, in the opening pages of the book, "What does 'do no harm' mean in a world where there are no free lunches and where all actions (including doing nothing) entail tradeoffs?" (DeMartino and McCloskey 2016, 7). In a separate essay in the book I argue that the Hippocratic directive "'first, do no harm,' if taken as an inviolable mandate or decision rule, has no relevance in economics since it would imply that economists can do nothing at all" (72). The development ethicist Des Gasper (535) writes that "often the do-no-harm principle cannot be fulfilled: not only cannot all consequences [of development projects] be foreseen, but ethically desirable material progress depends on development projects that inevitably displace some people, and full remedial compensation appears not always possible."

Krueger's mistaken belief that the only alternative to standard moral geometry is an inviolable Hippocratic principle that threatens economists' practice reveals the terribly undeveloped state of thinking in the profession concerning harm and harming. And so it bears emphasis: engaging economic and econogenic harm carefully does not necessitate the adoption of a new economic decision rule such as "first, do no harm." Economists very often face "tragic choices" (Nussbaum 2001) in policy formation where all options (including preserving the status quo) generate damage. Though decision rules are attractive and convenient for making tragic choices tractable, careful consideration of harm and professional harming leads us away from *any* moral geometry. Tragic choices are, in a word, tragic. They must be recognized as such, not converted by magical thinking into simpler problems.

A Harm-Centric, Ignorance-Based Economics

The foregoing yields a terribly difficult question, which this book seeks to answer: how might economists' practice be revised were they to pursue *harm-centric, ignorance-based economics*? If *harm-centric* economics rejects simplistic moral geometry, how does it proceed? An important requirement entails accepting the inherent complexity of harm, and the idea that not all economic and econogenic harms are reparable or compensable. A second requirement follows: the economics profession must accept the autonomy of those whom economists purport to serve but whom their practice also harms.

An *ignorance-based* economics builds upon the understanding that there is so much we cannot know in economics and so little we can control. It nevertheless seeks to apply economic expertise responsibly, *in concert with those whom economists seek to serve.* Recognizing irreparable ignorance with clear eyes opens the door to promising new thinking about policy formation that can achieve just what it is economists hope to achieve, the promotion of social betterment. In fields such as urban planning, water resource management, climate change, and security, we find important innovations today in policy formation that address irreparable ignorance. Economists can learn from other practitioners who also face severe epistemic limitations.

Plan of the Book

What are economic harms, and how severe are they? Why do economists cause harm as they aspire to do good? How do economists make sense of the harms their practice induces? And what can be done to improve how economists theorize and manage economic harm, especially to the most vulnerable? These are the organizing questions of the book.

This book can be approached as an integrated monograph that chapter by chapter builds a set of related arguments. Chapter 2 explores the deficient paternalistic ethos that guides economists' professional practice. Chapter 3 develops an account of harm that emphasizes its irreducible complexity, which presents challenges to all professions that risk harming. Part II of the book comprises three chapters that examine why even virtuous economists cause harm as they aspire to do good. Chapter 4 emphasizes the uneven impact of economic interventions, while chapters 5 and 6 explore the problem of irreparable ignorance in economics. Part III examines economic moral geometry. Chapter 7 presents and chapter 8 critiques moral geometry. Though the material in these chapters is a bit more complex, the presentation prioritizes clarity over technical precision. Chapter 9 then moves beyond moral geometry, offering a more adequate account of harm for economics. It expands the concept of harm to encompass setbacks to interests, social harms, and capabilities deprivation. Part IV examines how economic practice might be reformed to take better account of economic and econogenic harm. Chapter 10 presents a harm-centric approach to economic assessment. Chapter 11 highlights the epistemic problem, exploring how economists can promote social betterment when they cannot know the future impacts of the policies they propose. Chapter 12 concludes the book, returning us to the question of professional ethos.

Alternatively, the book can be approached as a series of essays that can be read independently depending on the reader's interests and purposes. The final chapters on *harm-centric, ignorance-based economics* provide the practical payoff. Practitioners might start with chapters 10 and 11 and then circle back to those chapters that are relevant to their work.

This book is a work in what might be called *critical economics*. It is not associated with a particular ideological position. The argument draws liberally on contributions across the political spectrum without passing them through an ideological filter. The new field of economic and econogenic zemiology marks a potential space for constructive dialogue across the profession, just as the study of iatrogenic harm is a shared venture in medicine despite physicians' respective worldviews. A subordinate goal of the book is to model the kind of discourse that welcomes conflicting perspectives. To that end the book raises far more questions than it seeks to answer. It should be read not as a treatise but as an invitation to contribute to a new conversation.

One terminological point might prevent misunderstanding. I principally use the term "economic harm" to refer to the *source* and not the *nature* of harm. Interventions that economists propose induce heterogeneous harms. Some harms are of a strictly economic character, such as increased unemployment. But economic interventions also induce physical, psychological, social, cultural, ecological, and political damage. Just as iatrogenic harm can be taken to reach beyond harms that are strictly medical in nature, so can economic harm (as cause) be associated not just with economic effects but also with the other harms that follow from economic events. For instance, economic policy can generate adverse health effects, including dramatic declines in life expectancy. We can therefore speak of "econogenic morbidity" and "econogenic mortality" in cases where economist-advocated interventions undermine public health.

That said, to avoid a proliferation of terms, I will also use the term "economic harm" in its more natural usage to refer to damage that is explicitly economic. The distinction between the two usages of the term (as cause and as one kind of effect) will be clear from the context in which the term appears.

A final preliminary: the book focuses solely on the damage associated with economic practice. It should not be inferred that economists only induce harm. My claim is that they contribute to deep, enduring harm as they promote social betterment. The positive side of the ledger has been well documented in work like Siegfried's. The negative side is too often overlooked by economists eager to apply their craft to social problems. This book tries to balance the scales.

2

Economic Paternalism, Heroic Economics

> [The "man of system"] is apt to be very wise in his own conceit; and is often so enamoured with the supposed beauty of his own ideal plan of government, that he cannot suffer the smallest deviation from any part of it. He goes on to establish it completely and in all its parts, without any regard either to the great interests, or to the strong prejudices which may oppose it. He seems to imagine that he can arrange the different members of a great society with as much ease as the hand arranges the different pieces upon a chess-board.
>
> —ADAM SMITH ([1759] 1976, 286)

Ten Million Missing Russian Men

"Ten million Russian men disappeared in the early 1990s" (Stuckler and Basu 2013, 21). The deaths occurred among working-age men. In just three years, from 1991 to 1994, life expectancy among Russian males fell from sixty-four to fifty-seven years.[5] A workforce projected to grow from 149 million in 1985 to 164 million by 1998 in fact shrank to 144 million in that year. The missing ten million Russian men accounted for 6.7% of the total Russian population.

Catastrophes of this magnitude typically occur only during pandemics and wars. Even by that standard, the Russian deaths are staggering. As of November 2021, the total number of people who have perished globally from COVID-19 is estimated at about 5 million, or .06% of the world's population. Even the flu pandemic of 1918–1920 killed far fewer in relative terms—about 2.8% of the world's population—compared to the Russian deaths. The deadliest war in US history, the Civil War, claimed the lives of about 2.1% of the US population. The total number of Americans who have lost their lives in war over the past 250 years is about 2.9 million—less than a third of the Russian deaths. France lost 1.9 million soldiers in WWI, representing 4.9% of its total population. So the loss of ten million working-age men in Russia over just a few years is stunning.

The Russian deaths were not caused by war or pandemic. The proximate causes included alcohol poisonings, suicides, homicides, injuries, and heart attacks (Stuckler and Basu 2013, 25). Many of the alcohol deaths involved the consumption of particularly lethal *odekolon* by men who could no longer afford vodka. Odekolon (a sound-alike for "eau de cologne") is "manufactured using aftershave, mouthwash, and other products that [contain] alcohol but were not meant for consumption." Odekolon consumption increased the rate of death from "alcohol psychosis, liver cirrhosis, and heart disease by a factor of twenty-six over not drinking these substances" (Stuckler and Basu 2013, 26).

How are we to account for these deaths? In 1991, under the tutelage of economists from Harvard and other Western institutions, Russia pursued a massive and unprecedented economic experiment (Wedel 2001; DeMartino 2011a). It sought to transform its state-directed economy into a market economy. Not over a period of decades, but immediately, all at once, at breakneck speed. "Shock therapy," as this kind of experiment came to be called. The government suspended economic subsidies to factories and the price controls on which the economy and living standards depended. Citizens were now to fend for themselves in the vibrant market economy that was expected to spring up spontaneously once the state stopped meddling in economic affairs. A key feature of the transformation was the privatization of massive state holdings. State-owned enterprises were transferred to politically connected "investors." Economic advisers called on Russia to privatize 200,000 firms in less than five hundred days. In fact, the state managed to transfer 120,000 firms to the private sector in under two years—an extraordinary feat never before imagined. In the context of severe economic turbulence, the new owners stripped the assets of unprofitable firms and laid off workers by the million. Entire towns were wiped out economically. In short order the economy collapsed. The Russian government reported that by 1995 one-quarter of its citizens were living in poverty, while independent researchers put the figure at over 40%—up from 2% in 1988. Officially, 22% of the workforce was rendered unemployed. In terms of purchasing power, the Russian economy fell to a level comparable to the US economy of 1897. The state responded with austerity, not assistance. State allocations to social welfare (including health care) were cut by 20%.

The ten million Russian men who died in the wake of these measures died deaths associated with despair—stress, social isolation, poverty, and desperation. The men had "no hope for the future, no work, nothing to do, nowhere to go" (Stuckler and Basu 2013, 27). The many "mono-industrial settlements," organized around one firm or one industry, faced extraordinarily bleak circumstances. In the face of abrupt factory closures, workers lost income and savings, but also their identities as providers for their families and productive members of their communities. Overnight they lost the social relationships that factory work had afforded. The outcome was alcohol consumption—with up to 25% of unemployed men drinking odekolon (in comparison with just 5% of employed workers) (Stuckler and Basu 2013, 27).

What does any of this have to do with econogenic harm? The issue is not whether the Russian economy needed structural reform. The issue is how well-meaning, well-trained economists could contribute to such extraordinary misery for those enduring the reform. What might the episode tell us about what is wrong in economics?

The Economic Ethos: Paternalism

Professions tend to adopt distinct views of their obligations to society and how to meet them. Each has a particular professional ethos. Ideally, professional sensibilities evolve over time as a consequence of learning and challenges to practice from beyond the profession. The ethos governing economic practice, however, has been stagnant for well over a century.

That ethos can be summarized as follows: on pressing policy matters, *economists know best.* A wide, unbridgeable epistemic gap separates the profession from laypeople who cannot begin to master the logic and mathematics of economic science. That epistemic gap engenders a paternalistic ethos. Paternalism is grounded in beneficence—the obligation of experts to do what *they believe* is best to promote the interests of others, even over the beneficiaries' principled objections. It is closely tied to utilitarian philosophy, which requires the professional to promote maximum happiness across society's members (see chap. 7). The paternalistic ethos in economics is surprising given the widespread antipathy in the profession toward paternalistic measures by other actors, such as the state, which are seen to violate individuals' freedom to choose for themselves (Friedman and Friedman 1980). Under the paternalistic ethos, if economists believe that a policy promises large aggregate gains even though it also induces substantial suffering for many, they are obligated to advocate for the policy despite the resistance of its victims. The greater the resistance to the correct policy, in fact, the greater the duty to advocate, and the more quickly the policy should be introduced, before its victims can mobilize to resist.

Jeffrey Sachs's work in the post-Soviet transition to market economies reflects the paternalistic ethos. Knowing that market liberalization would cause widespread harm, he emphasized the "need for speed" in the transition to market economies in the former socialist countries. His advice to officials was to "figure out how much society can take, and then move three times quicker than that." To drive home the point, Sachs cited approvingly the words of a Polish economist: "You don't try to cross a chasm in two jumps" (Sachs 1991, 236).

Sachs and other social engineers justified shock therapy on economic grounds, claiming that the success of reforms in one sector required simultaneous reform in other sectors. But there was no compelling reason to believe that the transition could not have been undertaken more gradually, with far less suffering. Poland pursued that course, and with much better results (Stuckler and Basu 2013, chap. 2). The economic argument for speed was a smoke screen. The key motivation for shock therapy was political rather than economic. It was intended to allow economists to implement their agenda before opposition could mobilize. Sachs (1991, 239) admitted as much, arguing that the reforms he advocated would "eventually produce great benefits, but they will be opposed by many in the shrinking sectors. Populist politicians will try to hook up with coalitions of workers, managers, and bureaucrats in hard-hit sectors to slow or reverse the adjustment." Shock therapy was intended to circumvent this problem.

Economists' paternalism vis-à-vis society parallels the paternalistic ethos parents carry vis-à-vis their children. It is associated with a heavy burden that the profession must bear if it is to fulfill its obligations to others—if it is to promote social betterment.

THE EVOLUTION OF MEDICAL ETHICS

Is paternalism an appropriate ethos for a profession with influence over the lives of others? We can usefully compare economics to the medical profession, where the risk of harm is acute and where a good bit of attention is given to the problem by medical practitioners and ethicists. While the economic ethos has remained tied to paternalism for over a century, medical ethics has evolved in response to shifting sensibilities concerning patients' rights.

The normative foundation of medical practice for centuries and up through the latter part of the twentieth century was deeply paternalistic. Under this ethos the physician was to be in charge of the clinical relationship. From the time of Hippocrates, patients were expected to defer to physicians' expertise and follow carefully their prescriptions. There was widespread recognition of the fact that patient harm was the price to be paid for medical benefit. Then, in the early nineteenth century, a rupture emerged in medicine over this matter. Benjamin Rush advocated a so-called heroic approach to medical practice. The "heroic healers" believed that radical interventions were often necessary to restore health. This was an era of unproven surgeries of all sorts, including gruesome amputations and other radical interventions that often induced shock and death. But the heroic healers were undeterred by pain and suffering: "According to the heroic healers, the harms associated with therapeutic intervention were necessary and thus justified. Harms of omission were, however, reprehensible" (Sharpe and Faden 1998, 8).

Jacob Bigelow led the opposition. He and his disciples emphasized instead the healing powers of nature. Whenever possible, nature was to be allowed to take its course. In this view, "restraint was laudable, intervention was culpable" (Sharpe and Faden 1998, 8). The debate over clinical intervention "centered largely on the propriety of competing therapeutic maxims—the heroic rallying cry of 'better something doubtful than nothing,' versus the more skeptical one of 'better nothing than something doubtful' " (Sharpe and Faden 1998, 130).

The dispute masked a unified professional ethos. Both sides held to the view that physicians' virtue legitimated their direction of the medical intervention. Physicians, not patients, were authorized to determine what counted as harm and benefit, assess their magnitudes, and decide when the harm was offset by the promised benefit.

By the end of the nineteenth century, the Rush-Bigelow debate had yielded to a shared faith in a new scientific, empirically grounded practice. Statistical methods came to infuse medical research. Physicians were now to heed the findings of the science rather than their intuition. Despite the empirical revolution, however, the profession remained firmly under the sway of paternalistic sensibilities. Medical science widened the epistemic gap between the physician and the patient, leaving even less room for patient input into treatment. Physicians' "presumed epistemic authority" was enhanced by the substitution of dependable, objective science for undependable virtue as a guarantor of appropriate conduct. Now more than ever the patient was to defer to medical authority—to the findings of medical research that the patient surely could not understand. At the same time, attention shifted away from the actual patient in the doctor's office to the average or statistical patient. The reports of the actual patient came to be discounted. As Sharpe and Faden (1998, 12) put it, "the individual patient became increasingly unimportant as a reporter of clinical signs. Harms and benefits began to be regarded as *objective* facts determinable only by the expertise of the physician."

The physician-knows-best conception of medical practice survived until the 1960s in the US (and survives up to the present in many other countries). As late as that, it was perfectly appropriate for physicians to engage in paternalistic deception, lying to patients when they thought it best to do so. But events in the United States in the 1960s upset this approach to medical practice. Trust in expertise began to give way in the face of movements for empowerment of nonexperts. Advocates for patients' rights arose to challenge what were increasingly seen to be illicit medical privileges. At the same time research demonstrated the extensive failures of the profession to actually heal patients.[6] Litigation led to a series of court decisions that substantially empowered research subjects and patients. In 1966 the US Food and Drug Administration called for prior informed consent by research subjects in medical experiments. Then, in 1972, the landmark *Canterbury v. Spence* decision by the US Court of Appeals for the District of Columbia overturned the physician's authority in treatment by finding that "the patient's right of self-decision shapes the boundaries of the duty to reveal." Two years later the National Research Act established Institutional Review Board procedures under which disinterested experts must decide what are and are not reasonable research protocols before research can proceed. Taken together, by the 1970s "professional paternalism was increasingly challenged by the publicly and politically-forged ethos of patient self-determination" (Sharpe and Faden 1998, 67). The patients' rights challenge had the effect of shifting the locus of decision making from physicians to patients.

Today, the paternalistic ethos has been displaced as the central guide to medical research and treatment. The 1978 publication of the Belmont Report by the US National Commission for the Protection of Human Subjects of Biomedical and Behavioral Research formalized the duties of medical researchers toward research subjects. Its core principles include respect for persons (autonomy), beneficence (including nonmaleficence), and justice. These principles soon came to govern medical treatment as well. Today physicians can no longer easily justify their manipulation of patients for the patient's own good by reference to beneficence. The duty to recognize patient autonomy implies a duty to inform patients of their conditions, treatment options and associated risks, and other salient aspects of the therapeutic situation. The therapeutic relationship is now ideally to reflect a patient-centered ethic. Patient autonomy is not absolute—it is to be balanced against beneficence and justice. The key point is to recognize that medical ethics and medical practice have evolved over the past century. Today neither physicians' virtue nor their expertise is taken to warrant unilateral authority to control the therapeutic relationship with patients.

The foregoing hardly suggests that medical practice is now beyond reproach. In the US, the profession's ethical commitments to patient autonomy and justice are violated in direct and indirect ways. For instance, medical specialists have exploited opportunities to establish for-profit private clinics that create conflicts of interest. The strategy enhances physicians' incomes but leads to overprescribing of medical services (such as imaging examination) and to selecting for treatment the healthiest patients with the most generous health insurance (Hillman et al. 1990; Gabel et al. 2008; Cole 2013). And yet, the evolution of medical ethics at least provides patients, ethicists, and government regulators with the foundations to challenge damaging medical practices.

THE STAGNATION OF ECONOMIC ETHICS

This detour through medical history leads to certain provisional insights into the economics profession. Economic practice of the last third of the twentieth century paralleled closely the heroic healing medical practice of the previous century. Leading economists in fact borrowed the language of medicine to justify dangerous policy interventions. As Milton Friedman put it in the case of Pinochet's Chile in the early 1970s, for instance, "The fact is, Chile is a very sick country, and the sick cannot expect to recover without cost" (cited in Cárcamo-Huechante 2006). Driven by heroic sensibilities, economists believed they were authorized to advocate terribly risky economic interventions despite the inevitable harms they would induce. Exploring that issue requires a quick look back at the origins of the modern economics profession.[7]

Eighteenth- and nineteenth-century classical political economists believed that their field could illuminate the workings of the economy and generate beneficial policy interventions. The goal was to inform economic policy making to promote social betterment. The approach of Adam Smith, John Stuart Mill, and their contemporaries blended moral, social, political, and economic concerns into multidimensional investigations of human affairs. Economic inquiry was typically grounded in moral philosophy as much as it was in scientific principles. As late as 1885, when a gathering of political economists created the American Economic Association (AEA), advocates of the social gospel who sought social reform in keeping with Christian principles predominated in the profession. Twenty of the fifty founding delegates at the convention were former or current Christian ministers. For them, economics could not be divorced from a social mission guided by the word of God. In the view of AEA founder and first secretary Richard T. Ely, the university economics departments that were just then emerging should be located in schools of theology. The goal of the emerging profession was to support the Christian effort to bring about a "kingdom of righteousness" on earth. For Ely the teaching of economics was to "provide the knowledge base for 'a never-ceasing attack on every wrong institution, until the earth becomes a new earth, and all its cities, cities of God'" (Nelson 2004, 60). Ely urged the AEA to emphasize "the positive role of the church, the state and science in the solution of social problems" (Coats 1960, 557–58; Furner 1975, 71). He advocated a "movement 'which will help in the diffusion of a sound,

Christian political economy'" (Crunden 1982, 13). Ely's *Statement of Principles* for the AEA incorporated these ideas. Among other things, the statement rejected laissez-faire economics as "unsafe in politics and unsound in morals" (Crunden 1982, 13).

THE NEW NEOCLASSICALS

A new approach, neoclassical economics, emerged toward the end of the nineteenth century. The neoclassical ascendance marked the professionalization of the field, which came to be dominated by full-time specialists. Despite sharing classical political economy's goal of social betterment, neoclassical thought broke with classical economics in fundamental respects.[8] The neoclassicals sought to narrow the field, grounding economics in scientific propositions and findings that could be verified or refuted by logic and evidence. The objective science was to be insulated from idiosyncratic normative judgments (Ross 1991; Sullivan 2005). From this perspective, Ely and his band of ministers were disqualified as economic scientists owing to their intermingling of economics, morality, and metaphysics. Prominent economist J. Laurence Laughlin, for instance, refused to accept an appointment to the advisory council of the AEA on grounds that he would not join any association that "has any constitution save love of truth" (Furner 1975, 78). The neoclassical revolution sought to sharpen and modernize economic practice just as the professional study of economics was migrating into the new universities (Larson 1977; May 1980; Ross 1991). The neoclassical vision of economic science was ascendant in the United States in the 1880s just as Ely sought to solidify the theological grounding of economics. Within a few years neoclassical economists had taken control of the AEA. Ely's *Statement of Principles* was dropped by 1888, and in 1892 Ely was temporarily driven from the leadership by economists who rejected his moralizing as harmful to the profession's progress and influence.

The early neoclassicals recognized that engagement in public policy entailed value judgments, however, and they were certainly unwilling to withdraw from the policy domain on those grounds. Their challenge was to find a way to maintain scientific objectivity while contributing to morally charged policy assessment. What could they offer that other policy partisans could not? How could their science—the study of *what is*—inform policy discussion—which necessarily involves *what should be*?

Various strategies emerged to square the circle. John Neville Keynes (1891) and Lionel Robbins (1932) argued for a sharp distinction between economic science and policy application. J. N. Keynes emphasized the distinction between the "positive science" and the "art" of economic practice; Robbins, between "economics" and "political economy." Economic science grounded in deductive logic and verifiable propositions was to be the physics of the social world, though Robbins thought the economic science of his day could yield only the most provisional conclusions. Economic science generated theorems derived deductively from first principles about which, it was thought, there could be little dispute. In contrast, political economy (the "art") engaged policy questions. In this view policy conclusions depended equally on inferences from economic science and on normative claims and practical judgments about the world. Economic practice of this sort generated what J. N. Keynes called "precepts." He defined a precept as a "rule of thumb that concerned policy; it followed from the art of economics and was not derived from economic theory but from introspection, induction, and an educated common sense" (Colander 2005a, 279). As David Colander (2009, 444) puts it, "For Robbins, as for Keynes, the science of economics was to be used as a backdrop for thinking about policy problems, useful to help organize one's thoughts, but was not to be directly applied to real-world problems."

The J. N. Keynes–Robbins position, that economists should maintain what Colander and Freedman (2018) call a "firewall" between economic science and policy prescription, was lost on future generations of economists. The profession instead embraced a view of economics throughout the twentieth century in which incontrovertible policy prescription could be deduced strictly from objective scientific claims about the nature of the world (Colander 2009). The field of welfare economics, where economists engage normative questions and evaluate policy, was increasingly formalized and understood as a body of strictly scientific propositions about policy (Colander 2005a). Robbins (1981, 7) objected, writing that "welfare economics conveys an impression of value-free theory which it should be just our intention to avoid."

Leading economists such as John Hicks (1939), Nicholas Kaldor (1939), and Abba Lerner (1944) helped to persuade the profession that policy assessment could be reduced to objective criteria (see chap. 7). For Lerner, "applied policy economics was the application of a scientific set of rules determined by economic theory to be followed by policy makers and by agents in the economy. . . . Economic analysis became *the* decision criterion, not an input into a broader decision process" (Colander 2003, 201–2). In Colander's view, Lerner's perspective involved a "control story in which there is a knowable social optimum that government policy is designed to achieve" (Colander 2005b, 254). That sentiment is reflected in the title of Lerner's important book *The Economics of Control*, which influenced the profession's thinking about policy interventions through the latter half of the twentieth century.

HEROIC ECONOMIC HEALERS

The self-conception of economists as objective scientists with their hands on the levers of social betterment produced a particular sense of the economist's responsibility to society. As in pre-1970s medicine, the predominant ethos in economics from the ninteenth-century neoclassical revolution into the twenty-first century has been paternalism grounded in economic expertise. That ethos has been widely shared across leading schools of economic thought, from the market fundamentalism represented by the Chicago School to the state interventionism of Keynesianism. It has been widely taken by economists to be appropriate to use all the means at hand to bring about what *the economists* know to be best. Such means have included extraordinary pressure from international financial institutions and leading governments (democratic and nondemocratic), the authority furnished by academic credentials, and even deception (Rodrik 2017; DeMartino 2021). The paternalistic ethos grounds what otherwise appears as inconsistencies in economists' practice. For instance, the eminent liberal economist Friedrich Hayek, who warned the profession of totalitarianism, embraced the Chilean military coup led by the murderous dictator General Augusto Pinochet that overturned the government of the democratically elected Salvador Allende in 1973. Hayek's justification was Pinochet's dismantling of Allende's socialist economic program in favor of economic liberalism. "I have not been able to find a single person even in much maligned Chile," Hayek wrote, "who did not agree that personal freedom was much greater under Pinochet than it had been under Allende" (cited in Farrant, McPhail, and Berger 2012).[9]

Like Hayek, other twentieth-century economists were eager to exploit their leverage to induce economic reform and even, sometimes, economic revolution. The most notable instance of economic adventurism concerned the effort of the world's most influential economists and economic institutions to promote abrupt, complete market transition in the Global South in the 1980s and then in the post-Soviet economies during the 1990s. Rather than tread carefully, searching for robust policy reform that might succeed under a wide range of unpredictable scenarios, the profession adopted the *maximax* decision rule—though no economist thought in these terms or would have dared to say so. Maximax urges us to choose the strategy that promises to provide higher rewards than any other strategy, provided everything goes perfectly well. Maximax does not consider the odds of failure; it considers just the maximum possible payoff of the available strategies on the assumption that each will in fact succeed. Maximax directs us to throw all of our savings into the lottery since, on the minuscule chance that we get the winning number, we will be better-off than we would have been had we put our savings in any other investment. In the case of post-Soviet transition, Jeffrey Sachs spoke for many of the world's most influential economists who presumed that they knew the potential payoff of shock therapy would be higher than that of any other, more prudent strategy. Their paternalistic ethos obligated them to press the shock therapy experiment on the governments they advised. To increase their influence, economists and government leaders asserted that the "body economic" was gravely ill and in need of emergency care (Stuckler and Basu 2013; Wedel 2001).

No sane economist could possibly endorse the maximax decision rule. It is the riskiest of all imaginable decision rules. But in fact, in the case of shock therapy, no other decision rule justified the strategy. Shock therapy was driven by the belief that the approach included among its possible outcomes one outcome that was better than the best possible outcome of all alternative policy regimes. As maximax dictates, there was no consideration of the risk profiles of the abrupt market liberalization experiment or any alternative regimes. Economists acted as if they were obligated to press for the policy regime that might generate the highest possible payoff.[10] The late twentieth century should be understood, then, as the heyday of *heroic economics*—a full century after the abandonment of heroic medicine. Just like heroic healers, the heroic economists were willing to risk all manner of harms resulting from extraordinarily risky interventions. They were not prepared to accept harms from more prudent strategies. Better, they thought, to cause even extreme and widespread harm by acting than to allow any harm by failing to act.

Adam Smith worried about the dangers of heroic interventionism, as the epigraph to this chapter demonstrates. His warning about the man of system is just as timely today. "Some general, and even systematical, idea of the perfection of policy and law, may no doubt be necessary," he wrote (Smith [1759] 1976, 234):

> But [for the reformer] to insist upon establishing, and upon establishing all at once, and in spite of all opposition, every thing which that idea may seem to require, must often be the highest degree of arrogance. It is to erect his own judgment into the supreme standard of right and wrong. It is to fancy himself the only wise and worthy man in the commonwealth, and that his fellow-citizens should accommodate themselves to him and not he to them.

Shock therapy was grounded in the mistaken conviction that a dynamic market economy would come to life as soon as the state removed itself from economic management. A comparison of the trajectories of the post-Soviet transition economies reveals instead that those countries, like Russia, that pursued shock therapy suffered severe economic crises and dire social and health outcomes. In contrast, those that instituted market economy at a more modest pace, such as Poland, had much better results. In fact, while Russia faced an unprecedented mortality crisis in the early 1990s, Poland's health indexes *improved* even though Poland, too, was undertaking market reform (Stuckler and Basu 2013). The comparison suggests that the ten million extra deaths in Russia were not inevitable but were the result of an extraordinary economic mistake launched under the tutelage of the leading lights in the Western economics profession. This was not the error of just a few economists, though Sachs and other economic heroes played outsize roles. At the time, despite the protests of most non-neoclassical economists, there was an extraordinarily widespread consensus among the most influential voices across the profession on the wisdom of shock therapy (Murrell 1995). Only later would some advocates come to recognize their error. By then, millions of lives had been needlessly lost.

Today, heroic economics is out of fashion. More economists are now willing to acknowledge what they don't know and to think carefully about how to apply economic theory in a world they can't control. In place of faith-based economics featuring simplistic blackboard proofs, the profession is now in a transformation to scientific economics defined, like the science-based revolution in medicine in the late nineteenth century, by empirical research. The new empirical research—some of it careful, too much of it deficient (Ziliak and McCloskey 2008)—recognizes that myriad unknown factors complicate economic causality. Thoughtful economists today recognize that policy effects are deeply context dependent (Rodrik 2017; Goldberg and Pavcnik 2007). The best applied economists today recognize that good policy decisions require deep, localized knowledge, and the art of decision making that J. N. Keynes and Robbins had urged on the profession a century ago. Even Sachs (2005, 78ff) has been touched by the reform. He now urges the profession to practice case-based "clinical economics" rather than to infer policy from blackboard proofs.

Conclusion

That's the good news. But just as in medicine a century ago, the new empiricism is taken to warrant economists' elevated authority in policy making. The economist is still taken to know best in matters of public policy. Economists today continue to believe it perfectly acceptable and perhaps even ethically required to advance policy that imposes harms on some members of society, even over public opposition, for the so-called good of society. We find too few efforts among the most influential economists to displace economic paternalism with a new ethos that recognizes and respects the agency and autonomy of those who will bear the consequences of economists' practice (cf. Easterly 2013). The profession continues to privilege the judgment of the economist over the judgments of the laypeople they serve.

But why do economic interventions cause so much serious harm? Why do even the brightest and most virtuous economists pursue strategies that yield anticipated and unanticipated damage, especially to the most vulnerable? Before answering that question it is essential to get a sense of the complexity of harm. That is the goal of the next chapter.

3

Harm's Complexity

> There is plenty of evidence that unemployment has many far-reaching effects other than loss of income, including psychological harm, loss of work motivation, skill and self-confidence, increase in ailments and morbidity rates (and even mortality rates), disruption of family relations and social life, hardening of social exclusion and accentuation of racial tensions and gender asymmetries.
>
> —AMARTYA SEN (1999, 94)

Austerity

National governments sometimes face substantial fiscal imbalances when public expenditures far exceed revenues over extended periods. Fiscal imbalances can come about for many reasons. Government officials often use deficit spending to sustain political support, providing government services and targeted benefits to privileged or vulnerable groups without being willing to impose taxes to pay for them. Other times deep imbalances are caused by exogenous shocks, such as the financial crisis of 2008 or the COVID-19 pandemic. In such cases governments are forced to deficit-finance social protection schemes, providing income guarantees to the suddenly unemployed and bailouts to businesses, and to augment the approach with expansionary monetary policy that ensures wide access to credit to prevent bankruptcies and protect the financial system.

Although most economists support short-term imbalances in response to crises, many take a dim view of long-term fiscal imbalances. Among economists' concerns is the worry that deeply indebted countries will face increasing costs of borrowing for government and businesses. Where an economy is incurring sizable deficits one year after the next, increasing national debt to levels that economists deem to be unsustainable, many economists advocate "austerity" policy. Austerity generally entails curtailing government expenditures. Social welfare programs that provide economic support to those in need, subsidies to businesses, price supports, and infrastructure expenditures and other public investments are all put on the chopping block. Austerity also generally involves raising tax revenues and imposing user fees for public services. The goal is to engineer a fiscal balance, even though doing so may induce a severe reduction in employment and per capita income. Ideally, the shock will be short-lived and the ensuing economic damage will be erased quickly by sustained economic growth. As with a painful but necessary medical procedure, the expectation is that the economic patient will be much better-off following recovery.

One notable case of austerity is the program pressed on Greece by the so-called Troika—the European Union (EU), the European Central Bank (ECB), and the International Monetary Fund (IMF)—following the financial crisis of 2008. EU rules require that budget deficits in any year not exceed 3% of a country's GDP and that accrued government debt not exceed 60% of GDP. Prior to the crisis of 2008 Greece's aggregate debt was about 105% of GDP, far exceeding the EU limit. The crisis hit Greece hard. In 2009 it faced a budget deficit of 15.4% of GDP, and by 2010 its total accumulated national debt had reached 142.8% of GDP. In 2010 it began to face spiraling borrowing costs. Interest rates on ten-year government bonds reached 30% in 2012. The austerity program imposed by the Troika included all the measures described above. Its economic consequences were so severe that even the historically pro-austerity IMF eventually raised concerns about its destructive effects. But in the standard economic view, the harms were necessary, temporary, and endurable. More to the point—the harms were understood to be largely if not entirely *economic* in nature. They amounted to a temporary reduction in the standard of living for many Greek citizens that would be compensated for by subsequent economic growth.

But is that belief warranted? Austerity typically generates widespread unemployment, as economists expect, but also substantial increases in violent crime and domestic abuse, divorce, infant mortality and low-weight births, and sometimes—as in the case of Russia—dramatic declines in life expectancy. Austerity can also induce social isolation and loss of social respect, loss of autonomy, deep shame and despair that result in dramatic increases in suicide, and erosion of political efficacy. Austerity can force vulnerable families to remove their children from school to help support the family. Those children, already disadvantaged, lose the opportunity to develop their skills, capacities, and talents; they face a lifelong reduction in what economists call their "human capital." That loss can carry forward deep into their lives, restricting them to lower-skilled occupations with lower wages than they could have otherwise secured. Inequality bears on the ability of individuals to weather the storm of austerity, while austerity policy in turn deepens inequalities in income and wealth, health, and other measures of well-being. The consequent inequalities are often transmitted from one generation to the next. These kinds of harms are not restricted to periods of austerity, but austerity substantially amplifies the risk that all these harms will manifest, with profound impacts on those suffering them.

What can we learn from the case of austerity about the nature of harm that people suffer as a consequence of economic interventions? Most immediately, what are the dimensions of harm? Is the concept obvious, such that we know it when we see it?

*

The concept of harm is exceedingly complex. Harm is internally heterogeneous. Harm manifests as damage to physical and mental faculties, psychological or emotional suffering, impairment in the pursuit of one's life plans, social isolation, stigmatization, loss of a valued way of life or political efficacy, and other forms. Distinct harms often occur in clusters rather than individually. Moreover, the way a particular harm occurs, such as a physical injury, affects its harmfulness. Complicating matters further, an event that is harmful to some people may not be harmful to others. For all these reasons, the concept of harm is contested. On questions pertaining to the nature, presence, and depth of harm, people often disagree. And on top of all that, some individuals whom observers view as harmed may not see themselves as harmed, while others might claim to be badly harmed when observers see little grounds for accepting that they have been harmed at all.

These are just a few of the issues that arise when we begin to explore the nature, presence, and depth of harm. The upshot is that the question "What does it mean to be harmed?" yields multiple answers that conflict in vital respects.

The complex and contested nature of harm might seem to present insuperable obstacles to ethical economic practice. For that reason economists might feel justified in working with a simplistic account of harm that allows them to get on with their work, but this view is wrongheaded. Concepts like rights, democracy, security, equality, justice, and sustainability, too, are complex and contested. Yet all these concepts nonetheless serve as standards for evaluating social arrangements, even as their advocates dispute their meanings and implications.

A Harm Taxonomy

Harm takes many forms. The taxonomy in table 3.1 maps some of those forms. Some of the listed harms are obvious; others are subtler. For simplicity the taxonomy groups harms to human beings into seven broad categories. The categories and the placements of elements are based on judgments of fit-for-purpose. Some of the harms listed here span categories; some appear in various specifications in multiple categories. The taxonomy should be taken as usefully imprecise in the sense that it corrals diverse harms into a manageable

TABLE 3.1. A taxonomy of harmed and harmful conditions

Physical	• Pain • Injury or dismemberment • Loss/diminution of physical or mental capacities • Death • Degradation of physical environment
Psychological	• Emotional or psychological suffering; depression • Becoming fearful, insecure, or anxious • Becoming ashamed • Loss of hope • Erosion of self-respect • Loss of capacity for creativity, playfulness, inventiveness, love, or fraternal feelings
Economic	• Loss of income, wealth, or welfare/utility • Loss of access to valued goods • Loss of genuine choice over valued goods • Loss of economic security • Loss of economic opportunities (e.g., to do, be, or become) • Loss of economic capacities (e.g., to earn a living) • Loss of control over one's economic activities • Alienation from one's labor, output, or nature • Subjection to exploitation, discrimination, or deprivation
Political	• Disenfranchisement • Loss of political efficacy • Subjugation
Social	• Loss of community • Loss of one's place in community (status, influence, or role as contributor) • Loss of respect, recognition, or honor • Loss of fraternity or meaningful connections with others • Erosion of social capital
Moral	• Erosion, inversion, and/or collapse of important ethical or spiritual values, systems, virtues, sensibilities, and norms
Autonomy	• Adaptive preference formation • Impairment in the pursuit of one's life plans • Treatment as means and not also as an end • Destruction of a valued way of life • Constriction of one's capabilities or feasibility set • Exacerbation of personal or systemic threats, risk, or instability • Assault on negative or positive rights/freedoms (coercion) • Denial of opportunity to participate in vitally important social, economic, or cultural processes

The taxonomy includes both obvious harms and others that are subtler and contested. Welfare and utility are meaningful within standard (neoclassical) economic theory but not within Marxian theory, while alienation has meaning within Marxian but not within neoclassical theory. This and subsequent chapters explore many of the harms listed here.

set of categories. It is also incomplete. Not least, it is anthropocentric, focusing exclusively on harms to human beings and taking account of other harms only to the degree that they affect humans.

PHYSICAL HARM

When we think about harm, damage to physical well-being comes most readily to mind. The category of physical harm comprises injury, dismemberment, the loss or diminution of physical or mental capacities, and death. Physical harm can also take the form of pain. When intensely felt or chronically endured, the experience of pain can be disabling. The degradation of the physical environment might also usefully be categorized as physical harm to humans, especially today when climate change is inducing diverse hazards, owing to the myriad and complex interactions between human well-being and the attributes of the physical world humans inhabit.

PSYCHOLOGICAL HARM

Psychological damage or emotional suffering can be as debilitating as physical harm. An individual in a state of psychological or emotional turmoil may find it difficult to pursue her life plans, earn a livelihood, or even manage the basics of daily existence. Severe depression can be more crippling than severe physical damage, not just preventing an individual from living her life but sometimes leading her to end it. The concept "deaths of despair" (Case and Deaton 2020) focuses attention on the depth of harm from psychological suffering.

Psychological harm can manifest in many other conditions. A person is harmed when she is forced to live in a condition of fear, insecurity, or anxiousness. She is harmed when she is made to feel ashamed—when she indicts herself inappropriately for responsibility for failures or deficiencies—or when she suffers a loss of hope or an erosion of self-respect. In racially divided societies, for instance, the victims of racism may internalize explicit and implicit racial biases. A person suffers harm when she is deprived of or loses certain capacities that we associate with a good human life, such as the capacity and opportunities for creativity, love, or fraternal feelings toward others (Nussbaum 1992).

ECONOMIC HARM

Economic harm also manifests in diverse forms. The loss of income and wealth are typically recognized as central economic harms. But so is the loss of access to highly valued goods, like health care, and the lack of genuine choice over those goods, which may be tied to access to income and wealth. An erosion in economic security, when a person's economic fortunes are unstable and undependable, or when she is forced to scramble from one job to the next in search of subsistence, can be particularly harmful since some degree of economic stability is a critical precondition for life planning and many other aspects of well-being. Being restricted to low-income, part-time jobs may require a person to work several jobs each week or even each day. Overwork impairs family life and can induce social isolation. People working long hours don't enjoy opportunities to participate in important social gatherings or to engage in political affairs. The loss of economic opportunities and capacities to do, be, or become can lock economic actors into modes of economic existence that represent less well-being, agency, security, opportunity, and freedom than might otherwise be available. The same is true, of course, of a person's loss of control over her economic activity, such as when there are no opportunities for employment that build on one's skills and training. The loss of economic autonomy can in turn undermine autonomy in other, noneconomic spheres of life. A related form of economic harm involves alienation, wherein a worker enjoys only a remote or tenuous connection to her work, her output, or the institutions she serves. Alienation can be associated with exploitation, defined as being taken advantage of or manipulated into situations or behaviors that are contrary to one's interests owing to various forms of inequality. Exploitation also occurs when a person is deprived of the output of her labors. A person can also suffer economic discrimination and various forms of deprivation.

POLITICAL HARM

The taxonomy oversimplifies the category of political harm substantially. Here in particular the taxonomy should be taken as merely suggestive. Political harm involves the complicated concept of power—its forms, exercise, distribution, and effects. At a bare minimum, political agency is eroded when people are marginalized in decision making that significantly affects their lives. Disenfranchisement can take the form of capture of governance structures and procedures by some groups at the expense of others, explicit voter suppression by in-groups, and informal arrangements that exclude groups from effective participation. The concept of subjugation captures central features of political harm, such as the explicit domination of individuals or groups by others and the implicit domination that results from social structures and practices. The loss of political efficacy is harmful in and of itself and can bring about a wide range of other kinds of harm. Moreover, other forms of harm can generate political harm. For instance, the loss of economic capacities that occurs as a consequence of prolonged unemployment may undermine political efficacy by inducing social exclusion of and lack of respect for the unemployed.

SOCIAL HARM

Since economic and political relations are subcategories of social relations, there is necessarily extensive overlap between the three categories in the taxonomy. But here we can add harms that affect relations among individuals constituting society. Social harm occurs when a community is undermined or destroyed. This is not to say that all features of communities are desirable, or that people don't suffer, too, by virtue of occupying disadvantaged positions in an ongoing community. It is to say that humans are inherently social creatures. Being torn from a community, or having one's community shattered by disruptive events, can be deeply harmful. An individual or group can suffer the loss of a meaningful position in a community, and thereby suffer a loss of status, influence, and role as contributing member of society. Individuals can experience the loss of social respect, recognition, or honor owing to events that bear on them individually, or that impact the community more broadly (Linklater 2011). Deterioration in social standing can be associated with the loss of meaningful connections with others (Nussbaum 1992; Marglin 2008). Finally, a community or groups within it may suffer the erosion of social capital, the networks that facilitate economic coordination, such as when the bases for trust are undermined.

MORAL HARM

Individuals can experience moral harm in many ways. Important ethical or spiritual values and sensibilities can be undermined by developments within society, such as new social movements advocating alternative moral frameworks. Moral values typically evolve gradually, and in such cases the effect may be disturbing for those who hold to the displaced values, but not traumatic. On the other hand, moral values can suddenly be inverted or collapse abruptly, owing to external shocks. Think of the effects of colonization, military occupation, or globalization that undermines indigenous social norms and value-laden practices. In such situations individuals who have constructed identities based on those values may be bereft of a moral compass or moral sense of self. Moral beliefs should evolve, of course, since established moralities can prevent human flourishing, especially among those devalued by dominant moral systems. Widely shared moralities sustained slavery and racial segregation for centuries, denying recognition as equals to members of oppressed groups within society. But when moral transformation is abrupt owing to exogenous shocks, the harm can be deep and enduring. The cause and speed of transition can be just as important as the trajectory of change for the community experiencing the transformation (Polanyi 1944).

AUTONOMY

Autonomy is a particularly complex and contested idea, but it can be defined simply as genuine freedom to live a life that one values rather than living a life imposed by coercion, deprivation, insecurity, psychological impairment, or other factors. Assaults on autonomy therefore entail undue or unjust impairment in the pursuit of one's life plans (Hausman and McPherson 2006). Some theorists discuss the idea in terms of the constriction of individuals' positive freedoms or capabilities (Sen 1992). Sometimes people are used by others in ways that deprive them of their chance to follow their own life plans; they are treated as means and not also as ends (Kant [1785] 1993). Autonomy is also undermined by the destruction of community and a valued way of life (Marglin 2008); the exacerbation of personal or systematic threats, risk, or instability; assaults on negative freedoms, defined as freedom from physical coercion by others, including the state (Nozick 1974; Friedman 1962; Hayek [1944] 2007), and the denial of opportunities to participate in vitally important social, economic, political, or cultural processes.

Complications and Clarifications

The taxonomy raises as many questions as it answers, some of which will be explored in subsequent chapters.

ARE THESE "ECONOMIC" HARMS?

Here we are interested in the kinds of harm that result from economic events and from economists' practice. Many of the harms listed in the taxonomy are not typically understood to be economic in this sense and are thought to be only tangentially related to economic events. But all of the harms in the taxonomy can be induced, eliminated, or ameliorated by policies about which economists have a lot to say. Consider industrial safety regulations, health care policy and public-health measures, liberalization or regulation of markets, privatization, environmental and resource use policies, taxation and subsidy policies, regulation of trade union and worker rights (including equal opportunity measures), education, incarceration and criminalization policies, procedures for enlisting individuals to fight a nation's wars, monetary and other macroeconomic policies, and the myriad other policy interventions on which economists pronounce and, sometimes, exert significant influence. Taken together, these policies shape what I call an economy's "harm profile," which comprises the harms that those inhabiting an economy face as they pursue their lives (see chap. 10).

MISALIGNMENT OF OBJECTIVE AND SUBJECTIVE HARMS

Harm comprises objective and subjective components. The two may not always align in the ways we might expect. Individuals can suffer a profound loss of autonomy without any awareness of the harm. The paradigmatic case involves deception. A deceiver conveys false information about the world to induce the deceived to act in accordance with the desires of the deceiver (Bok 1999). If the deception is successful, the deceived lose autonomy yet do not recognize the harm, no matter how profound it may be. They are in fact harmed doubly—deprived of both autonomy and the opportunity to recognize and resist the assault on their autonomy (DeMartino 2021).

HARMING AND HARM

The taxonomy is intended to catalog harms as outcomes. It is not a list of the actions, processes, mechanisms, or other factors that generate harm. Often in contexts in which we are inclined to examine harm, we are also apt to want to understand the causes or inducements of the harm—the processes of *harming*. Harming, too, can take multiple forms and would require a taxonomy of its own. For example, public shaming and social exclusion of people experiencing homelessness in wealthy societies might bring about all at once many of the harms that appear in the taxonomy (Desmond 2019). Moreover, how a harm arises matters. The loss of employment owing to a natural disaster may be experienced as less psychically damaging than unemployment brought on by termination for cause or by a corporate strategy to increase profit. The point is fundamental: *how a harm arises alters the nature of the harm itself* and even affects whether the condition should be recognized as harmful at all.

These simple examples convey the idea that the complexity of harm is amplified by the diversity of ways that individuals, institutions, and structures induce harm. Taking a harm-centric approach to economic practice requires paying attention to the ways that economists induce harm and to economists' judgments about the ethical status of distinct harm-generating mechanisms in the economy. Important distinctions concerning harming have been explored carefully in moral and political philosophy and law and in some bodies of professional ethics. Many of the distinctions have largely been overlooked in economics. One of paramount importance is the distinction between *harming* and *not benefiting* (see chaps. 7–9).

CASCADING AND COMPOUNDING HARM

Some harms *cascade*, inducing and amplifying other kinds of harm. This is particularly true of economic and econogenic harms. For instance, austerity induces unemployment. The harm from unemployment can be theorized strictly as loss of income. But that view is deficient, as Amartya Sen's catalog of the grave harms of unemployment, provided as the epigraph to this chapter, demonstrates. It is not difficult to trace other linkages from unemployment to most other harms listed in the taxonomy. What appears in the first instance as a simple loss of income, then, can cascade into a wide range of other economic and noneconomic harms that undermine individuals' quality of life.

Some harms diminish over time, like ripples on a pond. Physical wounds often heal; individuals often adapt to changed circumstances in ways that overcome harm. But many harms instead *compound*, intensifying over time like an avalanche that grows as it moves down a mountain. Policies like austerity induce compounding harms. When children are removed from school to reduce family expenditures and generate income they can suffer permanent loss of income that exceeds austerity's harms to their parents. Harms that are transmitted across generations, such as harms from racial discrimination, can compound over decades and even centuries (Darity and Mullen 2020).

The risk of cascading and compounding harms bears on economists' responsibilities. While many harms are not preventable, the second-order effects of particular harms might be manageable. Policies that create new productive opportunities for displaced workers, for instance, can dampen the knock-on effects of unemployment. And if that is the case, then economists have an opportunity to promote social betterment by designing strategies that interrupt the circuits by which one localized harm sets off a deleterious cycle of cascading and compounding harms.

RECOGNITION OF HARM AND HARMING

Hidden harms of which an individual is unaware, such as autonomy harms stemming from deception, complicate judgments about the incidence and extent of harm. Harm that goes on behind our backs raises the thorny question of who should be authorized to ascertain whether, when, how, and how badly someone has been harmed. Should an individual herself be uniquely authorized to reach judgments about whether she's been harmed? Should we look to the judgment of those closest to her, who might be able to see what she herself cannot? Or does the complexity of harm, including the disjuncture between its objective and subjective components, warrant the transfer of responsibility for reaching harm judgments to detached "harm experts"?

The incidence of harm sometimes follows immediately on the heels of a harming event. Such is the case with the inducement of serious pain, injury, and dismemberment, and many other harms listed in the taxonomy. But harm can also be deferred, emerging only long after the harming event. Deferred effects, such as the appearance of cancer long after exposure to a carcinogen, can confound linking cause to effect. As difficult as it can be to trace cause to effect in cases of cancer, the problem is more acute in economics. In the social world, assessment of the cause-effect connection is confounded by the presence of innumerable intervening events that contribute to outcomes.

Harm recognition comes up against other difficult analytical problems. One is this: what is harmful to one person may prove to be benign or even ultimately beneficial to another. Individuals vary in innumerable characteristics, including their values, membership in privileged and disadvantaged groups, age, physical attributes, intellectual abilities, educational attainment, familial obligations, degree of resilience and initiative, integration into the community, and social networks. The differences among individuals bear directly on how events affect them. For instance, unemployment may severely damage many people who lack the attributes or opportunities to respond productively to the change in circumstances. But it may at the same time provide the impetus for others to attain new skills, start their own businesses, relocate to vibrant regions, or otherwise change their lives for the better. Divergent effects complicate the matter of assessing the occurrence and causes of harm, the causal significance of any harm-inducing event, the severity of the consequent harm, and the responsibility for the harm suffered (and for harm avoidance and amelioration).

The normative nature of harm implies that any taxonomy of harm is subject to critique on grounds that it includes outcomes that are not in fact harmful, omits outcomes that should appear, and misallocates the harms across the taxonomy's categories. Many non-neoclassical economists reject the neoclassical concept of welfare and so do not recognize a diminution in welfare so defined as harmful (see chaps. 7–8). For their part, neoclassical economists would reject the inclusion of the concept of economic exploitation in the taxonomy. Although the concept plays a central role in radical and especially Marxian political economy, it does not appear in neoclassical thought.

Contending accounts of harm yield deep disagreements about economic arrangements. Those grounded in the neoclassical tradition, for instance, posit a view of the rational human actor who seeks to satisfy preferences, *homo economicus*. In this account, work is theorized as an unpleasant experience that rational individuals endure to secure income to permit consumption of the goods they desire. The content of the work, the governance structure of the workplace, control over the work, and workplace relationships have no effect on the individuals who operate within them. What happens at work stays at work. In contrast, certain approaches within the Marxian tradition posit an alternative notion of human nature, *homo faber*, emphasizing the human being as maker rather than as consumer (Avineri 1968). In this conception, human laboring is an essential activity in which individuals work on their environment in accordance with preconceived plans, and in changing that environment they alter their own nature. Work is therefore central to human evolution and emancipation. Governance structures that separate workers from control over their own labor stunt the process of human development. Even when workers secure higher incomes through greater productivity, they cannot be adequately compensated for the harm of diminished agency. "We saw . . . that within the capitalist system," Marx ([1867] 1977, 799) wrote,

> all methods for raising the social productiveness of labour are put into effect at the cost of the individual labourer; that all means for the development of production undergo a dialectical inversion so that they become means of domination and exploitation of the producers; they distort the worker into a fragment of a man, they degrade him to the level of an appendage of a machine, they destroy the actual content of his labour by turning it into a torment.

The point is not that Marx was right about the centrality of work to human development and neoclassicals wrong, or vice versa. The point is that harm assessment requires attention to complex, contested ideas about human existence. But by whom? To date the economics profession has presented itself as uniquely warranted in defining and measuring harm. Given the complexity and contested nature of harm, might not those who face the risks of economic harm rightly claim to have much greater say in the matter?

Greek Austerity

Austerity generates most if not all of the harms included in the harm taxonomy. Austerity is an economic policy designed to treat an economic malady, and its first-order harms are indeed economic. For instance, austerity induces widespread unemployment and a reduction in wages of public employees and pensions, which entail a loss of income. Under normal circumstances some or even all lost income might be offset through social welfare payments. But under austerity, the social safety net is slashed to help close the budget deficit at precisely the moment it is most needed. Those harms affect in particular those already most vulnerable. But as we noted above, economic harm is just the beginning of the story. Unemployment and reduced income in turn generate other types of serious harms across the full range of the harm taxonomy, regardless of the presence or absence of social welfare support.

Greece received bailouts from the Troika in 2010 on condition that it undertake drastic fiscal reform. It was required to reduce public sector pay by 20% and pensions by 10% while increasing taxes and imposing user fees for public services, including co-payments for medical treatments and pharmaceuticals (Blyth 2013). Between 2009 and 2014 Greece reduced public expenditures by 36% (Karanikolos and Kentikelenis 2016). The Troika confidently predicted that the shock, though sharp, would be short, and that the Greek economy would return to growth by 2012. Instead the economy contracted sharply and then stagnated. In May 2008 the unemployment rate was at 7%; by the end of 2011 it had reached 21%. By 2016 Greek GDP had decreased by 29% relative to its 2008 level, with unemployment stuck at 26.5% (Karanikolos and Kentikelenis 2016; Cavero and Cortés 2013). Unemployment for youth seeking their first posteducation jobs rose from 19% in 2008 to 40% by May 2011. Exacerbating the crisis, Greece was forced to negotiate successive bailouts that imposed further cuts in public expenditures and increases in tax and fee revenues.

Austerity destroyed economic security for many Greek families. By 2011 Greece had the highest rates in the EU of people at risk of poverty and social exclusion. By 2012, more than one-third of Greeks fell below the poverty line (Cavero and Cortés 2013).

The knock-on effects of the economic crisis and the ensuing austerity measures were diverse and severe. Estimates put the increase in homelessness between 2009 and 2011 at 25% (Cavero and Cortés 2013; Stuckler and Basu

2013). Homelessness typically induces a broad range of harms to health, educational attainment, family stability, and autonomy that persist across generations. Prior to the crisis Greece had the lowest suicide rate in the EU. Between 2007 and 2011 suicides in Greece increased by 45% (Economou et al. 2015); by 2012, suicides had doubled. The Greek homicide rate doubled in just one year, from 2010 to 2011 (Stuckler and Basu 2013). The health impacts of the crisis were particularly severe and shed some light on the interconnections between economic and noneconomic harms. In Greece access to public health care is often tied to employment. The austerity-driven rise in unemployment undermined the provision of health care. Making matters worse, austerity policy reduced expenditures on public-health measures, such as HIV prevention, and increased user fees and co-payments for pharmaceuticals, putting them out of reach of many Greeks, especially undocumented immigrants. The effects were pronounced. Between 2008 and 2011 Greece experienced a 40% rise in infant mortality and a 47% increase in unmet health care needs (with 62% of undocumented immigrants experiencing unmet needs). Cuts to HIV prevention programs resulted in rapid increases in HIV rates among intravenous drug users, who also faced a doubling in the rate of tuberculosis. Surveys revealed substantial increases in self-reported untreated physical and mental health problems and deaths tied to austerity. A particularly pernicious effect of austerity was the extent to which it exacerbated inequality in access to health care and other government services, as well as educational and economic opportunities (Karanikolos and Kentikelenis 2016).

The chief implication is clear. Economic policies can and do induce a very wide range of deep, lasting harms that reach far into the future. The first-order damage is economic, which can be devastating. Subsequent economic improvement often comes too late to offset the costs, and misses those who need its benefits. But the effects of economic policy are not just or even primarily economic. Tracing through the cascading effects we find that economic policy also induces damage to physical and mental health, as well as political, social, moral, and autonomy harms. That obvious fact, as we'll see, undermines the standard way that economists make sense of, account for, and manage the harms their practice induces.

Conclusion

Appreciation of harm's complexity should be central to economic policy assessment. This complexity represents a difficult challenge to economists whose work promises to promote social betterment but also risks harming. It would seem that the concept of harm must be rendered tractable in some way or other, so that economists risking harm can nevertheless reach harm judgments while designing and assessing policy. The appeal of the predominant approach to harm in economics stems from its apparent tractability (see chaps. 7–8). But this tractability is achieved through conceptual strategies that grossly oversimplify and dismiss harm. Doing better requires reaching beyond standard economics to find better accounts of harm grounded in interests and capabilities that avoid both mistakes.

First, though, we need to explore the sources of econogenic harm. *Why do economists necessarily cause harm as they aspire to do good?* What is it about the impacts of economic interventions on the one hand and the nature of economic expertise on the other that induce harms alongside benefits?

PART II

The Origins of Econogenic Harm

4

The Unevenness of Econogenic Impact

> The concentrated adverse effects of trade on adult local labor markets spill over into worse educational outcomes for children in affected families, increased crime rates and worse health outcomes in affected communities, and lower provision of local public goods. While there are few studies of the effectiveness of the social safety net and other policies aimed at mitigating such adverse effects, the existing evidence is not encouraging.
>
> —NINA PAVCNIK (2017, 4)

The Downside of Trade

One of the most cherished beliefs in economics over the past two centuries is that trade liberalization generates enormous benefits. When two countries open their borders to trade, economists claim, both countries enjoy rising standards of living. The intuition is simple. Under "autarky," where countries are entirely self-sufficient, each country must allocate some resources to industries for which it is not well suited, where efficiency is low. Coffee trees could perhaps be grown in Sweden, but its climate does not predispose it to be an efficient coffee producer. Under free trade each country can specialize in the industries for which it is best suited given its resources, technology, and preferences—where it has what economists call a "comparative advantage." It can then trade with other countries to secure other goods for which it does not have a comparative advantage. Sweden can exchange machinery for coffee from Ethiopia, which is far better suited to produce coffee. As a result, the allocation of resources across both countries improves, total output rises, and both countries experience rising consumption. On the basis of this logic, generations of economists have preached free trade.

But economists know there is a downside. Even if trade liberalization increases total consumption, there will also be many people in each country who suffer losses. The standard account relies on the Stolper-Samuelson theorem, which finds that those who supply the relatively scarce "factor of production," such as labor or land, will face diminished rewards owing to foreign competition. In advanced economies, for instance, Stolper-Samuelson predicts that relatively low-skilled workers will face falling compensation because they are thought to be scarce relative to skilled labor in comparison with their numbers in low-income countries. The gains from trade in advanced economies accrue instead to skilled workers. This account predicts the opposite effects in low-income countries where unskilled labor is the relatively abundant factor of production. In those countries, unskilled workers should benefit, while skilled workers should see their compensation fall. An implication is that trade liberalization is expected to exacerbate income inequality in advanced economies but reduce inequality in the Global South.

New evidence contradicts these predictions. From the latter decades of the twentieth century to the present, opening economies to trade appears to exacerbate inequality *everywhere* by increasing wage inequality between skilled and unskilled workers. The new evidence has pushed trade economists to search for new theoretical models of the distributional effects of trade. A new account, sometimes referred to as the "new-new" trade theory, claims that trade-induced competition within an industry will have differential effects across firms in the industry. The most technologically advanced firms will thrive, while firms with outdated technology will contract and even collapse. And since technologically advanced firms typically employ more skilled labor, while technological laggards employ more unskilled labor, intensified competition from trade will benefit skilled workers and harm unskilled workers everywhere. In short, trade economists now recognize that trade liberalization tends to induce an increasing skilled-unskilled wage gap in both high- and low-income economies (Goldberg and Pavcnik 2007).

Though the new-new trade theory models imply different causal mechanisms and predict different outcomes than the old models, they nonetheless carry forward the very same insight: trade liberalization has uneven effects. Trade benefits some groups while threatening others with severe harm.[11]

In light of the new evidence that trade promotes wage inequality everywhere, noneconomists might expect trade economists today to be wary of trade liberalization. In fact, some leading economists are more circumspect about trade's benefits than they were even just a decade ago. But by and large trade economists continue to advocate further trade liberalization. The allure of a globally integrated economic system in which productive resources are allocated efficiently, and in which world production rises, remains strong in the profession even as it acknowledges that the free-trade utopia will induce widespread damage for many whose lives are already precarious.

*

Causes of Unevenness of Econogenic Impact

Any profession whose practice radiates out across society, altering the life circumstances of large numbers of people, faces the prospect of uneven impact. Even when an intervention goes just as planned, it may generate harms for particular groups. Economics is no exception to the rule. Economic practice that benefits some members of society often induces harms for others. Economists have wrestled with this problem for over a century. As John Hicks (1939, 706) put it, "Under private enterprise, any ordinary change in economic policy involves a change in the price-system, and any change in prices benefits those on one side of the market, and damages those on the other." Here we explore why unevenness of policy impact is the rule in economics.

SOCIAL DIVISION AND UNEVEN IMPACT

In very simple economies one might reasonably hypothesize that many economic interventions generate uniform impact. Consider a relatively homogeneous hunter-gatherer society in which the produce of the hunt and other resources are centralized and distributed according to some socially sanctioned criteria, such as household need. The discovery of water purification practices might reduce everyone's chance of contracting waterborne diseases. Similarly, a new technology that improves hunting efficiency, such as the displacement of spears by bows and arrows, might increase food consumption or time for nonhunting pursuits, or both. Even here, however, there are reasons to be sensitive to the possibilities for uneven impact. In the event of any division of labor in the economy there is the possibility for differential impact of technological change across community members. There could very well be a shift in relative labor burdens as those responsible for processing carcasses from the hunt might find that the labor effort required to keep pace with improved hunting efficiency increased, perhaps substantially. If the division of labor is gendered then the new hunting technology might yield increasing unevenness in labor burdens between men and women.

In complex economies, public-policy interventions and private-sector innovations are apt to induce disparate effects across society's members. This is true whether the economy features market mediation or extensive state direction of economic affairs. To explore this, presume for now counterfactually that economists have adequate knowledge of the impacts of economic interventions and the preferences and values of those who populate the economy. Let's also presume that economists enjoy control over policy. Even under these ideal conditions there are reasons to worry about differential impacts.

One cause of uneven policy effects is that people occupy distinct niches in the economy. For instance, they are distributed across the division of labor and have distinct purchasing patterns. Consider a potential reduction in the US tariff on sugar. The reduction would lower the market price of sugar, benefiting consumers, US producers of goods that require sugar as an input, and foreign sugar producers. But the reduction would harm domestic sugar producers. Alternatively, a decision by a local or national government to raise the minimum wage would benefit low-waged workers, who would experience rising wages, while harming those who would lose their jobs as employers tried to cut costs. A recent US Congressional Budget Office study of a proposed increase in the federal minimum wage illustrates unevenness: "In an average week in 2025, the $15 option would boost the wages of 17 million workers who would otherwise earn less than $15 per hour. . . . But 1.3 million other workers would become jobless. . . . The number of people with annual income below the poverty threshold in 2025 would fall by 1.3 million" (Congressional Budget Office 2019, 2).

A second cause of uneven policy effects is inequality in wealth, income, rights, privileges, and substantive opportunities. Capital gains taxes are taxes on increases in the value of assets, like stocks and bonds. In the US, capital gains taxes have been reduced several times over the past forty years. Today they are lower than the rate most people pay on their wage earnings. Who benefits? Today the wealthiest 1% of American households own 40% of US assets, while the bottom 50% own just 1% (Bricker et al. 2020). And so capital gains tax cuts generate enormous increases in post-tax income for the very wealthy but yield no appreciable benefits for the majority of US citizens. As for the harms, capital gains tax cuts reduce government revenues, placing pressure on government to reduce spending on programs on which the precarious are most dependent. Some gain, some lose—that's the norm in economics, and too often those who lose are those already worst-off.

THE CASE OF FREE TRADE

This discussion helps us to understand why trade economists continue to advocate trade liberalization despite its adverse effects. Economists recognize that most economic policies, even those that are taken to be widely beneficial, have uneven effects. It is in the nature of economic policy to generate losers as well as winners. To refrain from advocating any policy on these grounds would rule out most economic initiatives that economists believe promote social betterment. Moreover, trade economists have historically expected that in market economies the damaging effects of trade liberalization to any particular group would be shallow, temporary, and overwhelmed in the long run by the policy's beneficial effects. This belief is central to economists' moral geometry (see chaps. 7–8).

The argument in favor of that view is appealing. Economists have historically thought in terms of national markets. If there is a national market for unskilled labor, say, then the harmful effects of trade will be widely dispersed among those workers but relatively insignificant for each of them. Moreover, economists theorize those displaced by trade in dying industries as "freed up" to pursue better opportunities in robust industries and firms that are benefiting from trade. High wages in information technology (IT) industries will incentivize displaced textile workers to invest in their human capital, for instance, acquiring the skills that are now in increasing demand in IT owing to trade. If need be they will also relocate themselves and their families to be able to participate in the trade-induced economic bonanza in IT. Fortunately, wages in the expanding sectors will be higher than those in the senescent sectors, and soon the displaced workers will be better-off than they were previously. Ultimately, everyone will benefit from trade liberalization. In this account the harms of trade liberalization are nothing more than short-term adjustment costs to a new equilibrium of increased prosperity for all. This reasoning gives economists license to advocate free trade with little concern for those harmed.

That account is now in tatters. Recent research indicates that the harmful effects of trade are much deeper, more concentrated, and longer lasting than economists had assumed. The impact in the US of trade with China in the early twenty-first century, especially following China's accession into the World Trade Organization (WTO) in 2001, is now understood to have been particularly damaging while providing little net benefit to the US economy. The "China shock," during which China increased its share of total world manufacturing exports from 2.3% in 1991 to 18.8% in 2013, induced a loss of about one million manufacturing jobs and a total of about 2.4 million jobs across the US economy (Acemoglu et al. 2016; Autor, Dorn, and Hanson 2013; 2016). In the context of a national labor market of about 150 million workers in the early 2000s, the losses seem trivial. But industries are regionally concentrated. Job losses owing to trade liberalization are therefore also regionally concentrated, and the impact can be devastating for the affected cities. In the regions most affected by Chinese exports, such as the industrial cities of the Midwest, workers faced an average $549 in annual income loss, with the lowest-income workers hardest hit (Autor, Dorn, and Hanson 2016). These workers received on average just $58 in government payments to offset their losses. As averages, those figures do not adequately depict the situation of the worst-off, of course. Moreover, industries that expand under free trade can be thousands of miles away from industries that contract. When trade liberalization hastens the demise of the textile industry in North Carolina and promotes IT industries in California, those who lose their textile jobs are not apt to be recruited by IT firms. Those firms require workers with particular attributes that displaced textile workers rarely possess and find it difficult to acquire. They are hardly in position to compete against new college graduates for the new jobs.

Some displaced workers do in fact relocate to dynamic regions of the economy. But low-income, low-skilled workers are far less mobile, economically, socially, and geographically, than high-skilled workers. Low-income workers typically do not have far-flung social networks and are unlikely to be aware of the particulars of distant labor markets. They are often much more dependent on familial and other informal social support mechanisms that keep them rooted in their home communities. They also typically have industry-specific skill sets, acquired over their careers, that have allowed them to command higher wages in the firms from which they've been displaced than they would in new industries. And those in the middle or later stages of their working lives are also more likely than new college graduates to have family obligations that substantially limit their mobility (Goldberg and Pavcnik 2007).

Trade liberalization can also undermine wages relative to the income of investors. Trade liberalization alters the balance of bargaining power between workers and firms, not least by speeding up the cost-cutting technological change that displaces workers. Trade liberalization of the late twentieth century in particular was also associated with increased efforts of US manufacturing firms to shift production abroad where they could put the same technology to work with cheaper, more compliant workers. The service sector, too, offshored jobs to lower-wage countries. Moving abroad served as a potent weapon to undermine the power of labor unions in the US. In fact, the percentage of US workers represented by unions collapsed between the 1970s and the present. The unions that remain have far less bargaining power today than those of a generation ago, while workers threatening to organize unions face credible threats of factory closure and offshoring of jobs. In the context of the new trade agreements of the 1990s, like the North American Free Trade Agreement (NAFTA), many firms used the threat of relocation abroad to induce US workers to accept lower wages to hold on to their jobs (Bronfenbrenner 2000). When firms relocate abroad to improve their profit rates, US national income may rise, but the increases are monopolized by investors while displaced workers suffer deep losses.[12]

Are economists correct to presume that the damage from trade liberalization is temporary? The evidence is alarming. "Workers whose 1991 industry subsequently became exposed to higher import penetration accumulate substantially lower earnings over the period of 1992 to 2007, compared to their peers with similar demographic characteristics and previous labor-market outcomes" (Autor, Dorn, and Hanson 2016, 34). The displaced workers also face increased job insecurity and more time receiving Social Security Disability Insurance.

Multiple factors lead to a loss of income. Because of their industry-specific skills, low-skilled workers are more apt than high-skilled workers to search for new positions in the same industry from which they've been displaced. They remain tethered to sectors that are already under competitive threat. Low-skilled workers who leave the industry are less competitive in other labor markets. It's instructive that workers who lose their jobs during recessions typically lose three full years of lifetime income potential (Mian and Sufi 2015, 2).

The persistence of trade's damage is not just an American story. The China shock has arguably had greater impacts in middle-income countries than in the US. Research on Mexico finds that China's import penetration into the US following its accession to the WTO damaged Mexico's high- and medium-technology sectors (Gallagher, Moreno-Bird, and Porzecanaski 2008), effectively pushing the country back down the technology ladder. Brazil faced a similar threat (Leahy 2011). Moreover, research in Brazil finds that the concentrated harms from free trade have not just endured but compounded over long periods—at least twenty years (Pavcnik 2017).

Unfortunately, the economic effects of trade liberalization, just like austerity policy, can cascade. Pavcnik (2017, 4) summarizes recent findings in the epigraph to this chapter. She and other trade economists are coming to understand that communities hit by deteriorating economic prospects because of trade suffer a wide range of severe, long-lasting economic and noneconomic harms.

UNEVENNESS AND INEQUALITY

Trade liberalization and many other policies that economists have historically advocated induce inequality in income and wealth. Through the latter half of the twentieth century and until very recently, many economists dismissed the idea that inequality induces harm. Inequality has been widely taken to be the price to be paid for a dynamic, innovative economy from which even the relatively poor are expected to benefit. Economists like Deirdre McCloskey (2016a) argue that in fact it is principally the poor who have benefited from innovation that also generates inequality. The central ethical concern is not income gaps in the rich countries, she argues, but the persistence of absolute poverty in poorer countries. Some economists, like Milton Friedman (1962, 17) have gone further, arguing counterintuitively that inequality promotes democratic governance. Among those economists who have been troubled by inequality, most have placed faith in the Kuznets curve, which demonstrates that as economies develop, inequality initially increases but eventually declines, so that the long-run trajectory is toward more equal societies. Economic dissenters and critics in other disciplines who identified the harms and persistence of inequality have been routinely ignored by a large majority of economists (see Alacevich and Soci 2017).[13]

Over the past several decades, reaching back to the 1970s in the case of the US, inequality within countries has steadily deepened, contradicting economists' predictions about the equalizing effects of economic development. The US now faces extraordinary, unprecedented levels of inequality in income and wealth, with many other advanced and emerging economies also experiencing widening gaps between rich and poor.

Today, inequality is widely understood to generate a very broad range of damaging effects. At the macroeconomic level inequality is associated with rising levels of debt, which in turn makes economies more fragile and prone to financial crises. Inequality can also dampen economic activity. Hamilton et al. (2020) estimate that over the coming decade, for instance, the racial wealth gap across white, Black, and Latinx communities could cost the US economy $1.5 trillion (Hamilton et al. 2020). Inequality also opens the door to predatory lenders, like payday loan companies and pawnshops, that exploit the disadvantaged. Severe inequality undermines democratic governance and civic engagement by disenfranchising the relatively dispossessed while giving outsize influence to the wealthy. Severe inequality undermines the legitimacy of the market economy, which depends on widely shared beliefs that market outcomes are in some important sense fair (Boushey 2019). Inequality is also a driver of homicide and other violent crime, infant mortality, teen pregnancy, child poverty, alcohol and drug abuse and overdose, low educational performance, obesity, pain and poor health, financial insecurity, excessive working hours that undermine family sustainability for low-income groups, destruction of the "cultural fabric" and social cohesion that sustain communities, social isolation, decreased social mobility, and what Case and Deaton (2020) call "deaths of despair" (Pemberton 2015; Wilkinson and Pickett 2010; 2019; see also Alacevich and Soci 2017). Severe inequality is now understood to induce shame, stress, humiliation, degradation, and assaults on cherished identities. Economic and political inequality is also a primary driver of ecological degradation. Inequality allows the privileged to profit from ecologically damaging investments while offloading ecological damage onto others, while the disadvantaged lack the power to protect themselves or the environment (Boyce 2002; 2018).

Inequality harms everyone, not just those who face deprivation (Wilkinson and Pickett 2010). Everyone in unequal societies suffers from the risks of violence—though the risk is certainly not born equally—such that even the well-to-do feel deeply insecure and must take steps to protect themselves from physical and other threats. Everyone suffers from the erosion of fraternity and community institutions. Even the well-off face stress and anxiety driven by the fear of falling economically and losing their privileged positions, and the even greater anxiety associated with trying to ensure that their children are able to hold on to their social status. Children become investment projects from their preschool years right through graduate school. In more equal societies with strong public provision of valued goods, the threat of falling is softened by the fact that the landing spot is closer by. Losing one's job does not mean losing one's health care, for instance. In very unequal societies, like the US, the fall is potentially catastrophic. In an unequal society even the well-off suffer from extensive overwork owing to the enormous pressure to outperform their peers to ensure their economic security and the economic security of their families (Schor 1993). The collection of inequality-induced harms is evidenced in cross-national studies and also in studies that compare US states with different rates of inequality (see Wilkinson and Pickett 2010). With good reason do Wilkinson and Pickett (2019) argue that inequality gets "into our heads and spirits," distorting our sense of self and security and our relationships with others. Deeply unequal societies, they remind us, are "dysfunctional."

The foregoing implies that many economic policies that economists advocate, such as trade liberalization, generate wide, deep, and enduring harms that span the harm taxonomy. Even if the impacts of policy are in the first instance economic, those impacts cascade and compound in ways that touch all dimensions of people's lives. And that finding undermines the economist's claim that the harms of policies like free trade are simply economic, endurable, and brief.

DISPARATE PREFERENCES, VALUES, INTERESTS, AND LIFE GOALS

So far we've implicitly presumed that all individuals want and value the same things—that they have what economists call identical preferences—but that they happen to be differentially situated in complex economies owing to their location in the division of labor and their differential access to assets and opportunities. Even under the simplifying assumption of identical preferences we were able to see why policy typically induces harms alongside intended benefits.

The assumption of identical preferences cannot suffice when assessing harm, however. In diverse societies with complex social and economic arrangements, people vary considerably in their desires, needs, worldviews, values, and life goals. This implies that an economic policy that has the same objective impact on two individuals in identical economic circumstances may affect them differently. The policy might be experienced as beneficial by one and damaging by the other. Policy that promotes rapid economic growth might afford both individuals rising incomes but be opposed vehemently by one who values ecological protection over increased consumption. The example is paradigmatic: we often disagree passionately about policy owing not primarily to our different locations in the economy but to fundamental conflicts in values. The implication is that we cannot be so quick to read off benefits and harms from changes in economic variables. Engaging econogenic harm responsibly requires acknowledging interpersonal disagreements over values.

Conclusion

It might be inferred from the discussion that all economic interventions induce harm to someone. This was Hicks's own view, reflected in the passage cited earlier in this chapter, and it has been widely shared by economists in his day and since. Identifying the harm induced by economic policy and economists' practice was a notable achievement of early twentieth-century economists. It could have opened the door to the creation of a robust field of econogenic zemiology, similar to the study of iatrogenic harm. In fact, it did not. Instead, Hicks and the other new welfare economists were guilty of the "overrecognition" of harm (Shiffrin 2012, 372). Seeing harm everywhere contributed to a situation where economists, eager to advance the science of economic policy making in the face of pervasive harm, came to trivialize econogenic harm. We turn to this matter in part III. But first, we must explore one other set of reasons why well-meaning economists necessarily induce harm: irreparable ignorance.

5

The Specter of Irreparable Ignorance

> You may want to substitute the more familiar scientific words "theory and evidence" for "patterns and stories." Do not do that. . . . The words "theory and evidence" suggest an incessant march toward a level of scientific certitude that cannot be attained in the study of complex, self-organizing human system that we call the economy. The words "patterns and stories" much more accurately convey our level of knowledge, now, and in the future as well. It is literature, not science.
>
> —EDWARD LEAMER (2009, 3)

The Paradox of Knowledge Expansion: New Technologies

New technologies present an epistemic paradox. New technologies represent an expansion in human knowledge—knowledge about how to do things better or to achieve previously unattainable goals. Think of technologies like CRISPR and other gene therapies that are used to alter an organism's characteristics. Or artificial intelligence (AI) that replicates human judgment with the goal of transferring complex human tasks to machines, such as autonomous vehicles. Or facial recognition technology that is facilitating the shift to a cashless economy. Or blockchain technology that enables the construction and exchange of cryptocurrencies. New technologies embody expanded knowledge that promises to extend human capacities with the potential to enhance human well-being. It is generally presumed that the growth of knowledge diminishes the domain of human ignorance. When we *know more*, surely we *don't know less*. Our map of the terrain of knowledge expands, shrinking the domain of ignorance.

Were it only so. In fact, new technologies expand the domain of *salient ignorance*. AI, for instance, raises deep uncertainties about the consequences of transferring human "reasoning" and functions to nonhuman entities. AI also necessarily introduces *normative* uncertainty. When and how should the new technology be used, and when should it not? Science fiction has long speculated about the nature of machines with AI, about how they can help but also threaten society. Today those questions have moved from science fiction to science proper. As science develops the capacity to devise machines with AI, it also necessarily raises new pressing questions for which it cannot provide definitive answers.

The epistemic paradox arises whenever new knowledge is generated. In economics the problem is acute. New breakthroughs in economic knowledge generate new questions that cannot be answered prior to the application of the knowledge to policy interventions. The problem is ineliminable.

Economic Knowledge, Economist Hubris

Economists concern themselves with expanding the frontiers of economic knowledge, extending the map of the known, encircling and invading the remaining terrain of the not-yet-known. The profession presumes the increasing adequacy of economic knowledge over time. As economic knowledge advances, it is thought, the domain of ignorance necessarily shrinks, and the social benefits of economists' practice steadily increase. The economist's view of the potential of economic science and the capacities of the economics profession is abidingly optimistic.

Only infrequently do leading economists take note of the limits to economic expertise. Lionel Robbins's assessment of the state of economics in his day was particularly harsh: "What precision economists can claim at this stage is largely a sham precision. In the present state of knowledge, the man who can claim for economic science much exactitude is a quack" (Robbins 1927, 176). A half century later John Hicks could write, with justification, that "economic knowledge, though not negligible, is so extremely imperfect. There are very few economic facts we know with precision" (Hicks 1980, 1). Other economists have confronted the link between uncertainty and the limits to economic expertise. Frank Knight famously counterposed "risk" to "uncertainty." Risky activity, like betting at the roulette wheel, is characterized by a known probability distribution of outcomes. Under uncertainty, in contrast, there are no probabilities. Knight emphasized that uncertainty, not risk, characterizes much of the social world: "It is a world of change in which we live, and a world of uncertainty" (Knight [1921] 2014, 199). John Maynard Keynes concurred. Speaking of events like "the prospect of a European war . . . the price of copper and the rate of interest twenty years hence, or the obsolescence of a new invention . . .," he wrote, "about these matters there is no scientific basis on which to form any calculable probability whatever. *We simply do not know* . . ." (J. M. Keynes 1937, 213–14; emphasis added).[14]

These insights are inconvenient for a profession that has sought to increase its influence over public affairs since its emergence as a scientific enterprise during the late nineteenth century (DeMartino 2011a). The prevailing worry is that uncertainty would defeat the ability of economists to know the economy (cf. North 1999, 2). In response to Knight and Keynes the profession has repressed uncertainty, claiming that its knowledge is largely adequate to the task of promoting social betterment. Though economists understand that economic knowledge is incomplete, the profession nonetheless presumes steady progress of the science. Deepening expertise has been taken as warrant for increasing authority over public policy. In the pursuit of influence economists are abetted by the epistemic inequality between themselves and laypeople (Hardwig 1994). Laypeople find it difficult to assess what it is economists claim to know, not least owing to excessive formalization and the "mathiness" of economics (Romer 2015). Epistemic inequality has led to substantial deference to economists' judgment by noneconomists. That deference came to an abrupt halt with the election of Donald Trump as US president. President Trump's animus toward economic experts was galling for a profession that had enjoyed wide access to and respect from political leaders for well over a century. President Biden, too, relies on economists far less than previous presidents, owing to his awareness of the profession's repeated policy failures and his impatience with its inability to understand politics (Klein 2021).

Economists' optimism about their science too easily bleeds into hubris. Their arrogance reached extraordinary heights just prior to the financial crisis of 2008. Leading economists celebrated their ability to know the economy and to manage economic events (DeMartino 2011a). It is important to recall in this regard the so-called Great Moderation in macroeconomic affairs that was presumed to have settled in by the 1990s. Speaking in 2007 of the lessons learned over the previous decades, eminent macroeconomist Christina Romer, who would soon be appointed by President Obama as chair of the Council of Economic Advisors, had this to say, just as financial markets were about to fall off a cliff: "We have seen the triumph of sensible ideas and have reaped the rewards in terms of macroeconomic performance. . . . The costly wrong turn in ideas and macropolicy of the 1960s and 1970s has been righted, and the future of stabilization looks bright" (cited in Postrel 2009).[15]

Romer's view was widely shared in the profession. Federal Reserve Chair Ben Bernanke expressed unqualified confidence when speaking about financial trends right up to the onset of the crisis. In May of 2006 Bernanke (2006a) spoke of the virtues of "financial innovation and improved risk management," including "securitization, improved hedging instruments and strategies, more liquid markets, greater risk-based pricing, and the data collection and management systems needed to implement such innovations." He argued that "these developments, on net, have provided significant benefits. . . . Lenders and investors are better able to measure and manage risk; and, because of the dispersion of financial risks to those more willing and able to bear them, *the economy and financial system are more resilient*" (Bernanke 2006a; emphasis added). That June, Bernanke wrote: "Today, retail lending has become more routinized as banks have become increasingly adept at predicting default risk by applying statistical models to data, such as credit scores" (Bernanke 2006b). In response to a question about whether there was need for increased regulation of hedge funds, Bernanke (2006c) told Congress on July 20, 2006, that "the best way to achieve good oversight of hedge funds is through market discipline, through the counterparties, through the investors. . . . At this point I think that the market discipline has shown its capability of keeping hedge funds well disciplined." Two years later, on July 16, 2008, just weeks before the crisis emerged, Bernanke told the US House Financial Services Committee that "the GSEs [government-sponsored enterprises; i.e., Freddie Mac and Fannie Mae] are adequately capitalized. They are in no danger of failing" (Herszenhorn and Weisman 2008). Just two weeks later Warren Buffet issued a warning about the GSEs' fragility, and a month later, on September 7, the US Treasury was forced to purchase up to $100 billion in GSE securities to save the institutions and prevent global financial panic.

The Specter of Irreparable Ignorance

Whatever one's take on the exact drivers of the crisis, it is indisputable that the confidence of leading financial and macroeconomists in the precrisis period was wildly unwarranted. Economists' hubris led investors, lenders, and borrowers at all levels to trust the wisdom of financial markets and to take risks they otherwise might not have been willing to take even as a speculative bubble pushed asset prices to staggering levels. Robert Shiller (2009, 16) puts it bluntly: "This mania was the product not only of a story about people but also a story about how the economy worked. . . . *To a remarkable extent we have got into the current economic and financial crisis because of a wrong economic theory*—an economic theory that itself denied the role of the animal spirits in getting us into manias and panics" (emphasis added). Dani Rodrik (2017, 163) is equally direct: "Those who chalk up the global financial crisis of 2008–2009 to the power of big banks conveniently overlook the legitimizing role played by economists themselves. It was economists and their ideas that made it respectable for policy makers and regulators to believe that what is good for Wall Street is good for Main Street."[16]

The point bears emphasis. The economic crisis was a joint product of two reinforcing bubbles. The economics profession generated an intellectual bubble that celebrated deregulated financial markets. The intellectual bubble validated speculation in financial and housing markets (cf. Johnson 2009).

Rising asset prices in turn generated groupthink in economics. Economists treated as pariahs those economists who warned of looming danger (see Shiller 2008; Baker 2009; DeMartino 2011b; 2013a).

The triumphalist view of economics is now fading. The 2008 crisis shook the confidence of prominent economists, including some of the profession's leading public intellectuals (Krugman 2009a; 2009b; Shiller 2009; Stiglitz 2009). Reflecting the new attitude, Kenneth Rogoff (2018) writes, "As any academic macroeconomist will tell you, the global economy never ceases to be uncertain and unpredictable."[17] Peter Orszag, Robert Rubin, and Joseph Stiglitz (2021, 2) concur: "In our collective experience, fiscal policy should instead be informed by copious amounts of humility, particularly given the role of impossible-to-predict events (including pandemics, wars, and bubbles)."

Today, epistemically self-aware economists are beginning to discern a *specter of irreparable ignorance* haunting economics (DeMartino 2019; DeMartino and Grabel 2020). But epistemic self-awareness faces an uphill battle in economics. It is disturbing to economists to confront the fact that there are tight limits not just to what they know now and what they will know tomorrow, but to what they can in principle ever know. It is even more disturbing to accept that these limits crisscross the terrain of what economists need to know to do much of what they are currently doing. Forecasting, designing institutions and policies, and all other facets of economic social engineering run up very quickly against the currently unknown and the in-principle unknowable.

CATEGORIES OF IRREPARABLE IGNORANCE

The concept of irreparable ignorance requires specification.[18] Irreparable ignorance falls into three categories. The first includes what we don't know now and might someday know, but only after the moment the missing knowledge is needed for decision making. G. L. S. Shackle ([1972] 1992, 86) emphasizes this type of ignorance. "[The] validity of knowledge of general principles is independent of the historical calendar," he writes, "but the question: What is the best action? is wholly dependent on the unique historical situation; and any knowledge of that situation, which is lacking when it is needed, is effectively lacking for ever and is for ever too late."[19]

The second category of irreparable ignorance entails a cruel conundrum. It refers to knowledge that is vital to decision making but that can only be acquired by making the decision. The famished hiker lost in the woods asks, "Are these berries food, or are they poison?" Only the eating, when it is too late to change course, will provide the urgently needed information. In this kind of case, "'waiting for more information' is never an option since information has to be created with experimentation, monitoring, and analysis . . ." (Hallegatte et al. 2012, 12).

The third category encompasses the domain of the in-principle unknowable. This category captures what lies beyond the domain of economic expertise—not just at the rudimentary state of economic expertise yesterday or today, but at any conceivable level of the science as conducted by the smarter and better-trained economists of the future. This is the kind of ignorance that Knight, Keynes, Shackle, and Hayek warned the profession about when they spoke of the opacity of the future. About the future "*we simply do not know*."

The distinction between reparable and irreparable ignorance is crucially important for economic practice. If missing knowledge is discoverable, then it is sensible to allocate resources to discovering it. If, on the other hand, some unknown lies in the domain of irreparable ignorance, then resources put into knowing that unknown are wasted. Even worse, mapping what can't be mapped is dangerous. It deludes the profession and those who rely on its work into thinking it can know what it cannot in fact ever know. It is with good reason that Edward Leamer opens his macroeconomic textbook with the warning provided as the epigraph to this chapter. His plea to economists is to avoid deluding themselves into thinking they can know the unknowable. Irreparable ignorance forces economists and decision makers to act without the knowledge necessary to ensure good outcomes. If ignorance is irreparable, then the problem of expert-induced harm can only be managed; it can't be solved.

IRREPARABLE IGNORANCE IN ECONOMIC POLICY ASSESSMENT

How substantial is the domain of irreparable ignorance? Ecologists Wendell Berry and Wes Jackson emphasize that as concerns natural systems our ignorance is and will forever be vast. Berry (2005, 14) puts it evocatively by referring to the unknown as "mystery." Jackson (2005, 15) teases out the implications: "If we are up against mystery, then knowledge is relatively small" and we will always be "billions of times more ignorant than knowledgeable" about the world we inhabit (Vitek and Jackson 2008, 1).[20] The domain of irreparable ignorance is just as great in economics as in environmental science. Some of the unyielding uncertainty confronting both economists and natural scientists today stems from the tight linkages and complex interactions between natural and social systems. Both sciences founder on the unpredictable behavior of individuals populating the natural and social world.

PREDICTING POLICY EFFECTS

The economics profession has achieved authority in large part owing to its presumed ability to know today the future impacts of proposed policy interventions. But economic predictions are dependable only if several conditions hold. First, the decisions taken by individuals in the economy must outweigh the innumerable other exogenous factors that will influence the policy's effects. When exogenous events, those beyond the reach of economic science, overwhelm individual decision making in determining the effects of policy, predicting policy effects is impossible. And so the *convention* in economics is simply to presume that individual decision making is the key variable determining policy effects, overwhelming the causal force of exogenous factors. Unfortunately, that presumption is false. "It must be conceded," Hicks (1980, 22) argued, "that the abundance of exogenous elements in economics is no cause for congratulations; it is an indication of the modesty of the scientific status, if indeed it is a scientific status, which is all that economics can hope to achieve."

The second condition follows: economists must know how individuals make the decisions that will shape their behavior. If economists don't know that, then they cannot begin to tease out a policy's effects. But economic decision making is typically future oriented. Individuals investing in their skills and in other assets are concerned with their future returns. Individuals' decision making today depends on their expectations of the future. And that leads to the third necessary condition: to predict individuals' decisions, economists must know how individuals form their expectations of the future. But how are economists to know what expectations individuals hold and how those expectations will bear on their future-impacting behaviors? The profession has been obsessed with this question for well over a century, and with good reason. Without a compelling account of expectations and decision making, the project of predicting policy effects collapses.

DOMESTICATING EXPECTATIONS

The standard textbook approach predicts behavior by treating individuals as omniscient decision makers that respond rationally to economic stimuli. Rational economic actors are taken to make those choices that satisfy their self-regarding preferences. The influential nineteenth-century economist Francis Edgeworth (1881) put it best when he urged the profession to conceive of "man as a pleasure machine." Rationality also implies that individuals always choose correctly. To do so would require that they form correct expectations of the future since action based on incorrect predictions will lead to incorrect choices.

These conditions are simply assumed to hold in the standard textbook treatment of economic policy. In textbook models, rational economic actors always adjust their behavior in the ways specified by the economist in response to any policy-induced changes in their environments. If a carbon tax increases the cost of carbon-based fuel, consumers will find the cost-minimizing way to reduce its use. If monetary policy increases the interest rate, rational corporate managers will decrease borrowing and investment while households increase savings. And so it goes for every other conceivable policy proposal. Economists can ascertain in advance what will be the policy's effects since they have prescribed, before the policy is implemented, how economic actors will adjust their behaviors in response to it.

Economists rely on a range of modeling methods to achieve prediction. The simplest is "comparative statics," which attempts to sidestep the issue of expectations altogether. Here the economist takes a static snapshot of a simple hypothetical blackboard economy—*not* the actual economy—prior to a policy's introduction, and then takes another static snapshot of that hypothetical economy after the policy has worked its effects. The approach requires the presumption that the economy can and will in fact jump from one equilibrium to the other, without obstruction. Hypothetical economies can do that or, in fact, anything else the economist needs them to do. Throughout the exercise only prices and quantities are permitted to adjust. As every economics student learns, the economist assumes ceteris paribus, that all else remains constant, as the policy induces its effects on prices and quantities. But there is a fundamental problem here, which disqualifies comparative statics as a legitimate policy assessment tool. There is no *time* in the model and, hence, no consideration of how individuals' expectations affect policy outcomes. The policy-induced adjustment happens, as it were, in between moments in time. By this I mean that comparative static modeling does not specify the trajectory of the economy as it shifts from the pre- to the postpolicy equilibrium. It does not demonstrate the economic dynamics of adjustment. It simply presumes what decision makers need to know: that the policy will in fact have the anticipated effect.

Contemporary economic research features more complex, dynamic models. These, too, face the imperative to constrain individuals' behavior so that economists can derive definitive predictions of policy effects. This leads to desperate theoretical measures that rightly test the patience of noneconomists. An example is the late twentieth-century "new classical" model of "rational expectations." The approach posits that individuals know just which model to use in making their forecasts of the future. This is conveniently assumed to be the very same model that the economist uses to predict policy outcomes. Only on this basis can the approach generate policy predictions.

ECONOMIC TIME-TRAVEL MACHINES

The foregoing discussion leads to a fantastical conclusion. Economists seek to construct *time-travel machines*—economic models that permit them to see tomorrow, today. Good models, it is hoped, can tell us what the effects will be, tomorrow and beyond, of policy initiatives taken today. Building economic time-travel machines requires theoretical gymnastics that constrain agent expectations and behavior, so that individuals always act just as economists need them to (Grabel 2000). The economic agent must be endowed with the mind and tools of the economist—were the economist to be omniscient. The problem, of course, is that *the models presume what we need to know but which is, in fact, largely unknowable: how the actual people populating the actual economy at a particular moment in time will in fact develop their expectations in response to a particular policy innovation*. Economics succeeds in generating determinate predictions only by leaving real human beings, with their cognitive limitations and biases, completely outside the analysis. Leading economists tend to repress this fact. Thomas Sargent (2019), a prominent pioneer of rational expectations modeling, claims that "when we have good theories of other people, what they are likely to do determines what we expect them to do." In fact, much of economics works in precisely the opposite direction. It takes what economists need people to do for the sake of their time travel as determining what economists expect them to do.[21]

The problem with economic time-travel machines is that individuals who populate the economy, just like economists, face irreparable ignorance. They have limited knowledge of the economy at the moment they act. They can't know, for instance, what other individuals will do today and tomorrow and how that will alter the economic landscape. Their knowledge of the world is partial and often tacit (Hayek 1974). If they possess dependable knowledge at all, it is only of their immediate world. But events far afield will affect the outcome of their projects. The high school graduate forgoes college to take a high-paying job in the local industry, unaware of corporate plans to move its production abroad. The baker knows the current tastes of her consumers, but she doesn't know now next month's dieting fad that will discourage them from buying what she has to sell.

If individuals must act in the fleeting present to achieve future goals, then they need to know not just about the current state of the world but about the world as it will be tomorrow. That knowledge, however, is forever deferred. Individuals compensate for this epistemic limitation by making best guesses about what the future will bring. They rely on heuristics, like the presumption that the immediate future will be like the immediate past in relevant respects. Those expectations will bear on what they choose to do today. But in the aggregate, today's decisions shape tomorrow's world. So each individual faces the bewildering task of guessing what *other* individuals expect, how *those* expectations will affect *their* behavior, and how their collective behavior will affect the future (J. M. Keynes 1936, chap. 12). Only with that information can individuals be secure in their decisions today. But that information cannot possibly exist at the time decisions must be taken.

If we accept that individuals in the economy face irreparable ignorance owing to the simple truth that we "cannot have knowledge of what will be," then it becomes difficult to claim to know even probabilistically how they will respond to the complex stimuli they confront (Shackle [1972] 1992, xi; see also Nelson 2004). I have drawn on Shackle extensively here, and with good reason. Shackle recognized that economics is a study of *ideas* about the economy that inform economic activity rather than of brute objective forces that dictate outcomes. "Economics is about thoughts. It is therefore a branch or application of epistemics, the theory of thoughts" (Shackle [1972] 1992, xx). Rodrik (2017, 159, 163) emphasizes the same point today: "Yet without ideas . . . the concept of self-interest is empty and useless. . . . In truth, we don't have 'interests.' We have *ideas* about what our interests are" (cf. Knight [1921] 2014, chap. 7).

There is no escape from the problem. Individuals engage an unknowable future. Their behavior cannot be derived from a restrictive notion of rationality. Individuals are forced to rely on "images of a future state of affairs," "common sense," "intuition," "superstitions," "hunches," the "subconscious," "convictions or opinions" (Knight [1921] 2014, 201, 229–30), "trained instinct" (Marshall [1890] 1920, 337), "speculative hopes and anxieties, the expectations conjured from scarcely recognized suggestions and principles of interpretation" (Shackle [1972] 1992, 112), unacknowledged biases, and the judgments and anxieties of the groups in which they are embedded (Sommers 2011; Bazerman and Tenbrunsel 2011). Knight ([1921] 2014, 202) articulates the idea this way: "We do not perceive the present as it is and in its totality, nor do we infer the future from the present with any high degree of dependability, nor yet do we accurately know the consequences of our own actions." An important implication follows. In planning their strategies, individuals are engaged in the practice of *imagination* rather than rational calculation (Beckert 2016).

None of this implies that reasonable predictions can't ever be made. Behavioral conventions often induce practices that generate dependable results, which in turn sustain and enforce the convention. Once established, the convention to drive on the right-hand side of the road ensures that most drivers make it to their destinations safely. The result is to make the world navigable, secure, dependable. In the social domain, conventions make much of what is regular, regular. When conventions become institutionalized, such as in the law, they direct behavior and, to varying degrees, bring about the outcomes that the behavior was intended to secure. Conventions can convert an unknowable future into a knowable future. In economics, convention secures price stability, upon which economic survival depends. "Stability by convention, by indolence, by letting 'well' alone, by the strong instinct to preserve a frame of sanity, by the need of humanity's self-esteem to pretend to control its affairs, has to serve instead of stability determined by reason and knowledge" (Shackle [1972] 1992, 112).

All is well here—dependable, stable, secure, knowable—until, without warning, it isn't. Ruptures in behavior can suddenly and without warning disrupt the course of events and defeat expectations of the future. The belief that other drivers will stay on the right-hand side of the road is confirmed many, many times during many safe journeys, and then suddenly and without warning, it is shattered by a distracted driver. Knowing the future, then, requires far more than knowledge of existing conventions and institutional arrangements. It also requires a correct specification of the forces that disrupt those institutionalized conventions and behaviors (North 1999). We would need to know in advance when a behavioral convention was about to be shattered. But a successful theory of that sort would necessarily fail because it would change behaviors in the present as actors positioned themselves for the now-known disruptions ahead. The knowledge would not prepare us for the future so much as change it—in unknowable ways.

Common Epistemic Errors

THE LAW OF THE CONSERVATION OF TRUTH AND THE PROBLEM OF UNLEARNING

One can recognize the problem of irreparable ignorance and yet presume a progressive model of economic knowledge on the grounds that imperfect as our knowledge is, it is necessarily improving over time (see figure 5.1). In the progressive view of economic science, although there is no surefire test to judge contradicting economic theories, economists can be sure that today's economic knowledge is far more accurate than the economics of the past. Though the knowledge-generating project in economics is not finished, and

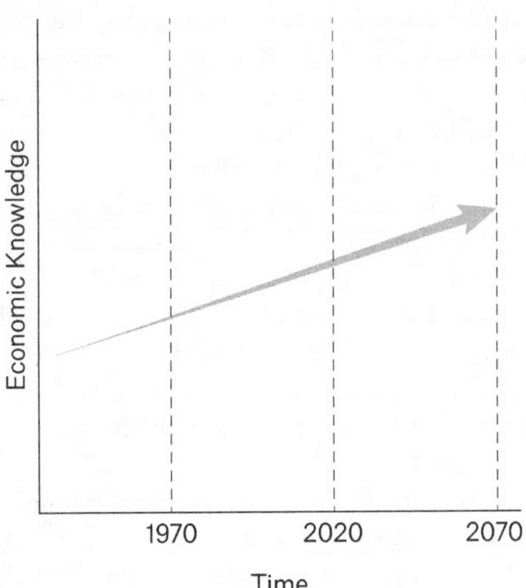

FIGURE 5.1. Knowledge expansion, standard view
In the conventional view, economic knowledge necessarily expands over time.

perhaps though there is no possibility of it being finished, economists at least are closer to dependable knowledge of causal mechanisms and have better access to the state of the world than in the past. We should carry on down this road, the argument goes, pursing the imperfect project of knowledge expansion, since it promises to get us there (or closer to there) better than any alternative path.

Faith in the progression of economic knowledge depends on what we might think of as a "law of the conservation of truth": the belief that we learn and we carry into contemporary economic practice only what is wise and correct in the work of our predecessors, while discarding only their errors. Taking this view, we can be assured that contemporary work is necessarily better than the work of previous eras. Deirdre McCloskey tells a story of what she calls a "Big Deal economist" (a Nobel Prize winner) who boasts that his syllabus includes only articles from the preceding five years. Why go back further, when the new represents an unambiguous improvement over the old?

This view is irresponsible.[22] The development of economics is marked by perpetual *forgetting*. I can't reproduce for myself Adam Smith's training or life experiences; nor can each generation of economists go back and duplicate the training of their professors before going off to contribute new thoughts. In proceeding to generate new knowledge economists do as much unlearning as learning, and as much forgetting as remembering. What economists have forgotten can harm those they purport to serve, especially during crises. In those moments economists must begin anew a process of unforgetting what they needed to remember in advance of the crisis.

But how are economists to know what exactly they need to take from their predecessors, and what they can safely leave behind? What should they take—their substantive claims, their concepts, or just their methods? The unsatisfying but inescapable point is that there is no dependable criterion for selection. Exacerbating the problem, the process of filtering past work is generally conducted implicitly, by what is put on and left off the syllabus, and by offhand comments by professors to their graduate students from which students infer which scholars and ideas do and don't deserve respect.[23] Economists lack dependable selection mechanisms that direct them to choose to remember and to forget just the right things. And so economists fight among themselves in perpetuity over what to carry forward from Adam Smith, say, or from Keynes, without a dependable standard for demonstrating that their selections are right or wrong. These selections are always influenced and sometimes driven by professional norms and conventions, by the sociology of the economics profession, the epistemic status of which is unsecure.

KNOWING MORE, NOT-KNOWING LESS?

The progressive view of economic science depends on further propositions that do not hold up to scrutiny. First, it presumes that because knowledge expands over time, ignorance necessarily recedes (figure 5.2). As we learn more about the world, isn't there less we don't know? Imagine, if you can, perfect knowledge. We can represent that spatially in a rectangle, divided into the domains of knowledge (what we know) and ignorance (what we do not—yet—know). It would seem that learning presses up against the boundary separating the two domains, expanding knowledge and shrinking ignorance. Or consider mapping a terrain. Over time, based on what we learn, we can improve the map intensively, adding contour lines, and extensively, expanding the borders of the known. The progressive view of economic science holds that this is precisely what happens. Our knowledge of the world extends and deepens; our ignorance shrinks. Today we are less ignorant than were our predecessors in 1970, say. And those who follow in 2070 will confront a world in which even less is unknown.

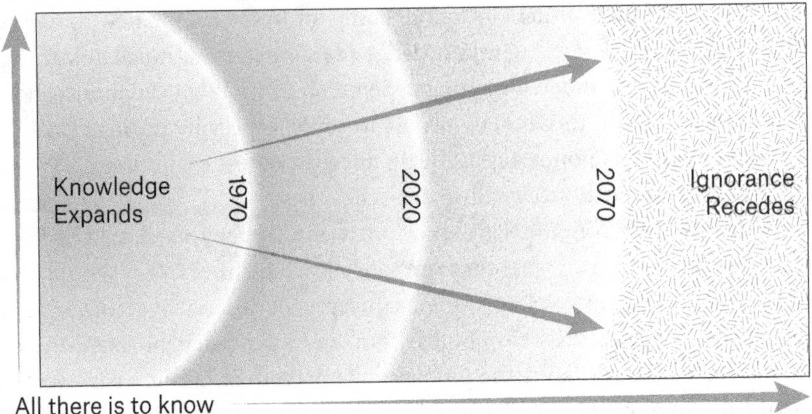

FIGURE 5.2. Knowledge and ignorance, standard view
In the conventional view, ignorance recedes as knowledge expands.

Episteme, Techne, Phronesis

But what if everything there is to know is not a finite quantity that can be represented by an enclosed space, like a rectangle, that can be increasingly filled in with knowledge? What if the terrain of the unknown is infinite? In this case, expanding knowledge doesn't reduce the domain of ignorance. Instead, expanding knowledge makes relevant and even urgent new domains of "unknowledge" that previously did not concern us. We did not need to know the effects of nuclear weapons before scientists developed the knowledge necessary to build them. We might say that nineteenth-century civilization was characterized by ignorance as concerns the effects of nuclear weapons. But that ignorance was irrelevant then and during the preceding millennia. It was made urgently salient by the new knowledge that permitted the construction of the bomb.

One way to grasp the issue is to recognize the distinct forms of human knowledge. "Episteme" refers to abstract, *scientific knowledge*, of the sort conveyed in textbooks, such as the principles that facilitate machine learning and AI. In contrast, "techne" (root of the word *technology*) refers to *how-to knowledge*. This kind of knowledge is often tacit and acquired through practice. Individuals may know how to do all sorts of things, like using AI, that they can't explain in terms of abstract principles. "Phronesis" refers to *practical wisdom*, defined as the capacity for good judgments about how to use the knowledge (episteme and techne) that humans acquire. Knowing when AI should and should not be used, by whom, and for what purposes requires phronesis, not just episteme or techne.

Distinguishing between various kinds of knowledge helps us appreciate the contradiction that new knowledge that expands human capacities also expands our *ignorance concerning things we need to know*. Think again of the advance of knowledge embodied in new technologies like genetic engineering, AI, information technologies, social media, financial trading algorithms, and blockchain technology. Each of these is associated with an expansion of human knowledge and each expands the domain of human capacities. But each brings to the fore new ignorance that was not salient before the arrival of the new knowledge. The invention of autonomous vehicles generates new uncertainties about how they will perform in complex driving conditions, the risk of cyberattack-generated accidents, and the number of serious injuries and fatalities they will both cause and avert (Kalra and Paddock 2016). New medical procedures, like genetic editing using CRISPR technology, raise difficult phronetic questions about the technology's potential use (and abuse), its intended and unintended effects, the nature and efficacy of its regulation, and the possible unintended consequences of any regulatory regime. Just as urgent are new moral questions that were simply not salient until the emergence of the new knowledge, such as when and for what purposes to use the technology. With good reason do Seybert and Katzenstein (2018, 127) argue that in the case of CRISPR "the quest for control has produced additional uncertainty." Once the technology comes into existence, the practical need arises to probe new questions that made no sense and perhaps could not even have been formulated beforehand.

Moral uncertainty is central to the ignorance-generating force of knowledge. A paradigmatic controversy today concerns how safe autonomous vehicles must be before they are introduced to the market. Is it morally sufficient that they reduce overall injuries and fatalities by a small margin, even if they cause some accidents that human drivers might have avoided? Or must they be proven to outperform human drivers by a wide margin before they are approved (Kalra and Groves 2017)? Another debate concerns the ethical algorithms that should ideally be embedded in autonomous vehicles that will guide their operation. In this case, as in so many others, lives are at stake. If a child runs out in front of an autonomous vehicle, should the algorithm cause the vehicle to careen off the road, risking the death of its passengers, when the vehicle calculates this is the only way to avoid hitting the child?[24] Whose lives should be prioritized in such situations: the vehicle's owners—the vehicle is *their property*, after all—or the lives of pedestrians? Should it matter if there are several passengers and just one child? What algorithm should the vehicle employ instantaneously in reaching its "decision" about whose lives take priority, if the vehicle's "brain" acquires the ability to make such distinctions? Answering these questions is emerging as an urgent matter for ethicists, designers of autonomous vehicles, and regulators. Complicating matters, evidence suggests that people disagree on these fundamental questions (Maxmen 2018).

Other confounding questions arise in the context of new technologies. How will the new knowledge be adapted by those using them? Will the consumers of AI hack the software, altering its decision-making algorithms to achieve some purpose or other? Will it be put to malevolent purposes? The people who designed the platforms for social media could not have anticipated the ways in which social media would induce public shaming and bullying of children, inducing anxiety and suicides, or how the technologies would be exploited by Russian hackers to alter the outcome of not just the US national elections in 2016 but the deeper trajectory of US politics for the foreseeable future. Nor did they anticipate the use of the new technologies to undertake "deep fakes" that provide new strategies to cause public confusion and serious harms. Finally, what further technological advances will a new technology enable; under whose control will those advances be made; and what will be the effects of these knock-on innovations?

Decision makers also face the "innovation dilemma" when confronting choices over technologies (Ben-Haim 2019, 108ff). A tried-and-true technology might generate a level of performance that is well understood. A new technology might emerge that offers a potential improvement in performance. Owing to its novelty, however, achieving that level of performance is uncertain. Should the technology be adopted? Uncertainty also arises about the technology's possible misappropriation, secondary and unintended effects, etc. These uncertainties and the decision maker's dilemma are *produced by the new knowledge* embedded in the new technology.

Social Technologies

Now consider another kind of discovery: the discovery of a new kind of policy that is intended to address a pressing social problem. This, too, amounts to a new technology: new how-to knowledge. Consider new neoclassical economic technologies that emerged over the past half century, such as the use of market mechanisms to improve public education or the social welfare system, or to promote ecological sustainability. One example is the use of transferable carbon emissions permits to address climate change. Or consider smart cities, climate-smart agriculture, geoengineering, and green growth. Each is intended to extend human control in ways that solve pressing problems. But predicting the effects of these expert-defined solutions requires oversimplifying the landscape in which they will work their effects:

> Conceived in narrow, technical terms, informed by relatively homogeneous, specialist views, these core organising ideas for high-level global policy-making typically emphasise aspiring control, asserting romantic visions of visionary leadership, heroic expertise, deterministic systems, orderly values, convergent interests, compliant citizens and expediently predictable futures. (Scoones and Stirling 2020, 1–2)

When any of the abovementioned conditions do not hold, the new social technologies generate new regions of irreparable ignorance and unforeseeable harm.

One final example will have to suffice. Blockchain technology has enabled the creation of cryptocurrencies like Bitcoin. Proponents see cryptocurrencies as creating efficiency and especially transparency in the payments system. They claim that cryptocurrencies promote freedom from government monopolies on money creation while offering safe opportunities to store wealth in countries where the central banks and the domestic banking system are prone to incompetence and instability (Seybert and Katzenstein 2018). Cryptocurrencies, proponents say, promise the average person opportunities for freedom and security that have long been available only to elite investors and large firms. The new monetary utopia marks a radical break with established strategies for addressing social problems. But like other innovations, cryptocurrency creates new urgent questions that could not have been answered before the technology's implementation. As critics of cryptocurrencies have by now demonstrated, the unintended consequences of this "democratizing" innovation include the unanticipated fleecing of naive investors and the monopolization of control by very few actors, the facilitation of organized criminal networks, tax evasion by wealthy investors, and the use of ransomware to extract untraceable payments (using Monero, a more anonymous alternative to Bitcoin; see Panda 2018). Taking stock of the situation, Nouriel Roubini (2018) concludes that "blockchain has given rise to a familiar form of economic hell" in which "a few self-serving white men (there are hardly any women or minorities in the blockchain universe) pretending to be messiahs for the world's impoverished, marginalized, and unbanked masses claim to have created billions of dollars of wealth out of nothing." Roubini points to "the massive centralization of power among cryptocurrency 'miners,' exchanges, developers, and wealth holders" to demonstrate that "blockchain is not about decentralization and democracy; it is about greed."

The startling conclusion to this line of argument is that new knowledge brings into play new domains of mystery. "We live on an island of knowledge surrounded by a sea of ignorance," writes physicist J. A. Wheeler. "As our

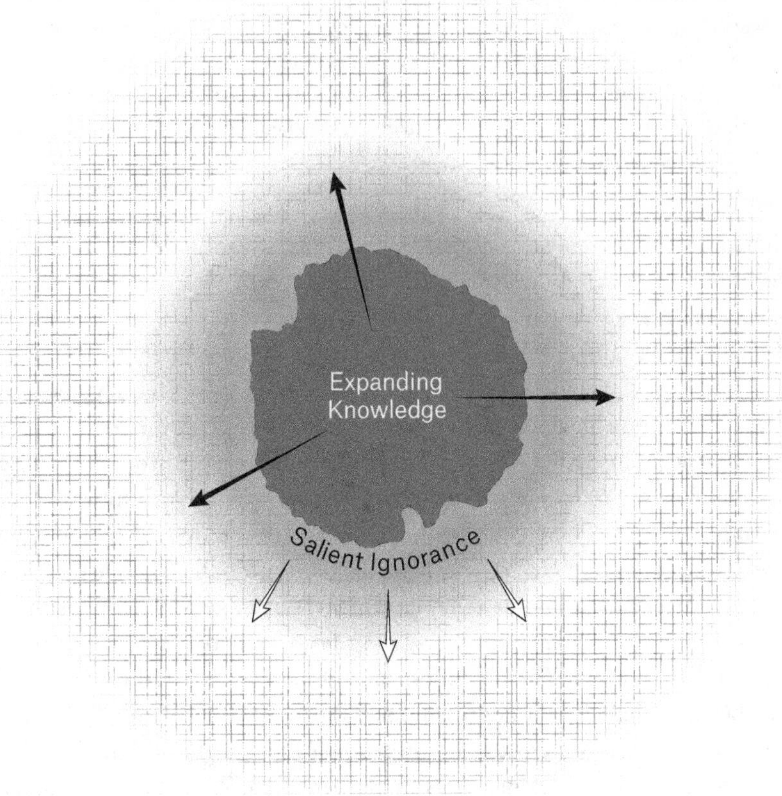

FIGURE 5.3. Expanding knowledge and salient ignorance
Contrary to the conventional view, new knowledge expands the domain of salient ignorance, represented by the shoreline separating the island of knowledge from the infinite ocean of ignorance.

island of knowledge grows, so does the shore of our ignorance" (Horgan 1992; cited in Ben-Haim 2019). The simple but arresting idea is reflected in figure 5.3. *The shoreline is where ignorance is salient. It is where what we don't know matters.* From this perspective, there is no guarantee that as the island grows, our new knowledge will ensure good outcomes. Instead, the newly salient ignorance that is brought into play by new knowledge can be very dangerous.

KNOWING MORE, HARMING LESS?

The progressive view of knowledge expansion is associated with a further proposition that is equally unsecure. The progressive view presumes a monotonically increasing function between knowledge acquisition and social benefit. As virtuous professionals learn more, their contribution to social betterment necessarily increases (see figure 5.4).

But if new knowledge expands human capacities while also expanding the domain of salient ignorance, then it is possible that new scientific or social technology might undermine the project of social betterment (see figure 5.5).

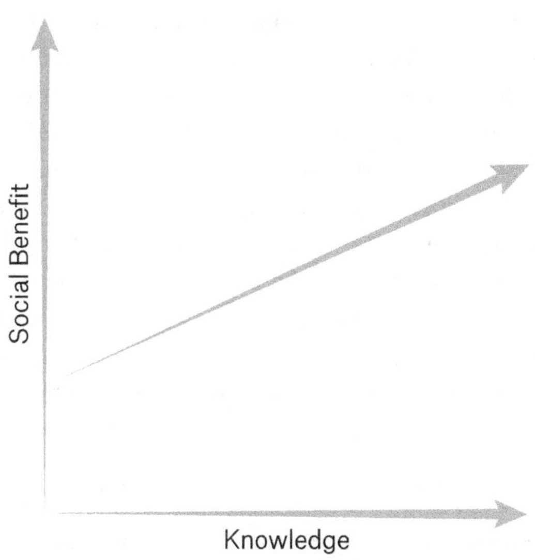

FIGURE 5.4. Expanding knowledge and social benefit, standard view
In the conventional view, expanding knowledge necessarily promotes social benefit.

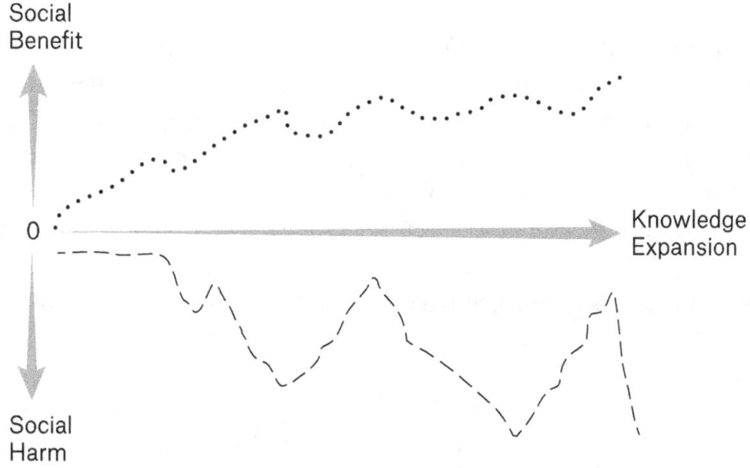

FIGURE 5.5. Indeterminate relation between expanding knowledge, social benefit, and social harm
Contrary to the conventional view, new knowledge promotes social betterment and induces social harm.

The relationship between knowledge acquisition and social betterment is, then, contingent, indeterminant, and, as a consequence, unpredictable (Derbyshire 2020).

As concerns its use, knowledge is typically indiscriminate. It allows for socially beneficial and socially destructive applications and effects. Social media and blockchain technologies are examples of a much more general problem. Moreover, the decision sciences, which explore how decisions actually get made, have come to find that "no simple relationship exists between more information and better decisions" (Weaver et al. 2013, 42). Complicating matters, knowing the right ways to use new knowledge often requires trial and error, the outcomes of which are uncertain and potentially damaging. And so it should be unsurprising that technologies that promise greater control over our environments, such as genetic engineering in agriculture, can leave us increasingly vulnerable to new sorts of threats. We can hope that the damage may be short-lived and quickly overcome by new increments of knowledge that teach us, say, how to use and protect ourselves from potentially dangerous technologies. But that hope often proves to be naive. Increments of new knowledge can interfere with rather than advance social betterment.

THE ILLUSION OF CONTROL

Economists construct very simple, imaginary model worlds in order to reason about policy effects. The imaginary model world of perfect competition featured in the standard textbook is ideal for this purpose. In that world, economic policy has knowable effects. In that world, for instance, the economist knows that an increase in the minimum wage will increase unemployment. And in that world, policy is implemented and enforced just as the economist intends. There is no slippage between policy design and application.

The device of imaginary model worlds provides the illusion of adequate knowledge. Economists constructing models impose sufficient conditions and simplifications so that they know all there is to know about the connection between a policy and its effects *in the model world*. Here, the economist can bring about good outcomes with no unanticipated consequences. Modeling of this sort is deeply gratifying. Within the model world the economist achieves absolute control. Why? Because the model is set up to provide that control.

An enormous, consequential mistake occurs, however, when economists carry forward the "control story" from the model world to the real world, the world where actual policy interventions occur (Colander 2005b). Control requires adequate knowledge of the world. But if economists face severe epistemic limits, then economists also face severe limits on their ability to exert control in the world. Absent adequate knowledge, the economist at best wields influence without control. Influence without control implies that each economic intervention that economists advocate is, essentially, a social experiment whose outcome cannot be ascertained in advance. We may hope that a real-world policy experiment will yield the same beneficial effects it yields in the model world, that most unintended consequences will be beneficial, and that harmful unintended consequences will be tolerable. But the fact of the matter is that none of those outcomes is assured at the outset of the experiment.

Influence without control is both the product and the source of epistemic insufficiency. Policy economists typically face the second type of irreparable ignorance specified above. They can learn what they need to know about a proposed policy intervention in the context it will be introduced only after the fact. Like the famished hiker confronting the berries, economists can make informed guesses but cannot know or control whether the "fruit" is harmful to society until a leap of faith is taken and the policy is introduced.[25] There is no other way to gain knowledge of the policy's effects at the time the policy decision must be made.

Economists face another domain of irreparable ignorance that undermines their control. The domain includes the myriad factors that bear on policy choice, implementation, and administration. Noneconomists weigh professional economic advice against many other considerations and often pick and choose which economic propositions they will draw on when deciding what to do, or when trying to justify decisions after they have been made. So do the administrators who are empowered to implement and manage policy. Legislation is never sufficiently comprehensive to anticipate all situations to which it applies. Decisions must be made about the rules that will be adopted to implement a policy, and about how to apply those rules (and what exceptions to make) in each particular situation. Administrators enjoy varying degrees of autonomy to interpret and implement legislation. They can seek to follow the letter of the law, pursue the spirit but not the letter of the law, or work to subvert the intent of the law. US President Biden's administrative appointees, for instance, are interpreting US law on immigration, public health, and ecological protection in ways that break decisively with the decisions of Trump appointees.

A sobering conclusion follows. Even if economists could predict the effects of a policy they advocate *were it to be introduced and managed just as they hope*, they cannot possibly know policy effects in a complex policy-making environment where their expertise is but one input. If they cannot know all the factors that go into the implementation of a policy, they cannot begin to control its ultimate impact.

ECONOMICS VS. OTHER PROFESSIONS

Many other professions risk harming, and for some of the same reasons. Physicians face severe epistemic limitations in their work. They harm by acting on the basis of imperfect medical science and mistaken judgments about the patients they treat. Epistemic limitations deprive them of control over therapeutic outcomes. Engineers, too, face epistemic limitations. Like economists, their projects affect large numbers of people extending over many generations. But professions vary in terms of their epistemic limitations and the harms those limitations induce. If we theorize a continuum ranging from those professional fields in which knowledge is largely adequate to those where it is deficient, we might place basic civil engineering near the pole of epistemic adequacy and medical practice at a middle point.[26] In contrast, economics resides in the zone where ignorance is extensive and deep (see figure 5.6).

If we construct a second continuum mapping the *risks resulting from epistemic insufficiency*, we are apt to place basic engineering in the benign zone, where the risks are well understood and manageable, medicine again at a middle point, and economics in the perilous zone, where dragons roam (see figure 5.7). Here ignorance is vast, influence is deep, and control is altogether absent. The risk is magnified by the proclivity of economists to pursue optimal outcomes that are extremely vulnerable to forecasting errors, rather than robust strategies that are apt to perform well enough under a wide range of unknown futures (see chap. 11).

Figure 5.7 would have appeared quite different were we charting the professions in, say, 1900 or even 1950. Over the course of the twentieth century the economics profession achieved tremendous influence over how other experts and policy makers approach most domains of social policy, ranging from health and education to environmental regulation. A direct link can be drawn from twentieth-century economic theory to policy innovations such as deregulation of transportation, finance, and telecommunications, the

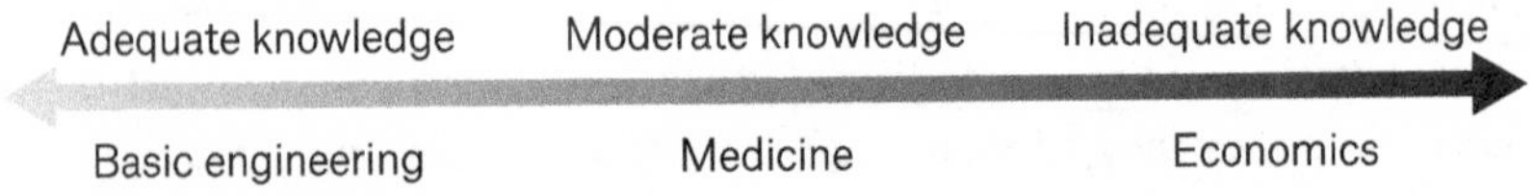

FIGURE 5.6. Severity of epistemic insufficiency
The epistemic problem is far more acute in economics than in many other professions.

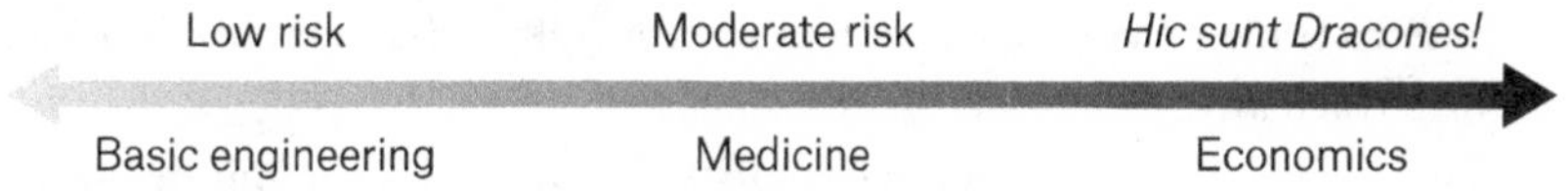

FIGURE 5.7. Risk associated with epistemic insufficiency
The risk arising from epistemic insufficiency is far more acute in economics than in many other professions.

introduction of school vouchers, the sale of visas, the marketing of pollution permits, and the privatization of prisons. In all these cases economists advocated the reforms on grounds of promoting social betterment by enhancing economic efficiency. At the same time, institutional reforms at the national and international levels provided economists with substantial new sources of influence. In this context we can think of the creation of independent central banks across the globe as banks were freed from oversight by political officials; and the empowerment of the international financial institutions, such as the World Bank and the International Monetary Fund, at a time when these institutions were becoming principal actors in economic policy making across Latin America, Africa, and Asia. By the late twentieth century economists had achieved unprecedented influence, which they happily exploited. But with that influence the profession did not acquire an ounce of control over policy decisions, modes of implementation, or policy effects. Not because it did not seek control but because control in the social world is unattainable. As its influence grew, then, the economics profession slid along the continuum to higher and higher levels of risk of inducing harm.

Conclusion

All economists, regardless of their theoretical and methodological commitments, face the problem of irreparable ignorance. And yet the profession emphasizes what it thinks it knows while suppressing what it does not and cannot ever know. Hubris spans schools of thought, and it is exceedingly dangerous. When combined with extensive influence, it can be deadly. The import of this insight is blocked in a profession where harm is weaponized rather than treated as a shared problem facing all economists.

Rectifying the problem in economics requires honest engagement with the limits to knowledge and the implications of that insight for professional practice. Scoones and Stirling (2020, 11) point us in the right direction. "In embracing uncertainty in modelling practice," they write, "the emphasis must therefore shift towards active advocacy of qualities of doubt (rather than certainty), skepticism (rather than credulity) and dissent (rather than conformity)—and so towards creative care rather than calculative control."

That seems to ask a lot of economists. But looked at in another way, it relieves the profession of burdens it has carried but should not: the burdens of trying to access the inaccessible, to know the unknowable, and to control the uncontrollable.

In this discussion of irreparable ignorance, I have sidestepped altogether a particularly acute epistemic problem. Economic explanation and policy design entail causal claims. But tracing causality in economics is an exercise that, ultimately, is grounded in fictitious counterfactual accounts of imaginary worlds. This issue is sufficiently complex and important to warrant its own chapter. This is the topic of chapter 6.

6

Counterfactual Fictions in Economic Explanation and Harm Assessment

> Nothing can ever happen twice
> In consequence, the sorry fact is
> that we arrive here improvised
> and leave without the chance to practice.
> —WISLAWA SZYMBORSKA, *Nothing Twice*

> [The] world we live in is not an ergodic world. . . . For an enormous number of issues that are important to us, the world is one of novelty and change; it does not repeat itself.
> —DOUGLAS NORTH (1999, 3)

The Trans-Pacific Partnership

In 2016 the Obama administration reached agreement with other countries over a massive trade deal, the Trans-Pacific Partnership (TPP). The agreement would have promoted trade among the US, Japan, Canada, Mexico, Australia, Singapore, and several other countries linked by the Pacific Ocean. In the run-up to congressional consideration of the TPP, economists generated predictions of its effects on the US and other countries. The most prominent study was conducted by Peter Petri and Michael Plummer (2016) of the Peterson Institute for International Economics. The study employed a massive "computable general equilibrium" (CGE) model. CGE models purportedly allow researchers to trace through the effects of any one economic change on other parts of the economy to derive the sectoral and overall aggregate effects. The model was complex, with "108,000 rows and columns, which are equations and variables" with "1.18 million data points." *How could it possibly have been wrong?*

The Peterson model predicted that relative to a world without the TPP, the trade agreement would generate a modest increase in national income for the US, with much greater increases for other TPP signatories (such as Vietnam—an 8% increase by 2030). The model predicted rising wages in the US, with no effects on US employment levels and no effect on income inequality. Immediately following the release of the Peterson study, economists at the Global Development and Environment Institute (GDAE) at Tufts University generated their own forecast of the effects of the TPP using the UN Global Policy Model (Capaldo, Izurieta, and Kwame Sundaram 2016). The GDAE economists used the Peterson predictions of the increase in trade flows under the TPP, but they dropped what they took to be several unrealistic assumptions embedded in the Peterson model. The GDAE model predicted that relative to the non-TPP scenario, the TPP would generate negative economic growth for the developed-country signatories, negative growth for non-TPP members, and increased income inequality in the US and other countries.

How could two models using identical projected trade flows reach such fundamentally different conclusions? The critical driver of their respective results was their conflicting assumptions about the way economies work. The Peterson economists simply assumed that trade does not affect employment levels. Their model also presumed that trade generates increases in labor productivity that automatically induce corresponding increases in wages, a central belief in neoclassical economics for over a century. They put it this way, without embarrassment:

> The model assumes that the TPP will affect neither total employment nor the national savings (or equivalently trade balances) of countries. This "macroeconomic closure" assumption allows modern trade models to focus on the goals of trade policy—namely sustained productivity and wage increases through changes in trade patterns and industry output levels.

The GDAE economists dissented. They dropped the assumption that trade has no impact on unemployment. They also assumed that intensified competition associated with trade liberalization depresses wages and promotes faster technological change, together reducing the share of national income that flows to workers. The GDAE economists assumed that the trade agreement would increase cross-national investment (called foreign direct investment, or FDI), to exploit higher potential returns on investment abroad. They assumed that increased FDI would increase the share of US national income that went to investors, at the expense of American workers.

Some economists rallied behind the Peterson study (see Lawrence 2016), while others sided with GDAE (see Drake 2016). But why? Shouldn't economists know by now how trade liberalization affects national economies? After all, countries have been negotiating trade agreements *for centuries.*

*

Trying to know the future is a daunting exercise. Not just the distant future; even next month is fundamentally uncertain in salient respects. Often the future unfolds just as we might expect—and then, without warning, events violate our expectations. But what about the past? Can't we at least be secure in our knowledge of what has already happened, and why?

Leading economists who have wrestled with the problem of ignorance have drawn a sharp epistemic distinction between the future and the past. Knight ([1921] 2014, 199) argued that "we live only by knowing something about the future; while the problems of life, or of conduct at least, arise from the fact that we know so little." In Knight's view, future economic events are characterized by uncertainty, where there are no probabilities to guide us. Drawing on Knight, Shackle ([1972] 1992, xii–xx) contrasted "the forward look into the *void of unknowledge*, and the backward look into the past with its *ascertainable history*" (emphasis added).

The distinction between an *ascertainable* past and an *unknowable* future has been readily accepted by those economists who probe the limits to economic knowledge. That seems to make sense. As concerns the past we have a good bit of information, imperfect though it is, about what in fact happened. By "what happened" I mean the occurrence and sequence of certain events and the approximate values of many variables at regular intervals. As concerns the future, on the other hand, we cannot know in advance of its arrival the occurrence or order of many events, or the values of key variables. The epistemic distinction between the past and the future, then, just seems to make sense.

But the distinction doesn't hold up under closer scrutiny. The kind of knowledge economists typically need to do their work is *causal* knowledge. They need to ascertain what causes what, or by how much the magnitude of one variable affects another, and why. Trade economists, as we've just seen, rely on causal mechanisms and pathways when trying to ascertain how a proposed trade agreement would generate and distribute benefits and harms. And when it comes to knowledge of causality, the basis for a sharp epistemic distinction between the past and the future evaporates. In *this* respect the past is just as inscrutable as is the future. Here we explore why.

Causality and Counterfactualization

Consider a simpler scenario than predicting the effects of a complex trade deal. Imagine that two economists are debating whether raising the minimum wage in New York City today will increase unemployment one year hence, and if so, by how much. We might expect their conclusions to conflict since they are trying to predict the future, but we might at least assume the economists would be sure about and agree on the effects of *past* increases in the minimum wage. This question, we might think, submits to certain, objective analysis, relying on well-established theoretical models and empirical techniques. As Fischhoff (1982, 335) put it, "Whatever the question we are asking, it is generally assumed that the past will readily reveal the answers it holds. Of hindsight and foresight, the latter appears as the troublesome perspective." Note, however, that the question of a policy's impact concerns causality. And I want to suggest that (1) the standard forms of causal knowledge in economics entail counterfactual reasoning; (2) all counterfactual reasoning is, by definition, fictitious; and (3) counterfactual-dependent causal claims are, then, likewise fictitious.

What are counterfactuals? A useful definition is this: counterfactuals "are subjunctive conditionals in which the antecedent is known or supposed for purposes of argument to be false (Skyrms [1980])" (Tetlock and Belkin 1996, 4). Consider the simple statement, "Had the minimum wage been increased last year, unemployment today would be 1% higher than it is." "Had the minimum wage been increased last year" is the false antecedent; "unemployment today would be 1% higher than it is" is the subjunctive conditional.

Counterfactual reasoning is inescapable in the social sciences, just as it is in daily life. We counterfactualize constantly as we navigate the world. I emphasize this point here so that I am not misunderstood as rejecting counterfactualizing. According to the influential computer scientist Judea Pearl, the ability to counterfactualize distinguishes human reasoning from the cognitive capacities of other species and represents the most formidable challenge to the realization of artificial intelligence (Pearl and Mackenzie 2018). Taleb (2010, 189) argues that "the ability to project conjectures into the future and play the counterfactual game" may be the "most potent use of our brain." Thus, even if we discover irresolvable problems with counterfactualizing, living without it is not an option.

Counterfactual reasoning applies equally to the explanation of events after the fact and to the prediction of future events. It informs judgments concerning our past actions and the future actions we contemplate (Lebow 2010, 276). But most causal accounts in economics do not explicitly construct counterfactuals.[27] Economists are less inclined to frame their causal arguments in terms of counterfactual reasoning than are those political scientists, historians, and other scholars who routinely examine an individual case, such as the causes of WWI, or comparativists who explore small numbers of cases. But economic explanation is just as dependent on counterfactual analysis as are political and historical explanations. Why is this so?

CAUSAL CLAIMS

The answer stems from the structure of causal claims that are routinely encountered in the social sciences, including economics, and that also underpin much of the theoretical work on counterfactualizing (Lewis 1973, 556). The influential philosopher and classical political economist David Hume ([1748] 2007, section VII) famously defined causality as follows: "We may define a cause to be an object, followed by another, and where all the objects similar to the first are followed by objects similar to the second. Or in other words where, if the first object had not been, the second never had existed."

As is widely recognized, Hume's statement conflates two distinct arguments concerning causality. The first sentence defines causality in terms of constant conjunction (Goertz and Levy 2007; Lewis 1973), which suggests a relation of sufficiency. The second sentence defines causality instead in terms of necessity. All of this requires some unpacking.

When economists claim that event *X* is causally related to outcome *Y*, they are typically making one of several kinds of claims, such as (a) through (c):[28]

a. that *X* is necessary for *Y*	(not-$X \rightarrow$ not-Y)
b. that *X* is sufficient for *Y*	($X \rightarrow Y$)
c. that *X* is necessary and sufficient for *Y*	($X \rightarrow Y$ *and* not-$X \rightarrow$ not-Y)

Proposition (a) is consistent with Hume's necessity definition: if *X* doesn't happen, *Y* cannot happen, though *X* happening does not ensure *Y*. For example, striking a match (*X*) may be necessary for the match to light (*Y*), but it will not suffice to light it if there is no oxygen present. Proposition (b) is consistent with Hume's constant-conjunction definition of causality. Whenever *X* occurs, *Y* will occur, though *Y* can occur without *X*. Being employed (*X*) suffices to ensure an individual receives income (*Y*), but she might receive income from other sources even if unemployed. Proposition (c) establishes the strongest causal connection between *X* and *Y*. Under (c), *Y* happens if and only if *X* happens. I receive the gold medal (*Y*) if and only if I cross the finish line first (*X*).

Now we can make sense of the connection between causal and counterfactual claims. Imagine that in the real world *X* occurs and is followed by *Y*. Is *X* causal? Answering the question requires consideration of an alternative, counterfactual world in which *X* or *Y* does not occur. Causal claims (a) and (c) entail the strong assertion that in an alternative world in which *X* does not occur, *Y* cannot occur (see Goertz and Levy 2007, 15; Lewis 1973, 557). Claim (b) equivocates, asserting that in that alternative world *Y* can happen even absent *X*. But (b) does assert strongly that if *Y* (earning an income) does not happen, *X* (being employed) cannot have happened. The truth of all three claims, then, depends on the truth of a counterfactual claim about what would have happened or could happen in an alternative counterfactual world in which *X* or *Y* does not occur.

Many scholars have argued that causal claims necessarily require counterfactualizing.[29] For instance, political scientists Philip Tetlock and Aaron Belkin (1996, 3–4) argue that "we can avoid counterfactuals only if we eschew all causal inference and limit ourselves to strictly noncausal narratives of what actually happened (no smuggling in causal claims under the guise of verbs such as "influenced," "responded," "triggered," "precipitated," and the like)." Economists, too, have sometimes theorized causality in terms of counterfactuals. William Stanley Jevons ([1888] 2010, 239–40), a nineteenth-century pioneer in mathematical economics, writes: "By the Cause of an event we mean the circumstances which must have preceded in order that the event should happen. . . . A *necessary or indispensable antecedent is* however *identical with a cause*, being that without which the effect would not take place." Hicks (1980, 7–8) explicitly centers his account of causality on counterfactualizing "For causality, we must be maintaining that if A had not existed, B would not have existed; if not-A, then not-B. But not-A and not-B . . . are events which have not happened. (In recent discussions among historians they are described as 'counterfactual.')"[30] The most influential advocate of the essential role of counterfactuals in economics today is the econometrician and microeconomist James Heckman. "A causal relationship is only well defined if a theory of potential counterfactuals is articulated and a mechanism generating variation in the causes is clearly specified" (Heckman 2001, 17).

THE FUNDAMENTAL PROBLEM OF CAUSAL INFERENCE

Why does specifying causality require counterfactualizing? Consider what statistician Paul W. Holland (1986, 947) called the "Fundamental Problem of Causal Inference" (emphasis in original):

> Causal inference is ultimately concerned with the effects of causes on specific units, that is, with ascertaining the value of the causal effect in (1) [$Y_t(u) - Y_c(u)$, which gives the difference in the value Y of unit u under a treatment (t) and nontreatment (c)]. It is frustrated by an inherent fact of observational life that I call the Fundamental Problem of Causal Inference.
>
> *Fundamental Problem of Causal Inference.* It is impossible to *observe* the value of $Y_t(u)$ and $Y_c(u)$ on the same unit and, therefore, it is impossible to *observe* the effect of t on u.

These abstract ideas can be put simply. To know whether a particular event ("treatment") caused a particular outcome, one would need to run history *twice*—once in which the treatment is provided, say, to a particular person, and a second time in which the *identical* person under *identical* circumstances is not given the treatment. For instance, inferring whether taking an aspirin causes Elise's headache to recede would require treating her with an aspirin and observing the outcome, then going back in time to the very same moment, this time not treating Elise with the aspirin, and again observing the outcome. We would then be able to infer the causal effect of the aspirin by observing any differences in Elise's condition under the two scenarios. But as Holland pointed out, it is impossible to do that. We can either treat or not treat Elise at any particular moment—we can't do both. That is the Fundamental Problem. Social scientists are aware of it. In the social sciences "we cannot rerun history at the same time and the same place with different values on of our explanatory variable each time" (King, Keohane, and Verba 1994, 91). Hence the need for counterfactualizing machinery to mentally *simulate* the rerunning of history.

So far, so good. Now imagine again that some event *X* actually occurred and was actually followed by another event *Y*. We may want to claim that *X* was necessary for *Y*. We now see that making that claim requires making the counterfactual claim that had *X* not happened, *Y* would not have happened. Since in the actual world *X* did happen, we are left to speculate about what would have happened in an alternative world—a world we cannot inhabit—where *X* did not happen. But here a new problem arises: the veracity of a counterfactual scenario where *X* does not happen cannot ever be confirmed or disconfirmed empirically *because that historical path was precluded when* X, *in fact, occurred*. When establishing a causal explanation, then, we must generate a *fictitious narrative* about *what would have happened* in an alternative world that was identical to the existing world in every respect but for the fact that *X* did not occur.[31] As Heckman (2001, 17) puts it, causal explanation requires "thought experiments involving counterfactuals in imaginary worlds." At the heart of an objective causal claim, then, is the construction of a *fiction* without which the objective causal claim cannot be sustained (cf. Beckert 2016, 51ff).

Fiction in social science: the claim strikes us as wrong. Surely there are some cause-effect linkages in the social sciences that we can *know*. Take the hypothesis that increasing the rate of taxation on tobacco will reduce cigarette consumption. The claim that if the tax had not been increased last year, cigarette consumption would be higher today, is *dependable* even if it is grounded in a statement about a hypothetical world. Typically, however, the social sciences concern linkages that tend to be far more complex and uncertain than the causal impact of a tobacco tax.

Those theorists who have examined causality in the social sciences most carefully have converged on the conclusion that causal claims require counterfactual projections. They have then had to grapple with the fictitious nature of counterfactuals to ensure that the counterfactuals used to sustain causal claims are dependable. Several theorists have advanced demarcation criteria to distinguish scientific from fanciful counterfactuals. For instance, Mary Morgan (2013) carefully probes the interpenetration of fact and fiction in economic models that permit counterfactual *what-if* analysis. *What* will happen to unemployment, say, *if* the minimum wage is increased? "*Imaginative stories* prompted by the what-if questions that economists like to ask about their model worlds are where we see *economists playing their games of make-believe*" (Morgan 2014, 235, emphasis added). In her view what distinguishes economic science from science fiction is the practice of "keying"—matching aspects of a fictitious model to facets of the actual world, so that inferences from the model can tell us something useful about the world. She urges us to think of models as *artifacts* rather than mere fictions—as useful tools for social investigation that nonetheless incorporate fictitious claims.

Morgan's approach is insightful. But good science fiction (and other forms of fiction) achieves the very same goal, as Morgan herself acknowledges. Good fiction often teaches us about our world by probing some imagined world that is very much like our own in most respects (keyed to our world), but unlike ours in one or more salient respects (Beckert 2016, 63–64). A narrative unfolds that permits us to see our own world differently, or more deeply. The power of good fiction depends in part on our ability to situate ourselves in the narrative. Perhaps, then, we should not search for unbending demarcation criteria to distinguish social science counterfactual fictions from other fictions. We might instead recognize the inherently fictitious qualities of social science (cf. McCloskey 1998; Leamer 2009). Ned Lebow (2010, 259) warns us that a failure to do so is harmful: "One of the more interesting—and ironic—findings in this regard is the degree to which a commitment to science and scientific methods by international relations scholars can constitute a major impediment to their practice of science."

CAUSAL FICTIONS SITUATED IN THE FUTURE AND IN THE PAST

We can now understand why economists debating the minimum wage might disagree not just about prospective impacts of proposed policy but also about the actual effects of past policy measures. The Fundamental Problem of Causal Inference undermines causal knowledge of the past and the future equally. Let's assume that the minimum wage was in fact increased last year, and that in fact unemployment rose this year. That series of events in itself tells us *nothing* about the causal relation between the two events. The risk of errant post hoc reasoning—inferring that because one event preceded another it caused the successive event—is ubiquitous in causal analysis. When economists adjudicate the matter of past effects of policy *they must put into the arena their contesting counterfactuals—their respective fictions of what would have been (or would be) but for the policy intervention* (cf. Tetlock and Belkin 1996, 4). But that historical path, the path involving no increase in the minimum wage last year, was foreclosed the moment the policy was implemented. Our economists cannot ever observe the simultaneous treatment and nontreatment of the same individual or community. *The resulting ignorance is irreparable.* It must be managed through counterfactualizing. But given the extent of human ingenuity and imagination, and the innumerable counterfactual stories that can be told and methods for generating them, we should have no trouble understanding why it is that the best minds with the best techniques in economics can and do disagree about something as apparently simple as the effects of increasing the minimum wage—its prospective effects, and even its effects in the past.

In *this* regard, then—in specifying causal relationships—there is no epistemic distinction between the past and future. As soon as we insert a counterfactual event like a policy intervention into the past or remove an actual event from it and ask what would have happened subsequently, we "are then telling an imagined story forward from that moment, time = T. *It is not a story that actually happened.* . . . All counterfactuals are histories of the future, even when they are situated in what we normally think of as past 'calendar' time" (Weber 1996, 276–77).

Counterfactuals set in the future are just as temporally complex. Imagine that a policy is to be implemented next month, and economists want to infer now its future causal impact. Drawing that inference requires economists to position themselves in the *future-future*: at a point in time by which (they presume) the effects of the policy intervention will have emerged. Economists must presume that from that vantage point they will know the course of history as it has actually unfolded with the policy. They must also presume that from that vantage point they can compare the actual history with how it would have unfolded without the policy. Heroically, they must also presume that their science provides them time-travel machines that allow them to mentally occupy that position in the future-future *today.*[32]

Counterintuitively, there is good reason to suspect that reaching good judgments about causal connections among past events is in some respects even more difficult than anticipating future causality. In scripting the past we are under the influence of hindsight and other cognitive biases that validate our worldviews and accord with our self-interests. Cognitive biases are particularly likely "in the most subjective of all methods of inquiry, the counterfactual thought experiment" (Tetlock and Belkin 1996, 37). "History is a terrible teacher," Tetlock and Belkin (1996, 9) remind us. "When we look back into the past from the present, we occupy a privileged but also easily abused position." Knowing about the succession of past events, "it becomes relatively easy to find antecedents that depict the consequence as the inevitable result of some 'inexorable' causal process."[33] In theorizing the future, on the other hand, we are far more willing to accept "the complexity and indeterminacy of possible relationships among antecedents and consequences" (Tetlock and Belkin 1996, 9, 31n4; see also Weber 1996, 275–79).[34]

An unwelcome conclusion follows. *Standard causal claims in economics are fictitious in the sense that they depend on the construction of fictitious counterfactuals.* The truth of the claim that raising the minimum wage last year induced higher unemployment today depends on the truth of the counterfactual claim that in a fictitious world just like ours in which the minimum wage was not raised, unemployment would now be lower. Counterfactuals are stories economists narrate to probe causal mechanisms and to convince themselves and others that they understand why things did and did not, or do and do not, or will and will not happen. In this fundamental respect the future and past are epistemically indistinct: we run up equally against the limits to knowledge in our confrontation with causal relationships in the past, and the future. What allows us to check off the past as "known" is a conventional exercise in which economists agree to subscribe to the same fictitious explanatory counterfactual.

CRITERIA FOR CONSTRUCTING AND ASSESSING COUNTERFACTUALS

Scholars who recognize the prominent role of counterfactuals in causal explanation and also the problems posed by the proliferation of counterfactual accounts must offer what they take to be scientific criteria for restricting the field of plausible counterfactuals (see Levy 2015). But given the nature of the problem—*knowing the unknowable*—there should be no surprise in finding that there is no consensus about what counts as legitimate counterfactualizing. The various criteria are also specified and applied in distinct and even inconsistent ways. Here I survey just two principal criteria.[35]

Historical Consistency

One attractive requirement for constructing counterfactuals is "historical consistency." A counterfactual must be consistent with well-established historical facts; it must involve only a "minimal-rewrite-of-history" (Tetlock and

Belkin 1996, 23). The criterion is widely accepted. It appears, for instance, in the "closest possible world" frameworks of Lewis (1973) and Stalnaker (1968).[36] The historical consistency criterion helps to explain why contingent events like assassinations are attractive subjects for counterfactualizing since it is easy to specify the world being identical in every respect to the actual world but for the fact that the assassination failed (the gun did not go off, the assassin missed the target, etc.).

The historical consistency criterion is deceptively complex. Alternative worlds may be like the actual world in some respects (e.g., sharing its laws) and unlike in others (e.g., different background conditions), as Lewis (1973) recognized. Deciding which of the alternative worlds is "closest" to the actual world is then a challenging, *theory-dependent* activity (Elster 1978, 187). Rigorous application of the criterion requires specification of *correct* theoretical claims that permit accurate measures of "closeness" between alternative worlds with "minimal" rewrites. But as concerns the social world, such theory remains elusive (cf. Lebow 2010, 285). One theoretical account might plausibly posit hypothetical world A′ to be closest to the actual world A, while another might plausibly hold A″ to be closer still. Steven Weber (1996, 271) concludes that causal complexity of the social world "butchers" the minimal rewrite rule. Heckman (2008, 16) concurs, arguing that discovery of closest possible worlds "founders on the lack of any meaningful metric or topology to measure 'closeness.'"

The historical consistency requirement faces a second challenge. Some particularly useful counterfactuals employ what Fearon (1996, 41ff) calls "miracle" causes (antecedents) that are explicitly inconceivable in the historical context into which they are inserted. A study of the connection between race and voting behavior concluding that the proposition that had "John Smith been Black, he would have been 30% more likely to vote for Clinton than he actually was" might be taken to generate useful insight, even though it is in fact impossible for non-Black Smith to be Black (Fearon 1996, 61). Similarly, it might be useful to theorize the trajectory of the Soviet Union had Trotsky somehow displaced Stalin, even though we may have good reason to believe "that Trotsky could never have been in Stalin's position" (Lukes 1980, 149). Hume exploited a miracle cause in a thought experiment that probed money neutrality. "For suppose, that, by miracle, every man in GREAT BRITAIN should have five pounds slipt into his pocket in one night," Hume wrote. "[This] would much more than double the whole money that is at present in the kingdom; yet there would not next day, nor for some time, be any more lenders, nor any variation in the interest [rate]" (Hume [1741–1777] 1985, 299; cited in Schabas 2008, 161).

Miracle causes often appear explicitly in fanciful speculations like Hume's. But they also appear implicitly within the most prosaic research methods.

Large-*n* statistical research that seeks to explore the logical implications of theoretical frameworks requires miracle cause counterfactualizing (Levy 2015, 383). As Fearon (1996, 56) points out, "authors estimating causal effects using regression analysis on nonexperimental data *never* ask whether it would have been actually possible for each case in the sample to have assumed different values on the independent variable." For instance, the results of a regression analysis of the link between national income and health outcomes might lead a researcher to conclude, counterfactually, that were Senegal to enjoy the same level of GDP per capita as Germany, its life expectancy would be 5.3 years higher than it is—without asking whether it is conceivable that Senegal could somehow have achieved that level of income.

Miracle causes are often legitimate and, as in the case of statistical studies, inescapable. But they nevertheless raise a confounding methodological question: just what limits should be placed on miracle causes, if any? The scenario "had Napoleon's arsenal included Stealth bombers he would have prevailed at Waterloo" (Fearon 1996) is sometimes cited by critics as an example of the problem of the undisciplined nature of miracle counterfactuals, and we should concede the point. It turns out that on the questions of when miracle causes are useful and what kinds of miracle causes are permissible, there is deep disagreement among counterfactual methodologists. There is no good reason to expect resolution to this problem—soon or ever.

Theoretical Consistency . . . and the TPP Controversy

For present purposes a second criterion for constructing counterfactuals, already suggested above, is most important and yet inescapably contested. It is the requirement that a counterfactual exhibit "consistency with well-established theoretical laws" (Tetlock and Belkin 1996, 25; see Heckman 2008, 3–4; Schabas 2008). This criterion is particularly problematic in the social sciences where such laws may be missing, contested, or, minimally, paradigm specific: "Different schools of thought in world politics [and, I would add, economics] have very different notions of what constitutes a theory or law or what is 'well established' " (Weber 1996, 285). Tetlock and Belkin (1996, 27) cast doubt on the criterion even as they offer it: "Consistency with *well-established* theory is a reasonable standard for gauging the plausibility of counterfactuals but we should expect disagreement about what counts as well-established theory in world politics" (see also Levy 2015).

The problem is on full display in the controversy over the TPP. The predictions of each model are baked into the cake. The initial assumptions in each model about how economies work shape the model's forecasts (Jackson

2016). Why don't the Peterson and GDAE economists begin with the very same assumption set? Because they hold to different theoretical frameworks. The Peterson economists hold to traditional neoclassical theoretical presumptions that trade flows do not cause unemployment, and that rising labor productivity automatically generates rising wages. The GDAE economists reject these assumptions. What is happening here is that the two approaches, grounded in alternative theoretical frameworks, are generating alternative counterfactual accounts driven by alternative claims of causality. And there is no epistemically secure reason why all economists should converge on any one theoretical framework, or why, even if they did, that they would land on the "right" framework.

Why is well-established theoretical law so rare in economics? Why have theoretical controversies between neoclassicals, Austrians, Keynesians, and advocates of other theoretical frameworks by now not been resolved once and for all, based on the empirical record? A common allegation among the partisans of diverse perspectives is that their opponents are prevented from seeing the evidence right before their eyes by a tangle of unacknowledged ideologies and incompetence. But the allegation is epistemologically naive. A better explanation recognizes that theoretical adversaries hold to distinct, theoretically driven, fictitious counterfactual narratives—*and the world can't ever tell us which fiction (if any) is correct*. Holland's warning is pertinent: world events unfold just once. Economists do not get to run the tape *n* times, alternately treating and not treating identical agents, to establish causal relationships. We can't inhabit a world in which the TPP is enacted and an identical world in which it is not, to ferret out its causal impact. Economists can adopt the convention that they can simulate multiple reruns with large-*n* studies, or multiple runs through the CGE machine. But each complex event in the social world is sui generis, occurring under innumerable unique, epistemically unavailable conditions that bear on outcomes.[37]

CIRCULAR REASONING

There is an inescapable epistemic conundrum regarding counterfactualizing that takes the form of a circularity problem. Generating dependable counterfactuals requires the right theory of causality, while establishing the right theory of causality requires the right counterfactual. Weber (1996, 272) makes the point while problematizing the minimal rewrite rule: "Once we knew what 'minimal' meant well enough to validate counterfactuals, we would no longer need to use counterfactuals because we would already know what we want to know and understand what we want to understand."

The circularity problem can be sidestepped but not resolved. It is sidestepped by a *convention* (Heckman 2008) that only one theoretical framework or method is legitimate, and so only its associated counterfactuals are appropriate when theorizing causal connections. But this requires that we presume what it is we think we are testing when we do empirical work—the adequacy of causal theory. Only if we are prepared to presume ex ante the unambiguous superiority of one theory over alternatives can we presume that its associated counterfactuals are uniquely correct. If we reject that presumption, as we should, then we are led to see that theoretical controversy is an inevitable feature of social science, not a pathology. Inevitable because *the fight is over what is not seen and can't ever be seen.* The fight is over the features of and outcomes in imaginary worlds. Sadly, there are no secure, scientifically unimpeachable means for sorting out which, if any, of the many hypotheses about that world is correct. How, after all, is one to do irrefutable, conclusive empirical research on worlds that do not exist?

Counterfactual Analysis of Harm and Harming

Let's turn now to normative matters—in particular, to the matter of harm. The standard approach to normative economics purports to render rigorous scientific judgments about what should be done to promote social betterment. The approach is "consequentialist." That is, it focuses exclusively on a policy's consequences, rather than on its inherent rightness or wrongness. The economic approach focuses on certain kinds of consequences: on the welfare benefits and harms that a policy induces. We will examine it carefully in part III. Here we focus just on the harms side of the ledger. Does harm assessment, too, require counterfactualizing?

Consequentialist policy assessment that examines harm requires counterfactualizing for two reasons. The first is that assessing policy consequences requires causal analysis, and as we've just seen, that exercise inescapably requires counterfactualizing. The second reason is more subtle. The standard literature in philosophy and law on harm and harming is *comparative.* Two comparative approaches predominate in the literature: the historical approach and the counterfactual approach.

THE HISTORICAL APPROACH

The "historical" approach compares how individuals are after an event with how they were immediately before the event (Shiffrin 2012). Are they now worse-off than they were before? If so, then there are grounds to suspect that

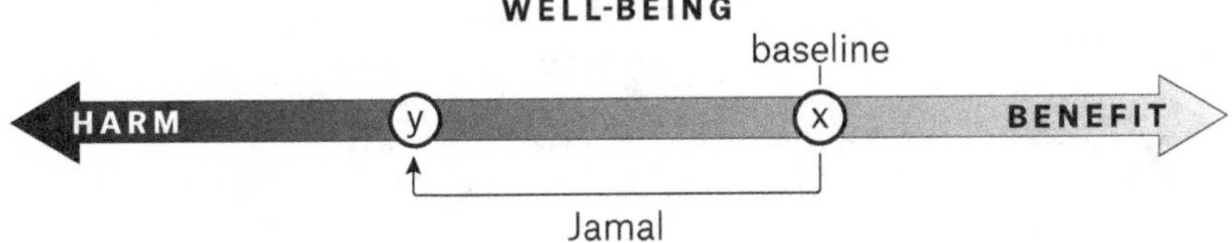

FIGURE 6.1. Historical account of harm
Under the historical account, any event that pushes Jamal to the left harms him. His current position *x* serves as the baseline for assessing harm when he moves to *y*.

the event has caused harm. In this approach, a person's current state prior to an intervening event serves as the baseline against which to assess and measure harm. Figure 6.1 conveys the argument. The continuum represents what we will call "well-being." Movements to the right indicate an improvement in a person's well-being. Movements to the left indicate a deterioration. Prior to some event, imagine that Jamal is at the level of well-being given by *x* on the continuum; *x* then serves as the baseline for assessing harm under the historical approach. Imagine that an event causes Jamal to shift to point *y*, where he experiences diminished well-being. For instance, imagine he has suffered a severe physical injury. By the historical approach we are led to conclude that Jamal has been harmed by the event since he is worse-off immediately after it than he was just prior.

In the historical approach, counterfactualizing is implicit. Even if Jamal is now worse-off than he was before an intervening event, we need to make a presumption that the intervening event was in fact what brought about the change in his situation; that the event was causal. And that returns us to all the problems we explored above as concerns the counterfactual in causal explanations.

The historical approach faces difficulties that are particularly relevant in economics. One is this: an event may not induce any diminution in individuals' well-being but might nonetheless lead to harm via "stunting" such that they do not attain in the future a level of agency, well-being, or capacity that they *otherwise would have attained* absent the event (Broome 1999, 173). In figure 6.1, imagine that Jamal never falls below his initial position *x* on the well-being continuum but instead remains stuck at *x* well into the future, when he might have been expected to experience increasing well-being. Relative to the relevant baseline *x*, Jamal has suffered no diminution in well-being. The historical approach concludes he has not been harmed.

But that can't be right. Persons who by virtue of a discrete event or persistent deprivation cannot develop their capacities and faculties as they otherwise would have been able to do are surely harmed. Children deprived of

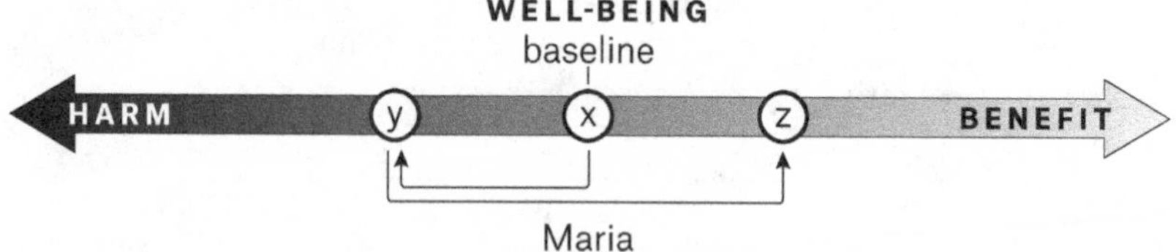

FIGURE 6.2. Historical account: benefitting from a harmful event
Under the historical approach, Maria is harmed by an event if the proximate effect is to push her leftward, from *x* to *y*, even if she ultimately benefits from the event (moving from *y* to *z*).

the opportunity to attend school may not have opportunities later on to earn livelihoods, achieve talents, or attain levels of autonomy that might otherwise have been available to them. In economic affairs in particular, stunting is a prevalent and pernicious form of harm, especially among those who face severe, persistent deprivation. An account of harm that doesn't recognize stunting is of little value in economics.

A second defect of the historical approach is the converse of the first. An event that initially shoves a person to the left on the well-being continuum may be converted by the "harmed" person into a long-run benefit. Imagine Maria has received a failing grade. Has she been harmed? She may as a consequence suffer embarrassment and be subjected to penalties such as the loss of a university scholarship. Under the historical approach we are encouraged to conclude that she has been harmed. But it would be prudent not to prejudge the matter in the immediate aftermath of the failing grade. Maria's failure might spark character improvement that redounds to her eventual benefit. What if Maria travels the path indicated in figure 6.2, from *x* to *y*, and then, as a consequence of learning, from *y* to *z*, achieving a level of well-being above the level she would have attained absent the causal event? Here we have good reason to reject the claim that the failing grade harmed her. Receiving instead an inflated grade above the F she deserved might paradoxically have had the effect of stunting her personal development in the same way that overprotecting children can stunt their maturation.

THE COUNTERFACTUAL APPROACH

The alternative comparative approach to harm assessment addresses these deficiencies. It is explicitly counterfactual. Here we compare how a person is at some point in the future after an event with *how she would otherwise have been at that point* had the event never occurred. In figure 6.3 we chart Jamal's actual life trajectory following an intervening event (or persistent condition) over an extended period. Then we counterfactualize, inferring the trajectory of Jamal's life as it would have been absent the event. In this account Jamal's future potential life, not his position just prior to the intervening event, serves as the baseline. If the event blocks his path to his potential life—if he remains stuck at *x* or any other point to the left of *y*—then the counterfactual approach finds he has been harmed.

Unlike the historical approach, the counterfactual approach is sensitive to stunting. The counterfactual approach therefore renders a far more adequate judgment in cases involving persistent deprivation. It also presents a more adequate account of events that entail surmounted adversity. Under this account, Maria is not deemed to be harmed by the failing grade. In fact, she benefits from it.

Except in simple or obvious cases, the counterfactual exercise comparing how individuals fare today with how they would have fared absent some intervening event in the past is daunting. This is true even when our focus is limited to a particular individual. The counterfactual approach requires the analyst to develop a compelling narrative about how an individual's life would have gone over time but for the event at issue. Without a compelling narrative we cannot assess whether harm has occurred, let alone measure its magnitude. Would an individual otherwise have completed secondary education, but for some damaging experience? To belabor the point, the counterfactual historical course absent the event is foreclosed in the moment that the event occurs. We must compare how Jamal's life goes against an irreducibly fictitious account of his life course absent the event. The baseline to make the comparison can't be seen; it must be inferred from some combination of data and subjective judgments. It is perhaps derived from how the "median" person's life goes in comparison with Jamal's. When the stakes are high, such as in debates over reparations for past injustice, for instance, there will no doubt be controversy rather than consensus.

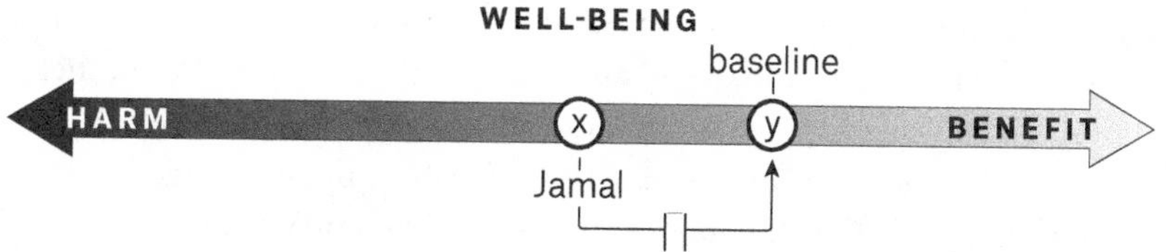

FIGURE 6.3. Counterfactual account of harm
Under the counterfactual approach, Jamal is harmed if any event or persistent condition prevents him from moving from his current level of well-being, *x*, to a level of well-being he would otherwise be expected to achieve. His potential achievement, *y*, serves as the baseline for assessing harm. The broken path from *x* to *y* indicates an insuperable obstacle.

HARM TO MANY

So far we have treated the simplest kind of case, in which an individual suffers harm. But economic policy decisions affect the lives of thousands and even millions of lives all at once. This fact greatly complicates harm judgments. One problem is this: what standard of reference should be used to assess harm when an intervention affects the lives of many? Should we assess a policy's impact by reference to its potential effects on the "representative" person? In this approach we are to insert the representative person into our counterfactual machinery and reach judgments based on how we think that person would be affected by the policy under review. But that approach raises difficult questions. Should we specify the representative person as white or Black; male, female, or nonbinary; able bodied or disabled in some way? Does that person enjoy a wide social support network, or is she socially isolated? What capacities should we attribute to this mythical person? The answer to these questions matters since the representative person will serve as the standard for harm assessment. Or, instead, is the right standard the *actual* persons who may diverge from the model of the representative person in vital respects, such as by being less resilient or fortunate than the standard?

There is no uniquely correct answer to this question, and it is not always obvious which is the right way to proceed. In medical practice, for instance, the physician must balance the median and variance of the effect of a treatment on large numbers of people against the particulars of the specific patient she is about to treat. If that physician believes that the patient she is about to treat diverges from the median patient in relevant ways, then the physician would be negligent if she ignored those differences and applied treatments that were appropriate for the median patient but not for *this* patient. But economics parallels public health more closely than it does clinical medicine. In economics, an intervention might have a neutral or even a positive effect on some members of society but induce severe harm to others who lack the privilege, resources, good fortune, ingenuity, or personal histories to respond effectively to the intervention. Some of the relevant characteristics of individuals may be known and observable, but many may not be. What, then, is the right standard to apply when evaluating counterfactually the effects of an economic intervention on the actual people who will be affected by it, and when probing whether the intervention should be pursued? While it might be convenient to rely on a conception of the representative person in these deliberations, that strategy should be recognized as a concession and not a solution to an insuperable epistemic problem.

The fact that economists treat large groups of people rather than individuals one by one raises another question that requires counterfactual reasoning. Often economists advocate policy that is expected to generate harm but that is deemed to be necessary for the achievement of some highly valued good. For instance, promoting economic efficiency is sometimes seen to require strategies that will increase inequality. Supply-side economists often promote tax cuts that favor the wealthy on the grounds that "society" as a whole will ultimately benefit. But in any individual case, is the harmful action actually necessary to achieve the goal, or is it gratuitous? Here we confront yet again the need for counterfactual reasoning. One plausible counterfactual account might yield the conclusion that efficiency could not be achieved by any viable alternative policy that avoided the harm. But another counterfactual account might find that the good could be achieved by an alternative policy that entailed no harm.[38] And this returns us again to the irresolvable epistemic problem in identifying causality in economics. We have no dependable means to ensure that we know which of the innumerable possible counterfactuals is, in fact, the right one.

There is much more to be said about the place of counterfactual reasoning in normative economics (see DeMartino 2021). It should suffice to say at this point that just like positive economics that explores causality, normative economics that explores harm depends on the confounding counterfactual. When it comes to harm assessment in particular, we must employ counterfactual fictions about the world as it is and as it would have been in the past, now, or in the future absent the event that is judged either to be or not to be harmful. The inescapable conclusion is that our most important normative judgments in economics depend on the particular counterfactual we choose to narrate. Normative economics, too, confronts the specter of irreparable ignorance.

The Extraordinary Virtues of Counterfactualizing

The epistemic iconoclasts are right to emphasize the limitations to what economists can know about the future. But the epistemic distinction many have drawn between an ascertainable past and the void of knowledge concerning the future fails. With Fischhoff (1982, 335) "we should hold the past in a little more respect when we attempt to plumb its secrets. While the past entertains, ennobles, and expands quite readily, it enlightens only with delicate coaxing."

The speculative freedom provided by counterfactual analysis is a bane to economists seeking causal certainty. But the very same freedom presents invaluable service to society if we know how to exploit it. Counterfactualizing helps us bridge the gap between finite realized worlds and infinite possible worlds. It does this by promoting scenario thinking that helps us prepare for and adapt to an unknowable world where things might go very differently than we expect, so that we can begin to imagine how we might adjust. Counterfactuals are instruments for managing better in a world that presents both opportunities and dangers that we cannot ultimately know, and that we can influence but never control. Good social scientific counterfactuals, Weber (1996, 268) tells us, "can be used to open minds, to raise tough questions about what we think we know, and to suggest unfamiliar or uncomfortable arguments that we had best consider." He emphasizes that "the diversity of ideas is a survival asset for a human society living in an uncertain environment with an uncertain future" (273).

Recognition of the speculative value of counterfactualizing provides the grounding for a defense of theoretical pluralism in economics. The existence of multiple contending theories in economics is inconvenient, of course. It casts doubt on the truth content of the counterfactual scenarios generated by the predominant approach and challenges the predominant causal claims. It's GDAE versus Peterson. But that is precisely the virtue of contending theoretical perspectives in economics. They serve to generate alternative possible causal linkages that are missed when a profession assembles within one particular church and professes the truth of its sacred texts. Convergence around one theoretical approach generates unwarranted confidence in theoretical propositions and empirical inferences, suppresses recognition of alternative worlds, and restricts the proliferation of alternative scenarios that just might prepare us for unwelcome futures. The consequence of groupthink is repeated surprise when the world takes an unexpected turn for which it is grossly unprepared.[39] The consequence is preventable human suffering, including the loss of ten million Russian men.

Is there a way to exploit the fertility of counterfactualizing even as it disrupts causal claims? The answer is, in fact, yes. New approaches to policy making that feature "decision making under deep uncertainty" (DMDU) foreground computational experiments that stress-test policy proposals under thousands of possible futures, without ever attempting to select the "right" forecast. We will explore this approach in chapter 11.

The epigraphs to this chapter provide a warning that illuminates the epistemic problem confronting economists. The pathbreaking economist Douglas North (1999, 2) warns that the social world is in most respects "non-ergodic"—that is, it lacks "a stable underlying structure, such that we can develop theory that can be applied time after time, consistently." The poet

Szymborska makes the same point lyrically.[40] The fact of the matter is that in the social world "nothing can ever happen twice," let alone $n > 2$ times. Our ability to navigate responsibly in the context of irreparable ignorance, "without the chance to practice," depends on our abilities to counterfactualize creatively, pushing back against the professional and psychological drive for theoretical closure and causal finality.

PART III

Economic Moral Geometry

7

Managing Harm via Economic Moral Geometry

> How are we to say whether a reorganisation of production, which makes *A* better off, but *B* worse off, marks an improvement in efficiency? The sceptics declare that it is impossible to do so in an objective manner. . . . In fact there is a simple way of overcoming this defeatism, a perfectly objective test which enables us to discriminate between those reorganisations which improve productive efficiency, and those which do not.
>
> —JOHN HICKS (1941, 111)

COVID-19 Containment Policies: Are They Worth It?

In the early months of the COVID-19 pandemic, economists published cost-benefit analyses in which they explored whether social distancing regulations in the US that would reduce economic activity in the short run were worth the cost to save lives. Thunström et al. (2020) estimated that successful social distancing measures could save 1.24 million lives at a cost of $7.2 trillion. Acemoglu et al. (2020) forecast that 8.7 million lives could be saved as the return on policy costs of $2.15 trillion (see also Robinson, Sullivan, and Shogren 2020; Greenstone and Nigam 2020; Silverman n.d.).

But what does it mean to say that the lives saved are worth the cost? Under cost-benefit analysis the assessment of policy requires translating all costs and benefits into monetary equivalents. It's not enough to know that an expenditure of $*X* will save *Y* lives. The economist wants to know whether that expenditure represents a rational use of scarce resources. And this judgment is thought to require placing the correct dollar value on each life saved. Today US government agencies that routinely conduct cost-benefit analysis use various estimates of the value of life. The Environmental Protection Agency (EPA) uses $7.4 million; the Consumer Product Safety Commission uses $8.7 million; the Department of Transportation and the Department of Homeland Security use $11.6 million. Economists assign much lower estimates in lower-income countries (Viscusi and Masterman 2017).

How are these figures derived? Under one commonly used approach the value of life is derived from studies that try to ascertain how much individuals would need to be compensated to accept small increments in the risk of mortality, or, alternatively, how much they would pay to reduce that risk. For instance, people often face a choice among occupations that vary in terms of how dangerous they are. Standard economic theory holds that individuals will be willing to enter hazardous occupations only if they are adequately compensated for the extra risk, or—what amounts to the same thing—they will be willing to sacrifice some amount of compensation to secure jobs in safer occupations. In this approach, then, the difference between compensation levels of riskier and safer occupations can be taken to provide reliable information about the risk-reward trade-off that individuals are actually prepared to make.

Imagine there are 100,000 people in a community where a new government regulation would reduce everyone's risk of mortality by 1/100,000 (or .00001) per year, on average saving one life in the community annually. Imagine that labor market studies find that these community members on average are willing to pay $100 per year for a risk reduction of this magnitude. Scaling up, we find that the community as a whole is willing to pay $100 × 100,000, or $10 million, to save that one life. This figure is called the "value of a statistical life," or VSL. Economists use the VSL to assess whether lifesaving policy is worth the cost; whether it will generate net benefits calculated in dollar terms.

Controversies over this approach abound. Is assigning the *same* VSL to all individuals, as the EPA does (see EPA n.d.), the correct method for measuring the value of human life? Standard neoclassical theory suggests that it is not—that the value of each life should depend on individuals' circumstances, such as earning capacity and level of risk aversion. Moreover, using the same VSL for all treats the life of a five-year-old and that of a ninety-five-year-old equally. But some economists object, arguing that the benefit to society of death avoidance is greater when children's lives are spared. To correct the problem economists sometimes use an alternative measure of value, a constant "value per statistical life-year," or VSLY. That strategy provides age-specific estimates of the benefits of risk reduction, most simply by multiplying an annual benefit from life by the expected remaining years of life. Many other methodological strategies, such as using a variable VSLY, also appear in the literature.

Cost-benefit analyses typically generate a very wide range of estimates of the effects of the very same policy. Robinson, Sullivan, and Shogren (2020) demonstrate that if we accept the accuracy of Thunström et al.'s (2020) predictions of economic costs of social distancing and lives saved but simply apply alternative valuations of human life that appear in the literature, the net benefits of the policy they investigate range from *positive* $6 trillion to *negative* $1.7 trillion. A finding of positive net benefit indicates that the policy should be pursued, while negative net benefit indicates that the policy should not be undertaken.

Noneconomists might be forgiven for raising a fundamental question that rankles many economists: *is this procedure morally legitimate?* Is it right to place a dollar value on human life? Is it appropriate to reduce all benefits and costs to the common denominator of money to assess policy that affects highly valued goods, like human life, that are not in fact economic?

The Emergence of Moral Geometry: From Utilitarianism to Welfarism

The neoclassical revolution in economic theory that unfolded in the late nineteenth century sought an objective science of human affairs (see chap. 2). But the new neoclassicals recognized that policy assessment depended on value judgments. Economists cannot weigh in on a policy like free trade, for instance, without some normative standard for reaching conclusions. The challenge was to figure out how to apply hardheaded economic logic to value-laden policy application. The approach that came to dominate the profession, *welfare consequentialism*, emerged in the 1930s. The approach entails *economic moral geometry* that was thought to largely sidestep nonscientific normative judgments. It evolved out of classical utilitarianism.

CLASSICAL UTILITARIANISM

The utilitarianism associated with Jeremy Bentham, Henry Sidgwick, and John Stuart Mill was taken by late nineteenth- and early twentieth-century neoclassical economists to provide an objective science of policy assessment (Weymark 2016). Bentham advocated the "principle of utility" as a universal decision rule. "By the principle of utility is meant that principle which approves or disapproves of every action whatsoever, according to the tendency which it appears to have to augment or diminish the happiness of the party whose interest is in question" (Bentham [1789] 1996, 1).

Bentham defined utility in "hedonic" terms, as the experience of pleasure and pain. He pointedly refused to judge the activities that gave rise to these experiences. Utilitarianism is consequentialist. No action is inherently good or bad—*only its consequences matter*. As Bentham (1830, 206) famously put it, the child's game of push-pin "is of equal value with the arts and sciences of music and poetry. If the game of push-pin furnish more pleasure, it is more valuable than either."

Bentham realized that a policy might benefit some individuals while harming others. His utilitarianism required a calculus to judge policy under these conditions. The adopted method is simple aggregation. The *social* impact of a policy is taken to be the *sum* of its utility impacts on all affected individuals (Sen 1987).

Aggregation of utility is tricky, however. It requires that there be a scale with fixed units to measure utility that is consistent across all individuals. That kind of scale is called an interval scale. Measuring the length or weight of objects, for instance, uses an interval scale. We can confidently compare the lengths of two objects in meters, and also sum their lengths. The early neoclassical economists assumed that utility could be measured in the same way, with a "util" as the basic unit of measure. The term "cardinal utility" was adopted to refer to utility measured on an interval scale. If Sara reports that she gets six utils from an apple, and Pierre reports getting just three, the utilitarian concludes that the apple better serves Sara than it does Pierre. If they both receive an apple, the aggregate utility is nine utils. Under utilitarianism, policy that maximizes total utils across society's members is deemed best.

Utilitarianism served the needs of an economics profession looking for a scientific grounding for policy design. It provided a very simple framework that judged policy by just the one criterion of aggregate utility. Good policy promoted pleasure and reduced pain, full stop. The approach appeared to require very few value judgments, which were taken to be unobjectionable: defining human well-being in terms of pleasure and pain, and treating all individuals equally. Up through the 1930s neoclassical economists grounded policy assessment in utilitarian calculation.

Early neoclassicals tended to presume that successive increments of income generated decreasing increments of utility. This idea is reflected in the "law of diminishing marginal utility" of money. Moreover, they presumed that the relationship between income and utility was the same across individuals. These presumptions led to the conclusion that an extra $15 in the pocket of a billionaire would generate infinitesimal extra utility, but in contrast, that $15 in the pocket of a poor person might mean sending a child to bed well fed rather than hungry. This reasoning implies that shifting that $15 from the rich to the poor will increase aggregate utility. On these grounds the early twentieth-century economic utilitarians tended to favor redistributive measures to promote income equality.

THE NEW WELFARE ECONOMICS

Critics of utilitarianism ridiculed the idea that utility could be measured on an interval scale. Eminent economists including Vilfredo Pareto, Francis Edgeworth, Lionel Robbins, John Hicks, and others argued that there were no standard units to measure utility. Utility measurements could not be verified objectively; therefore, they were unscientific (Robbins 1932, chap. 6). And without standard units, there was no basis for making interpersonal utility comparisons. How can we possibly know, when Sara reports six utils and Pierre three, that they are using the same measure of "util"? But if economists couldn't make interpersonal comparisons of utility, then they couldn't sum utilities across individuals. In that case, the utilitarian calculus of aggregation would collapse. How, then, could the profession ascertain whether one policy was better than an alternative?

What came to be called the "new welfare economics" developed during the 1930s in response to this challenge (Stigler 1943). The new approach abandoned the idea that utility could be measured like length or weight. In place of an interval scale they adopted an "ordinal" scale; utility measured in this way is called "ordinal utility." Ordinal scales do not include fixed units of measurement. They therefore only permit the *rank ordering* of objects. In judging an art contest, for instance, a judge ranks the works of art from best to worst without relying on any units at all. It would make no sense to say that this painting is five units better than that painting. Adopting an ordinal scale, economists could no longer say anything meaningful about the precise amount of utility Sara got from an apple, or whether she got more utility from the apple than did Pierre.

The implications of adopting an ordinal scale were dramatic. Without interpersonal utility comparisons there was no longer a dependable metric by which to decide whether transferring $15 from the wealthy to the poor would increase aggregate utility. In giving up utils the profession's commitment to income equality became theoretically unmoored.

A second implication was equally important. Under an ordinal scale individuals rank policy options from better to worse just as a judge ranks works of art. Imagine that Sally prefers a new policy to the status quo, while Pierre prefers the status quo. Lacking fixed units of measure, an ordinal scale precludes aggregating their individual utility levels to ascertain which is the best policy. The profession needed a new calculus to assess policy.

The critique was associated with another theoretical transformation. Economists came to be suspicious of the concepts of pleasure and pain, which they took to be unobservable and even fanciful. When football players crumble to the pitch in apparent agony, we have no idea how intense or mild is the pain, or if they are in fact faking the injury. In contrast, economists thought that *preferences* could be observed through individuals' market behavior. If Sara chooses an apple when an orange at the same price is available, she reveals her preference for apples over oranges. Neoclassical economists came to presume that individuals, being rational, made all decisions in accordance with their "preference orderings," their rankings of likes and dislikes. As a consequence of these insights, economists substituted *preference satisfaction* for pleasure and pain as the appropriate measure of well-being. While the term "utility" continues to be employed in economics today, it now typically refers to preference satisfaction. In addition, many economists came to hold the view that preferences were self-regarding—that Pierre's welfare depended only on the goods to which he gained access and not on his consumption levels relative to others.[41] Hence relative inequality itself was taken not to induce any harm of moral concern. Although people who are left behind financially while others enjoy rising income might feel envy or spite, those sentiments are not taken by most welfare economists to be valid (see McCloskey 1982, 181).

WELFARE CONSEQUENTIALISM

These theoretical innovations led the new welfare economists to adopt welfare consequentialism (hereinafter, welfarism). It remains the pillar of economic policy assessment even today in the branch of economics that evaluates policy, aptly called welfare economics. Welfare economics flourished through the 1960s and then disappeared from graduate economics curriculum. That omission is extraordinary given that the profession offers policy assessment in virtually every area of public policy, often with significant influence, and those assessments are grounded in a normative framework that economics students no longer study.

The contemporary welfarist framework insists that all goods, economic and noneconomic, are *welfare commensurable*. That is, all goods are theorized as nothing but transmitters of welfare, where welfare is defined in terms of preference satisfaction. Luxury yachts, insulin, environmental quality—the value of each good derives from the welfare it generates for individuals. Goods are not permitted to have value that is not translatable into welfare. The presence of other kinds of value would subvert the welfare commensurability that is vital to the normative framework.

Welfare economics makes a range of technical assumptions that permit simple mathematical calculations concerning welfare that in turn generate unambiguous policy assessments.[42] One technical assumption is that a person's preferences must be "continuous." Continuity ensures that small changes in the amount of any one good generate small changes in the individual's preference satisfaction (Adler 1998; Boadway and Bruce 1984, 34). The continuity assumption is thought to be a matter of simple mathematical convenience. In fact, it represents a terribly important *normative* leap. Here's why:

continuity rules out what is called a "lexicographic" ordering of preferences, where one or more goods are considered to be nonsubstitutable (Boadway and Bruce 1984, 146–47).[43] In a lexicographic ordering that prioritizes apples, for instance, no number of oranges could substitute for the loss of a single apple.

Continuity implies *substitutability* among goods, such that the loss of a finite amount of one good can always be fully offset by the provision of a finite amount of some other good. The assumption assures us that workers will always be willing to accept small increases in the risk of injury or death, for instance, provided they receive small increases in wages.

NEW WELFARE ECONOMICS DECISION RULES

The Pareto Criterion

The new welfare economists of the 1930s needed new decision rules to assess policy that avoided utility aggregation. The concept of Pareto efficiency introduced by Pareto around the turn of the twentieth century provided a first-best test of policy. The Pareto criterion holds that a proposed policy is better than an alternative policy—say, the status quo—provided at least one person prefers the policy and no one prefers the status quo. If some members of a community support building a water treatment facility that will prevent waterborne illnesses, and no one opposes it, then the Pareto criterion recommends constructing the facility.

The Pareto criterion appears to supply economists with an elegant test of policy. In fact, it is largely useless in policy assessment. Economic policy interventions typically generate uneven effects, benefiting some members of society while harming others (see chap. 4). In the context of uneven impact, the Pareto criterion has nothing at all to say about which policy measure is best. The new welfare economists needed a decision rule that could adjudicate policy even when it would benefit some and harm others. Ideally, however, the new decision rule should build on the Pareto criterion. Let's see how this goal was achieved.

Kaldor-Hicks Potential Pareto Test

Two of the earliest solutions to the problem of assessing policy that generated benefits and harms came from Kaldor (1939) and Hicks (1939; 1941) in parallel innovations that are now typically referred to as the Kaldor-Hicks compensation test (see also Hotelling 1938). Imagine a proposal to build a highway through a neighborhood that will benefit commuters but harm those whose community is destroyed by the project. Those who will win under the new policy prefer it; those who will be harmed oppose it, preferring instead the status quo. The Kaldor-Hicks test claims simply that the project is better than the status quo if the gains to those who benefit from the new highway are more than sufficient to fully compensate those harmed by it. In Hicks's words, "if *A* is made so much better off by the change that he could compensate *B* for his loss, and still have something left over, then the reorganisation is an unequivocal improvement" (1941, 111).

In the view of its advocates, the compensation test provides a mechanism for generating objective judgments on policy, as Hicks argued in the passage used as the epigraph to this chapter. That view is still widely shared today. The emphasis on productive efficiency is important. Productive efficiency entails generating greater output of goods that society wants relative to available productive resources. Shifting resources from the production of manual typewriters to that of personal computers enhances productive efficiency, for instance. So does new technology that increases the number of computers that can be produced given available resources. Policy that achieves productive efficiency is consistent with Kaldor-Hicks because some of the surplus can be reallocated to compensate anyone harmed by the policy.

More is going on here than meets the eye. Kaldor-Hicks requires that all benefits and harms be convertible to monetary measures. Let's assume that the gains to the winners from the proposed highway project are greater than the losses to the losers. *If some of the gains from the policy were used to fully compensate the losers*, then after compensation was made, *there would no longer be any losers*. This is the key point. The project *with full compensation* therefore represents a Pareto improvement, with the winners supporting it and no one opposing it. But here's the trick. Kaldor-Hicks does not require that compensation be made. It concludes that even if compensation is not made, the project still represents a *potential* Pareto improvement because it *could* generate a Pareto improvement were the losers to be compensated. The test is therefore better described as the Kaldor-Hicks potential Pareto test rather than the Kaldor-Hicks compensation test because in fact the test does not require compensation.

Noneconomists often find it difficult to accept the brazen attitude of economists who advocate policy that harms some members of society on grounds that it benefits others more. Hicks, too, worried about the willingness of economists to induce harm for the sake of economic efficiency. He criticized the "hard-boiled attitude" of economists of his era who believed that individuals who were harmed by policy should have prepared for an adverse policy shift by salting away savings to tide them over (Hicks 1939, 711–12). Hicks worried that the failure of policy makers to compensate losers from beneficial policy reforms would interfere with economic progress. He wrote that "economic progress has accumulated a roll of victims sufficient to give all sound policy a bad name" (1939, 711). Kaldor dismissed the matter of compensation as a noneconomic question. "[Whether] the landlords, in the free-trade case should in fact be given compensation or not, is a political question on which the economist, *qua* economist, could hardly pronounce an opinion" (Kaldor 1939, 550–51). Economists largely followed Kaldor's lead, advocating policy that would harm members of society without requiring compensation. While others might flinch from growth-promoting policies that put nineteenth-century handloom weavers or twentieth-century machinists out of work, or that would devastate communities through forced relocation to make way for infrastructure projects, economists armed with Kaldor-Hicks rise to the challenge.[44]

Kaldor-Hicks was (and is) intended to permit considerations of efficiency separate from matters of equity (Hicks 1939; Mishan 1960; Boadway 2016). Trade liberalization, for instance, is sometimes defended on the basis of Kaldor-Hicks. Trade liberalization is taken to increase a nation's aggregate income even though it often benefits high-waged workers and punishes low-waged workers. Kaldor-Hicks nonetheless advocates trade liberalization. All that matters under Kaldor-Hicks is the relative magnitude of the gains and losses.

Cost-Benefit Analysis

Kaldor-Hicks is operationalized through cost-benefit analysis (CBA; Dasgupta and Pearce 1972, 69).[45] Though for convenience I elucidate it here separately, CBA is the method utilized to ascertain when the Kaldor-Hicks test is satisfied, rather than an independent test of policy.

CBA is among the economist's chief contribution to policy formation. US federal agencies are required by executive order to apply CBA to proposed regulations (Executive Order 12866, 1993). The order states that "in deciding whether and how to regulate, agencies should assess all costs and benefits of available regulatory alternatives, including the alternative of not regulating." There are many methods for conducting CBA (see Dorfman 1993). Here I present the intuition underlying just one.[46]

CBA assesses a proposed policy, such as new government regulation that will reduce emissions of industrial pollutants, relative to a baseline, typically the status quo. A comprehensive CBA requires tracing all the effects of the regulation, including all its costs and benefits, and then placing dollar values on each. CBA approves of the project if the aggregate benefits exceed the aggregate costs.

The simplicity of that description belies the daunting complexities associated with identifying and measuring in dollar values all benefits and costs. Consider a very simple regulation, one that would require utility companies in a municipality to invest in smokestack scrubbers to reduce the emission of various pollutants into the atmosphere. Estimating monetary costs in this case might be fairly straightforward, provided the technology required to do the job is already available in the market and there is already sufficient experience with the technology so that economists know how much it reduces productive efficiency. But what about the benefits? Each pollutant entails distinct damages to human health and to the natural environment. Evaluating the policy's benefits requires assessing how much the reduction of each pollutant diminishes those damages. If the damages include morbidity and even mortality, a price must be placed on human health and even human life. Beyond all that, those affected by the pollution may value environmental quality. They would therefore benefit from reductions in damage to the environment. But how is the economist to calculate the magnitude of these kinds of "nonmarket" benefits so that a full comparison of costs and benefits can be made?

One approach to this assessment, known as contingent valuation, dispenses with some of the technical analysis. With contingent valuation, economists survey a sample of the individuals who will be affected by the policy, asking whether they support or oppose the policy. For those who support the policy, economists attempt to elicit their "willingness to pay" (WTP), the amount they would pay to have the policy introduced.[47] For those who oppose the regulation economists instead attempt to elicit their "willingness to accept" (WTA)—the amount they would have to be compensated to accept the regulation. The presumption underlying contingent valuation is that individuals can properly "price" the regulation's effects on their well-being. The approach relies on those who would be affected by the regulation to monetize the benefits and harms to them, freeing the economist from having to price nonmarket goods like human health.

Imagine that in the case of the smokestack scrubber initiative, people in the survey on average are willing to pay $150 to see the initiative introduced. If there are 200,000 people in the affected population, then the aggregate benefit measured in terms of WTP is $30 million. If the total cost of implementing the initiative is below $30 million, then the net benefits—total benefits minus total costs—are positive, and the project satisfies the Kaldor-Hicks test.[48] In that case, the winners (those who support the initiative) could fully compensate the losers (those who oppose the initiative, including, perhaps, those who oppose government regulations on ideological grounds) from the gains the policy would afford them. If instead the net benefits are negative, then the policy fails Kaldor-Hicks.

But what if a policy measure stands to save or threaten lives? Those whose lives are spared would surely report that they would pay an infinite amount for the policy, while those who would be killed would not accept it at any level of compensation. But infinite magnitudes wreck CBA. CBA economists often seek to resolve the problem through the kind of calculation presented at the outset of this chapter—inferring the value of a statistical life (VSL) from labor market studies that compare wage rates in riskier and safer jobs. Under the contingent valuation approach, survey respondents, rather than economists, are expected to do the difficult work of pricing life by reporting their WTP or WTA for a policy that entails a change in risk. If the smokestack scrubbers are expected to reduce the risk of death by 1/100,000, respondents are asked to take that fact into account when pricing the benefits to them of the scrubber initiative. When they on average report a WTP of $150, the economist presumes that respondents have priced in the value of the reduced risk to their lives, along with all other benefits. In this way, it seems, the procedure allows economists to price the priceless (see Viscusi 2014; EPA n.d.).

CBA follows Kaldor-Hicks in all important respects. It focuses on *potential* compensation; it does not require that the winners from policy actually compensate the losers. CBA is satisfied provided the policy yields a *potential* Pareto improvement. Moreover, CBA typically does not consider the distribution of benefits and harms across society's members. Following Kaldor-Hicks, the focus is on aggregate net benefits. In the words of the EPA (n.d.),

> Of course in most cases where the total benefits exceed total costs, it will *not* be true that the benefits exceed the costs for each and every person affected by the policy; rather, some individuals will gain and others will lose. However, if the total benefits are greater than the costs, then it is *in principle* possible for those who gain to compensate those who lose so that everyone could be better off with the policy. This is what it means for a policy to pass a benefit-cost test.

Distributional effects are sometimes tacked on to CBA as a secondary consideration. Alternatively, they are taken up separately, supplementing CBA.

The use of money as the metric in CBA has a notable consequence. If money is subject to declining marginal utility, an increment in income has a decreasing effect on utility as individuals' income rises. As individuals become wealthier, then, they will need to be compensated more to accept projects that harm them. Now consider the question of where to build a municipal trash incinerator. An incinerator generates serious health effects for its immediate neighbors, such as increasing the incidence of respiratory illness. If we apply CBA to the problem it will generally be the case that the wealthy will demand more in compensation to accept the incinerator in their neighborhood than will the poor, even though the health effects may be more detrimental to the poor, who are more likely to lack adequate medical care, than they are to the wealthy. Why? Because each dollar of compensation generates less utility for the rich than for the poor. If decision makers use the results of a CBA without adjusting for the declining marginal utility of money, they will be led to site the facility in the poor rather than the rich neighborhood.

We can now understand why economists rushed to produce CBA of COVID-19 containment measures in the early days of the pandemic. CBA economists think it essential to compare the monetary costs of pandemic control measures with the monetary value of lives saved. Especially when lives are at stake, these economists claim, good policy must be informed by the dispassionate policy assessments that CBA uniquely provides.

Social Welfare Functions[49]

Some economists are unpersuaded by the argument that utility can't be compared interpersonally. Following Abram Bergson (1938), these economists have developed "social welfare functions" (SWFs)—mathematical equations that combine levels of individual well-being into aggregate measures of welfare for society. From the 1950s through the 1960s (and again very recently—see Adler 2019) welfare economists wrestled with the challenges associated with constructing SWFs that assess policy by the metric of aggregated well-being levels. Today the SWF approach is employed in policy areas ranging from macroeconomics to trade, taxation, health care, and climate change.

The SWF approach to policy assessment involves several steps, each of which requires value judgments. The first step entails deciding what determines an individual's welfare. The range of options in the literature include utility, defined in terms of preference satisfaction, health status, educational attainment, and longevity. Once that decision is made, welfare levels are estimated for each member of society under a baseline scenario, like the status quo, and under a proposed policy. Next, a measure of *social* welfare must be constructed for each policy option from the individual welfare levels. This is the job of the SWF. The literature comprises many alternative SWF equations to achieve this result. Should the SWF simply add up the unadjusted individual welfare numbers to generate a measure of social welfare? If Maria gets ten units of welfare from a policy, while Salvador gets six, simple aggregation generates total social welfare of sixteen. That approach should sound familiar. Aggregating individual welfare levels returns us squarely to Bentham's utilitarianism, yielding what is called the "utilitarian SWF." But there are other options. For instance, individual welfare numbers can be adjusted before aggregating. One option is to adjust the numbers to give greater weight to the welfare levels of the relatively worse-off members of society. Under what Adler (2019, chap.4) calls the "continuous prioritarian" SWF, for instance, redistribution of income from high- to low-income individuals generally registers as an increase in aggregate social welfare.[50]

Once all these decisions are made and the measurements are taken, two policies can be compared based on their aggregate social welfare. If a policy promises greater social welfare than the status quo, the SWF economist endorses the policy on the grounds of social betterment. If instead the status quo outperforms the proposed policy, the policy is rejected.

DISCONTINUITIES BETWEEN SWFS AND KALDOR-HICKS/CBA

The SWF approach breaks with Kaldor-Hicks/CBA in important respects. The SWF approach accepts interpersonal well-being comparisons (Adler 2019, 14, 41ff, 76ff). Even if it is not always clear how to make fine-grained welfare distinctions among people who are about equally well-off, SWF advocates argue that it is certainly appropriate to distinguish the welfare of the well-off from the welfare of the deprived (Sen 1992). The approach also can prioritize the welfare of those who are worse-off, overcoming the bias in favor of the privileged that exists under Kaldor-Hicks/CBA.

Adler (2020) and Adler and Hammitt (2020) have attempted to demonstrate the discontinuities between SWFs and CBA in their examination of COVID-19 containment policy. They argue that under CBA, economic theory would have us value more highly the lives of high-income individuals owing to the declining marginal utility of money. High-income individuals require much greater compensation to accept risks to their health than do low-income individuals. That defect generates the indefensible conclusion that COVID-19 containment efforts should be biased in favor of protecting high-income individuals from the virus. CBA is also insensitive to who is most burdened by policies like social distancing to contain the pandemic. Adler and Hammitt argue that the SWF approach can resolve these deficiencies by giving greater weight in COVID-19 policy assessment to those who are worse-off.

SHARED FOUNDATIONS: THE THEORY OF HARM

Kaldor-Hicks/CBA and the SWF approach nonetheless share important theoretical foundations. First, we explore their common conception of harm. We then turn to ancillary matters.

The most important connection binding Kaldor-Hicks/CBA and SWFs is that they both enact welfarism, which shapes their conception of harm. The logic is straightforward. Welfare consequentialism treats all goods as welfare commensurable, as nothing but welfare transmitters. Individuals benefit when they gain access to more of the goods they prefer. The approach generates an extraordinarily elegant account of harm. *Harm is defined here as the loss of welfare that is consequent upon the diminution in an individual's access to one or more goods she values.* Harm can be represented simply as a leftward shift on a welfare continuum from *x* to *y*, depicted in figure 7.1, that is caused by a reduction (from *a* to *b*) in access to a valued good.

The simplicity of this definition of harm obscures the complexity of its implications. Since goods are substitutable welfare transmitters—recall that the standard approach rules out lexicographic preferences—any harm to an agent owing to reduced access to goods she values can be fully offset via increased access to other goods. There will always be some finite amount of an alternative good that, once provided to the harmed agent, will leave her as well-off as she was prior to the harm.

That argument involves two distinct claims that are often conflated. The first is that all harms are *reparable* in the sense that a harmed agent can always be made whole. An agent who slides leftward on the welfare continuum can

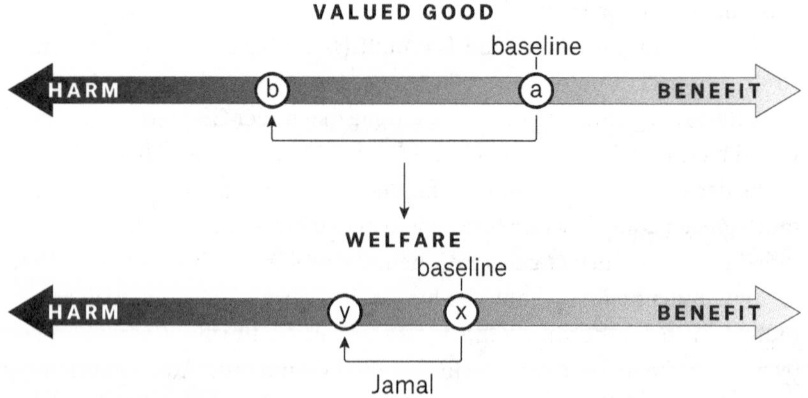

FIGURE 7.1. Harm as welfare loss
Under standard moral geometry, Jamal is harmed—his welfare is reduced—when he suffers diminished access to one or more valued goods.

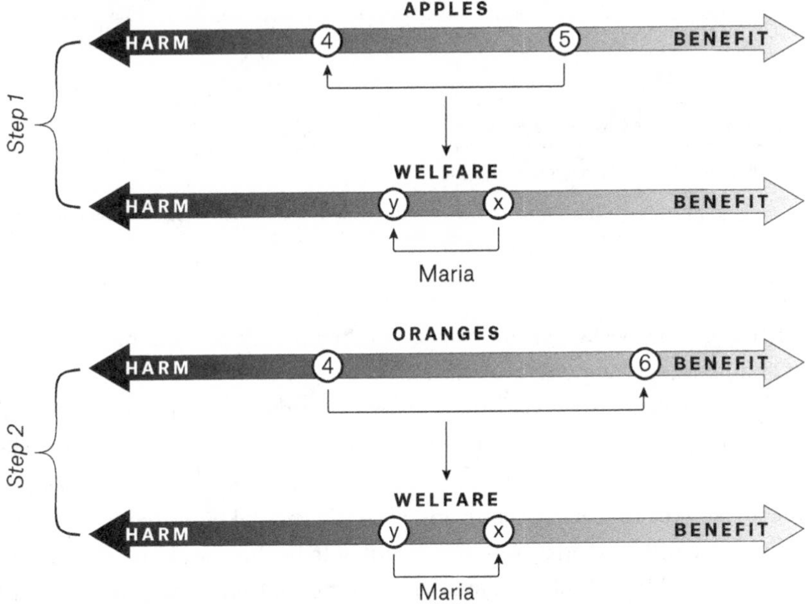

FIGURE 7.2. Compensation through substitution
Under standard moral geometry, Maria's harm from diminished access to apples (step 1) is offset by increased access to oranges (step 2). Potential harm from the loss of an apple—moving Maria from *x* to *y* on the welfare scale—is repaired by "compensation" in oranges that returns her to *x*.

always be restored to the preharm position. She is no worse-off after repair than she was prior to the harm.

But how does repair take place? The second claim concerns the *mechanism* of repair. Under moral geometry, repair occurs only via *compensation* (Adler 1998; Adler and Posner 2006). The loss of some amount of one good is compensated for by increased access to another good, where the amount of compensation necessary to do the job is determined by the person's willingness to trade off one good for another. If she is indifferent between having one apple and two oranges, two oranges will suffice to compensate her for the harm she suffers from the loss of one apple. With either bundle of goods—the one with one more apple and the other with two more oranges—she is equally well-off. The situation is reflected in figure 7.2. Initially, Maria has access to a bundle of five apples and four oranges. If she loses access to one apple, her welfare falls from *x* to *y*. But that harm can be fully compensated by access to two additional oranges. Compensation in oranges returns her to her previous level of welfare. She is indifferent between the two bundles—the first that includes five apples and four oranges, and the second that includes four apples and six oranges. If we take money as providing general access to

TABLE 7.1. Compensable vs. noncompensable, reparable vs. irreparable harm: The standard view

	Reparable harm	*Irreparable harm*
Commensurable, substitutable goods	Compensable harms	
Incommensurable, nonsubstitutable goods		

If all goods are welfare commensurable and substitutable, then all harms are reparable through compensation.

other goods, as welfare economists generally do, then we can theorize harm as compensable via monetary transfer.

Table 7.1 elucidates the relationships between the relevant concepts. Moral geometry presumes that all harms are reparable. Under this approach the cells in the right-hand column of 7.1, which denotes irreparable harm, are empty. But are all reparable harms compensable—can they all be erased through the provision of other goods, or money? For that to be the case, all goods must be commensurable and substitutable. The assumptions underlying the standard approach ensure these conditions are met. In fact, all goods are treated as nothing but substitutable welfare transmitters. The cells in the table's lower row, which denotes incommensurable, nonsubstitutable goods, must also be empty. The elegant result is this: all harms that humans suffer must reside in the northwest cell of table 7.1, which designates compensable harms.

The standard welfarist approach to harm entails other conceptual building blocks. First, it rejects the idea of "harm's priority" (Shiffrin 2012): it requires that *benefits* and *harms*, too, be mathematically and morally commensurable. Commensurability implies that they can be adequately compared on the same scale. Commensurability was implicit in our discussion of figure 7.2, where we combined harm and benefit into one welfare outcome. Second, on the welfare continuum, individuals are benefited by *any* move to the right and harmed by *any* move to the left, irrespective of the magnitude of the shift. In figure 7.3 both Jamal's decline from x to y and Maria's decline from x' to y' indicate harm, even though Jamal faces a much greater decline in preference satisfaction (in absolute and relative terms) than does Maria. Third, both Jamal and Maria are harmed by the declines they experience even though Maria is far better-off than Jamal before and after the shift.

Fourth, the standard approach also holds that *not benefiting* is equivalent to *harming*. Imagine a situation in which a proposed policy would benefit some individuals but harm others. Think of a tax cut for the wealthy that will necessitate cuts in social welfare payments to the poor. The alternative is to

FIGURE 7.3. Welfare, magnitude of shift, and inequality
Under moral geometry, no distinction is made between Jamal's and Maria's situations. Both suffer harm when access to valued goods is diminished, even though the magnitude of Maria's welfare loss is far less than that of Jamal's, and even though Maria is far better off than Jamal before and after the loss.

maintain the status quo. In this case can all harm be avoided simply by retaining the status quo? The answer given by moral geometry is "no." The approach holds that those who would have benefited from the policy are harmed if the status quo is maintained. *Their forgone benefit is treated as harm.* This theoretical maneuver is not obviously correct, though moral geometry depends on it. Without commensurability between harming and not benefiting, the moral foundations of Kaldor-Hicks/CBA and SWFs would collapse (see chaps. 8 and 9).

Finally, standard moral geometry does not recognize absolute welfare thresholds. It allows for no welfare level at which a reduction in individuals' welfare precipitates an abrupt or catastrophic decline in their quality of life. Let the vertical line on the welfare continuum in figure 7.4 indicate a threshold such that Jamal's move from above to below it is experienced as catastrophic. The line might designate zero welfare, a point below which life is not worth living (Broome 1999, chap. 10; Adler 2018). The assumption of continuity in preferences implies that *there is no such threshold*—that there is no point distinguishing a life worth living from one that is not.

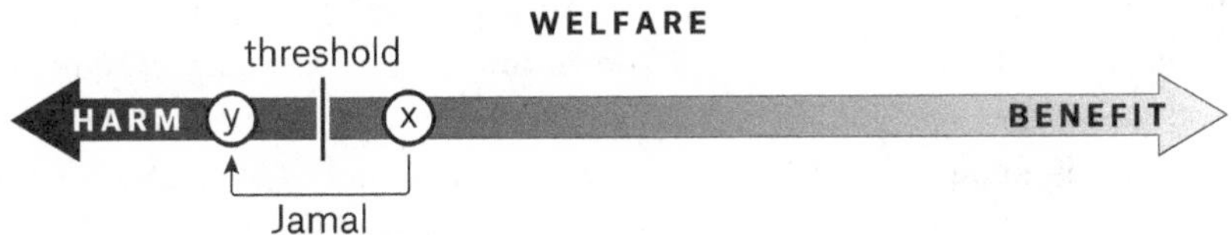

FIGURE 7.4. Welfare threshold
Under standard moral geometry, there is no threshold signifying a catastrophic deterioration in the quality of life.

OTHER CONTINUITIES

Kaldor-Hicks/CBA and the SWF approach face a range of common problems that they largely manage identically. Here we survey three.

Uncertainty

Since all these approaches are consequentialist, they must come to terms with the problem of uncertainty of future policy effects, including both costs and benefits. How confident can we be that we know the impacts of policy that must be factored into the consequentialist accounting? Predicting policy impact, as we have seen, requires time-travel machines that allow us to see tomorrow, today.

Moral geometry seeks to eliminate uncertainty by treating the future effects of policy as *probabilistically knowable*. Moral geometers must presume that a policy option could generate any one of a range of possible outcomes—some better, some worse—depending on the "state of nature" that emerges in the future after the policy is implemented (Boadway and Bruce 1984, 10). They must also presume that they can identify the full range of possible policy outcomes prior to policy implementation. The geometers must also presume, finally, that they can know the probability of each possible outcome. Matthew Adler (2019, 19), certainly among the most sophisticated contemporary welfare economists, explains the strategy clearly:

> I'll generally conceptualize uncertainty about the outcomes associated with policies by thinking of each policy as a *probability distribution* across outcomes. Policy *P* is one such probability distribution, assigning to each outcome *x* some numerical probability, the probability of *x* given the choice of policy *P* (these probability numbers summing to one); policy *P** is a different probability distribution.

The US Office of Management and Budget (OMB) provides guidance to government economists on CBA, including on complications stemming from uncertainty. It claims that "the precise consequences (benefits and costs) of regulatory options are not always known for certain, *but the probability of their occurrence can often be developed*" (OMB 2003, 38; emphasis added).[51]

What is going on here? Moral geometry thinks of policy outcomes like the outcomes of throwing a die.[52] We know the full range of possible outcomes of throwing a normal die (1–6). We do not know whether the next roll of a die will come up 4, but we know with certainty that there is a one-sixth chance of it coming up 4. This kind of a system—wherein all the possible outcomes and their probabilities are known and remain stable over time—is called "ergodic." Now think of policy outcomes. Just like the gambler throwing dice, the moral geometers generally presume they can know the full range and probabilities of possible future outcomes of any policy, and the economic value of those potential outcomes. With that information in hand, we can then compare policies by reference to their respective probability distributions. For instance, we can pursue one widely accepted approach of calculating the weighted average of each policy's possible outcomes. For a normal die, the weighted average is (1 × ⅙) + (2 × ⅙) + . . . (6 × ⅙), or 3.5. The weighted average yields the policy's *expected* level of social welfare, denoted in the literature as "expected utility," or E(U). We can undertake the same exercise for all other possible policy options, including the status quo. We are then directed to choose the policy with the highest E(U). The approach can be described as *optimizing over potential outcomes*—implementing the policy that appears to promise maximum social welfare (Lempert and McKay 2011).

Let's extend the analogy to clarify how the procedure works. Think of two policy options where the potential outcomes of the first are reflected in a normal die, numbered 1–6. Imagine that the possible outcomes of the second policy are reflected in a die numbered like this: 2, 2, 2, 2, 3, 7. Keep in mind that each number indicates the level of social welfare that *could* arise from each of the two policies. A policy maker must choose one die (policy) over the other, and then she can roll that die just once. Which "policy" should the policy maker choose? We've just calculated the E(U) of the first policy; it is 3.5. The E(U) of the second policy, calculated the same way, is 3.0. The E(U) decision rule dictates selection of the first policy.[53]

What has been done here is ingenious. Moral geometers are treating a *changing, unknowable* future characterized by Knightian uncertainty as if it were a *stable, probabilistically knowable* future characterized by Knightian risk (see chap. 5). They're assuming the future effects of alternative policies are as knowable as the outcomes of throwing dice. The strategy lets us believe that if it were possible to enact the policy options repeatedly under identical circumstances, we would know the frequency with which each outcome would occur. We have *domesticated* irreparable ignorance, eliminating it from view by treating policy choice just like throwing dice, where we *do* know the probability of each outcome. The heroic assumption that policy choice is just like throwing dice enables economists to utilize moral geometry even in cases where economists acknowledge limitations to their knowledge of the future.

Discounting the Future

Moral geometry that compares benefits and harms requires judgments about how to balance the welfare of people alive today against the welfare of future generations. The thorny problem of time discounting arises in this context. Imagine that a policy is expected to impose a cost of $1 billion on the present generation while generating a benefit of $2.5 billion for those alive thirty years from now. If we were to treat the present and future generations as if they were both present today, the policy would almost certainly pass the Kaldor-Hicks/CBA and SWF tests. But economists don't proceed that way. Instead, economists typically "discount" future benefits and harms. There are several justifications for the practice. One follows reasoning associated with "pure time preference." Individuals typically prefer receiving a dollar today to waiting five years for the dollar. Receiving the dollar today, the recipients can invest it at the going rate of return, for instance, and receive back more than a dollar five years out. Moreover, people don't know if they will even be alive in five years. Recipients would typically need to be promised more than the dollar in the future to forgo receiving the dollar today. How much more they would need to be compensated for waiting depends on how much they discount the future. If an individual discounts the future by 4% per year, she would need to be promised $1.22 five years from now to forgo the dollar today. To put it another way, $1.22 five years from now is equal to just $1.00 today. We say that the "present discounted value" of the future $1.22 is $1.00.

Now consider policy assessment. For the moral geometer, $1 billion today counts for more than $1 billion five years from now. The moral geometer must discount future sums of money to make them comparable with current sums of money. But discounting biases moral geometry toward the interests of the present generation. At a 4% discount rate, $1 billion today equates to $3.24 billion thirty years from now. That means that a policy that imposes a cost of $1 billion on those living today and that yields any amount of benefits below $3.24 billion for the generation thirty years hence fails under moral geometry. The intensity of the bias in favor of the present generation depends on the choice of the discount rate that is used in the assessment. The higher the rate at which the future is discounted, the greater will be the bias.

Much is at stake in the selection of discount rates. In assessing climate change, Nicholas Stern, who headed up the *Stern Review on the Economics of Climate Change* for the government of the UK (2007), argued for an effective discount rate of zero to balance current costs against future benefits. The *Review* (31ff) accepted the long-standing ethical critique of relying on pure time preference to discount the welfare of future generations. The *Review* concluded that 1% of world GDP should be invested immediately to reduce the rate of climate change. In response one of the world's leading environmental economists, William Nordhaus (2007, 1), challenged what he viewed as the *Review's* alarmist findings. He argued that "the *Review's* unambiguous conclusions about the need for extreme immediate action will not survive the substitution of assumptions that are consistent with today's marketplace real interest rates and savings rates." Nordhaus's critique was grounded in established moral geometry that insists on setting a discount rate that reflects economic fundamentals (the "real interest and savings rates"). The logic is that since future generations will be better-off than the current generation, there is good reason to discount benefits that will flow to them (see OMB 2003, 32).

Laundering Preferences

All preference-based approaches to welfare must reckon one way or another with inappropriate preferences. Individuals may be misinformed and so prefer something that will reduce rather than enhance their welfare. This problem is acute in contingent valuation surveys, where the replies of ill-informed respondents can determine whether a policy passes the CBA test. Individuals may also have antisocial preferences. A sadist prefers that others suffer. Should that preference count in moral evaluation of outcomes? If not, what about the widely shared preference today for watching American football, where the players risk severe injury, including brain damage and premature death? Individuals may also have conflicting preferences that complicate moral geometry. I might prefer that you get a good while you prefer that I get it. And what is to be done with "remote" preferences—preferences over aspects of the world that have little or nothing to do with a person's actual life? I might prefer the preservation of a distant national park that I will never visit. Should that preference count? Finally, individuals facing sustained deprivation may come to devalue important goods, including basic freedoms, to which they will never gain access (see chap. 8). Should the preference for those goods be eliminated from policy assessment?

Which preferences should count, then, in moral geometry? The standard approach is to accept most if not all preferences. That is the case in contingent valuation surveys. The surveyor typically does not inquire why people prefer one policy over another. OMB's guidance to federal government economists does not raise the matter at all (OMB 2003). Instead, consumer sovereignty reigns, where, as Bentham said, push-pin is just as good as poetry. Some economists are reluctant to accept all existing preferences, however, and argue for amending preferences to ensure that social assessment is based exclusively on *appropriate* preferences (Adler 2019). After all, people may in fact hold racist and other antisocial preferences that run contrary to social betterment. In principle, "laundering" (or "idealizing") preferences makes sense. But laundering preferences risks substituting economists' value judgments for the judgments of others. This is troubling to many economists given the degree to which the exercise potentially compromises the sovereignty of the individuals whose welfare the economist seeks to enhance. When preferences that are deeply held by individuals are ignored in the welfarist exercise, is the assessment of welfare grounded in individuals' preferences or in the preferences the economist wishes individuals had? Laundering preferences places economists' values at the center of an evaluative exercise that was intended to remove economists' values from social accounting.

Taking Stock, Looking Ahead

We have covered a lot of ground here. A quick summary is in order. Table 7.2 presents the central aspects of the standard welfarist decision rules as they are most commonly specified in moral geometry.

Moral geometry reduces complex ethical deliberations to simple math problems, the solutions to which purport to convey what we need to know to make the right policy decisions. The Pareto criterion avoids difficult ethical questions by refusing to judge policy that induces any harm whatsoever. It need not make a series of contentious assumptions that are required by the other tests. But it is largely useless in policy assessment. Kaldor-Hicks/CBA and SWFs seek to judge policy even in the face of harm. Those theorists who reject the validity of interpersonal welfare comparisons employ Kaldor-Hicks/CBA. Those who instead accept the validity of interpersonal comparisons adopt SWFs. Typically, the tests do not prioritize the welfare of the worst-off, though the SWF approach can do so. Both tests are grounded in welfare consequentialism, where goods are nothing but commensurable welfare transmitters. Harm, then, is simply the reduction in welfare caused by diminished access to one or more goods that individuals prefer. Both tests require continuity in preferences, which rules out lexicographic orderings of goods, and also require the substitutability of all goods, which ensures the reparability and compensability of all harms. The tests also require the commensurability of benefits with harms and of harming with not benefiting. They avoid welfare thresholds, though the SWF approach can incorporate them. They reduce uncertainty to calculable risk, and they discount future benefits and costs. And to the degree possible they avoid laundering preferences. The procedures all yield rigorous yet tractable judgments about even the most complex policy questions, like how to respond to COVID-19, that involve monetary and nonmonetary benefits and costs, including the protection of life.

The field of welfare economics exhibits extraordinary intellectual virtuosity in pursuit of the "right" moral geometry to evaluate policy. I have been able to convey only a small amount of the subtlety and creativity of the field here. But the literature tends to pass far too quickly over the most important

TABLE 7.2. A comparison of decision rules

	Pareto	*KH*	*CBA*	*SWFs*
Managing harm	No one is harmed	Gains to winners > Losses to losers	Applied KH	Aggregation of individual welfare
Interpersonal comparisons?	No	No	No	Yes
Prioritizes worst off?	No	No	No	Can but need not
Welfare commensurability of all goods?	NA	Yes	Yes	Yes
Welfare reductionism of all harms?	NA	Yes	Yes	Yes
Substitutability of goods?	NA	Yes	Yes	Yes
Reparability of all harms through compensation?	NA	Yes	Yes	Yes
Commensurability of benefits with harms?	NA	Yes	Yes	Yes
Equates not benefiting with harming?	NA	Yes	Yes	Yes
Recognizes welfare thresholds?	NA	No	No	Can but typically does not
Managing uncertainty	NA	E(U)	E(U)	E(U)
Discounting the future?	NA	Yes	Yes	Yes
Laundering preferences?	No	No	No	Can but typically does not

KH = Kaldor-Hicks; CBA = cost-benefit analysis; SWF = social welfare function; E(U) = expected utility; NA = not applicable.

questions that normative economics should examine. Should welfare consequentialism be taken as the singly appropriate normative standard for policy assessment? And is any sort of moral geometry an appropriate approach for a profession that induces harm as it promotes social betterment? We now turn to these questions.

8

Moral Geometry: An Assessment

> Unfortunately, principles, rules and commandments are built on the assumption that they don't conflict with each other and that moral ideas can be made "clear and distinct." Sadly, however, moral "geometry" fails us. Just when we most need to be unconflicted things turn out to be ambiguous. So, we twist and turn to get principles, rules and commandments to fit the situations we meet or we blind ourselves to the thickness of experience in order to get principles, rules and commandments to work out. [We] simplify what cannot really be simplified. We miss the clue of the parable, the fable, the story.
>
> —HOWARD B. RADEST (1997, 111)

The Sioux Nation and the Treaty of Fort Laramie

The 1868 Treaty of Fort Laramie guaranteed the Sioux Nation tribes—the Lakota, Dakota, and Nakota—"'undisturbed use and occupation' of an enormous swath of land that included the Black Hills, a resource-rich region of western South Dakota" (LeGro 2011). In 1874 miners discovered gold in the Black Hills. The US violated the treaty by refusing to deter the influx of thousands of white prospectors, who joined the gold rush and appropriated the land. A century later, the Lakota Dakota Nakota Nation (LDN) sued the federal government for the return of its lands. In 1980, the Supreme Court ruled that the LDN was due compensation in the amount of $102 million. Although lacking further legal recourse, the LDN refused the payment. The funds have remained in a trust, accruing interest. Today the fund totals $1.3 billion.

The LDN reconvened as the Confederacy of the Black Hills in 1991 to officially reject the compensation because the "land [was] not for sale." The rejection document states:

> This land was put here by the Supreme Being and he also put the Indigenous race here with its own form of government suited to its own religion, traditions, culture, and environment within which to base its social modes and jurisdiction of government on, since time immemorial.

Moreover, the land is "an indefinite and indefinable commodity that cannot be equated with the value of money as money is man-made" (LDN 2012).

The LDN demands repatriation of the land, restoration of the original boundaries of the 1868 treaty, *in addition to* monetary compensation for economic losses. Although tribal members face high levels of poverty, unemployment, and morbidity, and although they have virtually no possibility of repatriation, the LDN constinues to refuse to accept the money without it. They are unwilling to give up their claim to the land. "That's when the Sioux will become a defeated people" (Streshinsky 2011).

What might the LDN's refusal to accept compensation for their stolen land tell us about the adequacy of moral geometry?

*

Here we explore whether moral geometry is ethically appropriate for managing the harms associated with economic policy. For the sake of brevity I focus primarily on Kaldor-Hicks/CBA, noting when the critique also applies to the SWF approach.

Kaldor-Hicks: Benthamite and Paretian Defenses

The most common defense of Kaldor-Hicks appeals to intuition. If, in comparison with the status quo, a policy promises gains to the winners that are so large that the winners could fully compensate the losers and still benefit, then we might have reason to believe that the policy would enhance social welfare. I will refer to this defense of Kaldor-Hicks, which focuses on each individual policy innovation in isolation, as Benthamite. Recall that under Bentham's utilitarianism we are directed to pursue maximum aggregate utility even if the policies that achieve that goal induce harm. The Benthamite defense accepts that some will be harmed from Kaldor-Hicks-consistent innovations on grounds that their suffering is the price to be paid to promote social betterment.

The Benthamite defense has been subjected to a range of ethical critiques.[54] First, critics argue that the insensitivity of Kaldor-Hicks to inequality invalidates it as a decision rule (Bhagwati 1994; Sen 1987). Under Kaldor-Hicks, a policy that punishes the poor while generating benefits to the rich might very well be deemed worthy of support. Second, the Kantian objection notes that Kaldor-Hicks violates the "Dignity of Persons" by treating the individuals who will be harmed merely as a means for the benefit of others (White 2006). Third, Kaldor-Hicks justifies an *actual* policy outcome in which some individuals are harmed by reference to a *hypothetical* scenario in which compensation is paid to those who are harmed. But why should the fact that the winners *could* compensate the losers have any bearing at all on our evaluation of the policy when in fact the winners don't provide the compensation (Sen 1979; Adler 2012)? Sen (Sen, Deaton, and Besley 2020, 17) notes, sarcastically, that under Kaldor-Hicks the Bengali famine that killed three million people "might have been a compensation test victory, because quite a lot of people gained a lot in 1943, and they could have compensated the new destitutes. They did not have to do it, and the destitutes mostly died—*but was there a social improvement there*?"

THE LONG-RUN, PARETIAN PROMISE

These critiques demolish the Benthamite defense of Kaldor-Hicks. Is there a compelling response that overcomes them? The strongest defense of Kaldor-Hicks takes a long-run view. It draws on the Pareto criterion, not Bentham. It is predicated on a Paretian promise that *all of us* will be better-off living in a world in which Kaldor-Hicks-consistent efficiency-promoting policies are always enacted, even if each policy causes uncompensated harms to some of us. The "Kaldor-Hicks test is sometimes defended . . . as a decision procedure which, in the long run, yields Pareto-superior outcomes," Adler (2015, 330) writes. "If government repeatedly makes choices that are Kaldor-Hicks efficient (by repeatedly using CBA), everyone will be better off." Why might this be so? The claim is that over time, if economic efficiency is advancing, everyone will enjoy economic improvement. Peter might be harmed by today's Kaldor-Hicks-consistent policy innovation, but as with everyone else, the gains he has enjoyed in the past and will enjoy in the future from efficiency-promoting innovations will more than offset today's losses. If, instead, efficiency-promoting policies that generate uncompensated harms are not permitted, economic progress will stagnate, leaving everyone (including Peter) worse-off. Economists can therefore presume that everyone has consented to endure short-run harms from application of a decision rule that permits uncompensated efficiency-promoting harms.[55]

The long-run Paretian defense of Kaldor-Hicks claims influential defenders. Deirdre McCloskey (2010, 84) deserves to be quoted at length:

> [The] gain since 1800 from economic change has massively outweighed in monetary and ethical terms the loss to English woodmen disemployed by Swedish timber, or American blacksmiths disemployed by automobiles, or Indian bullock-drivers disemployed by motor trucks. The Win-Win-Win-Win-Wins far outnumber the lone Lose. To put it back in terms of rule utilitarianism and constitutional political economy, what sort of society would you rather be born into: one that forbad every innovation that resulted in any loss whatever to anyone, and rested therefore at $3 a day, and held that the sun "rose" and that painting must always be representational, or one that allowed

> innovation, perhaps with a social safety net like Norway's, and resulted in $137 a day, and allowed Copernicus and Picasso to make old ideas obsolete?"

We are urged to accept that there is no reasonable basis for rejecting a decision rule that ultimately benefits everyone, including the disadvantaged, more than would any other viable policy decision rule.[56]

ASSUMPTIONS, ASSUMPTIONS

Like the Benthamite case, the Paretian case invokes consequentialist welfarism and the associated neoclassical assumption set. Doing so enables the presumption of universal reparability of harms through compensation, which is even more vital to the Paretian than it is to the Benthamite case because the Paretian case needs to be able to claim that everyone is *in fact* compensated in the long run. Reparability through compensation is assured only by theorizing harm exclusively in terms of the loss of welfare associated with decreased access to one or more goods, and by treating all goods as commensurable and substitutable. Absent these assumptions the compensation test would fail as an ethical decision rule in the Paretian just as in the Benthamite account. Moreover, the Paretian promise, just like the Benthamite defense, accepts that all harms and benefits, and the act of harming and the act of benefiting, are commensurable, permitting ethical evaluation through mathematical calculation of the "Win-Win . . . Lose" sort.

The Paretian promise requires additional assumptions that need not concern the unrepentant Benthamite. First, all harms must be minor relative to the flow of gains that individuals secure. Second, the Paretian promise requires some degree of randomness in the distribution of harms and benefits. Only if losses are small relative to gains *and* if instances of winning and losing from successive policy innovations are distributed fairly randomly can we presume that there will be no losers in the long run (Hotelling 1938; Coleman 1980; Posner 1980).

ASSESSING THE PARETIAN PROMISE

The Paretian promise is impervious to the criticisms of Kaldor-Hicks presented above. If the Paretian promise is realized, then the critique that Kaldor-Hicks is insensitive to inequality is somewhat less urgent. Moreover, the Paretian promise can survive the Kantian objection that Kaldor-Hicks treats individuals merely as means to others' ends since it presumes that everyone has consented to the arrangement. Sen's complaint concerning the absence of actual compensation also falls away since everyone *is* compensated in the long run. *If the Paretian promise is realized*—if everyone actually gains in the long run—then the critiques lose their ethical force.

A persuasive challenge to the Paretian defense of Kaldor-Hicks persists, however, which applies also to the SWF approach. It entails demonstrating that its welfarist conception of harm is deficient. Since the Paretian promise also depends on auxiliary assumptions, those assumptions also bear scrutiny.

On Welfarism

A range of moral and political philosophers and economists across the political spectrum, such as John Rawls, Amartya Sen, Martha Nussbaum, Seana Shiffrin, Bernard Williams, and Robert Nozick, have subjected welfarism and utilitarianism to intensive critique. Much of the critique concerns welfarism's inadequate treatment of rights and autonomy (e.g., Williams 1973). Welfarism generates a paternalistic ethos associated with professional privilege that is insensitive to layperson rights (see chap. 2). In many professions over the past fifty years we find growing recognition of the autonomy of clients that overrides professionals' authority to decide how to promote client welfare. Emphasis on autonomy acknowledges the fact that distinct individuals do and are entitled to hold diverse and often conflicting aspirations and values, including beliefs about which value criteria to employ in policy assessment. Recognition of that fact undermines the selection of policy based on moral geometry. Though consequentialist welfarism and utilitarianism continue to be advocated by first-rate scholars (see Adler 2019; Sumner 1996; Griffin 1986; Smart 1973), outside of economics these approaches are widely taken to be insufficiently sensitive to the rights of laypeople.

Our focus on harm leads us to a different critique. Recall the taxonomy of harms that appears in table 3.1. Perusing the list we confront the extraordinary diversity of harms that individuals suffer, ranging from assaults on their physical bodies and mental capacities to damage to their psychological states; economic, social, and moral conditions; and autonomy. Economic interventions that economists propose can induce most if not all the harms listed in the taxonomy. This is especially true of large-scale projects that reach across national borders, like trade and financial liberalization. Moreover, harms cascade, such that one discrete harm (like the loss of economic security) can induce a wide range of other kinds of harms and can compound over time.

Recognition of the internal heterogeneity of harm suggests a methodological choice, one with wide practical and ethical implications. With the moral geometers we can choose to insist that it is appropriate to reduce all forms of harm in the taxonomy to one simple metric, the loss of welfare typically defined in terms of preference satisfaction. We can presume that much is gained and nothing of moral significance is lost when we translate all the harms in the taxonomy into one metric so that we have just one measure of human well-being to maximize in economic policy formation.

Welfare reductionism has seduced a profession that craves authority in public policy. It permits definitive judgments about policy that are endorsed by economic science and derived from objective mathematical formulas. It allows economists to believe that someone suffering the loss of one good can be rendered whole provided she is able to extend her access to other goods. But the approach serves the economics profession far more than it serves society. Reducing all harms to the one metric of welfare entails indefensible ethical compromises. Not least, welfare reductionism leads the economist to take an extraordinarily casual view of harm and harming. Each of the harms in the taxonomy is recognized as harmful only because and to the degree that it diminishes welfare. The geometer's simple taxonomy, then, includes just one category, welfare diminution, that covers the entire harm domain.

It should be clear that welfarism is grounded in a narrow conception of human existence. It presents an impoverished conception of what it is people value and what it takes to live a good life (cf. Atkinson 2009). In reality, a good life expands beyond people getting what they prefer. Harm, too, must then reach beyond diminished preference satisfaction. The loss of honor, or a sense of self as a provider for one's family, or a loved one, or a valued way of life is distorted and diminished when theorized simply as people not getting what they prefer. Welfarist accounting trivializes what it *means* to be harmed while ignoring the diverse *forms* of harm and *ways* people can be harmed. A richer account of harm that respects those who suffer harm needs to accept harm's complexity and internal diversity.

A preference-based account of harm is also undermined by the problem of "adaptive preference formation." Preferences adapt insidiously when disadvantaged individuals or members of oppressed groups come to believe that they do not value important goods that are systematically denied to them (Elster 1982). Preference adaptation is an unconscious coping strategy for dealing with deprivation. The dependent servant who subordinates his life plans for the sake of his overseer might think that his life is just as it should be only because he has lost sight of his own aspirations. That forfeiture represents a profound loss of autonomy *especially* when not experienced as such. Once preferences have adapted in this way, deprivation no longer registers under neoclassical welfarism as harmful.

Harm's Priority

Liberal philosophy provides the basis for another kind of critique. Liberal thought embraces the concept of "harm's priority." This is the idea that "stronger moral reasons are generated to refrain from inflicting this harm on a person, to prevent it from occurring . . . and to alleviate it than are generated to confer [a comparably sized] benefit (to that person or another)" (Shiffrin 2012, 362). The point is that harming requires special justifications beyond the fact that harming some might allow for benefiting others. From this perspective harming and benefiting are incommensurable. Harm's priority precludes treating harms and benefits on the same scale, using the harm/benefit continuums that we have drawn on extensively in explicating moral geometry. It precludes the math that directs us to approve of policy provided only that the benefits are greater than the harms, or that it increases social welfare.

Harm's priority finds substantial support not just in philosophy but in everyday life. In fact, social intercourse requires it. We do and must constrain what we do to benefit some individuals when doing so would significantly harm others. The alternative is to be at risk of assault on our person, property, or projects whenever others could benefit more from what we possess. In that world kidney snatching would be justified whenever the recipient would gain more from the theft than the victim would lose. Surely economists, too, especially those working in the liberal tradition that emphasizes personal freedoms, must embrace harm's priority. But doing so would disrupt moral geometry. How do the geometers handle the problem?

Conflating Not Benefiting *with* Harming

We noted in chapter 7 that moral geometers equate *not benefiting* with *harming*. We now see why this assumption is crucial to moral geometry. The conflation allows economists to conclude that those who would benefit from a feasible policy intervention are *harmed* if the policy is not implemented. It transforms a situation in which economists are comparing harming with not benefiting into one in which they are only comparing rival harms—the harm to those who will suffer if a policy measure is introduced, and the harm to those who will benefit from the measure if it is in fact not introduced. The stratagem is intended to allow the economist to evade entirely the normative problem posed by harm's priority.

In fact, the stratagem depends on our willingness to accept the conflation of not benefiting with harming. Moral, legal, and medical philosophers tend to refuse that conflation, and with good reason. If we accept it, we are back in the world of kidney snatching. Fortunately, medical practice does not accept the conflation, and so our kidneys are safe when we enter the doctor's office. Shiffrin argues that we should give weight to our moral intuitions. And those intuitions push back against the conflation of not benefiting with harming. In chapter 9 we will return to this issue, to see how legal philosophy distinguishes between harming and not benefiting.

Moral Plurality

The alternative methodological choice is to push back against mechanical thinking, acknowledging the essential complexity, heterogeneity, and incommensurability across harms. The alternative is grounded in "moral plurality," the acceptance of competing conceptions of what it means to live a good life, and what it means to be harmed (Sen, Deaton, and Besley 2020, 4). This route complicates greatly the assessment of the presence and extent of harm, responsibility for harm (and harm aversion), reparability of harm, and other harm-related decisions. It places a much heavier burden on the shoulders of those, like economists, who are in position to induce significant harm to those they purport to serve. It suggests the need for multi-objective social assessment, where we consider a policy's distinct, incommensurable harmful effects. Doing so can lead to what economists call "incomplete orderings" of available policies, where many policies can't be ranked as better or worse than others because one option may outperform another in preventing one kind of harm but underperform in preventing other kinds of harm, where the harms can't be reduced to a common metric (Sen 1992). Incomplete orderings are inconvenient for a profession trying to reach unambiguous policy decisions. Those who reject moral geometry must also face the question of who should decide which option to choose when there is ambiguity in policy rankings (see chap. 11). Refusing welfare reductionism, then, generates a host of thorny problems that are papered over under moral geometry. And yet the refusal is necessitated by the stakes involved in economic practice. The sacrifice of tractability is the price to be paid for responsible professional practice that can withstand close ethical scrutiny.

Moral geometry cannot tolerate the moral ambiguity associated with moral plurality. It banishes moral plurality by reducing all goods to the welfare they induce, and harms to diminished access to goods. The strategy implies that whatever harms the fates may bring can be corralled under the category of welfare losses. But this feature of welfarism, taken by moral geometers to be a principal virtue, in fact represents its central deficiency.

On the Scale of Harms

The Paretian promise requires that all harms are relatively trivial relative to the benefits everyone will enjoy from a long series of Kaldor-Hicks-consistent policy decisions. If the harms are not trivial, we can't conclude that the benefits that flow to individuals over time more than compensate for them. But are the harms people suffer from policy trivial, always? Moral geometers handle the problem in the established way of standard welfare economics: by simply *assuming* that there are no catastrophic harms. "It will be assumed that no negative reward is so large as to 'bankrupt' the individual at some point and end his participation in the 'game,'" Polinsky (1972, 414n6) writes. "This assumption will also be made for bankruptcy occurring through the accumulation of negative rewards, none of which would be sufficiently detrimental alone."

Is the assumption warranted? A cursory review of the harm taxonomy should disabuse us of the notion that the economic arrangements that economists endorse impose no catastrophic harms. Employees who lose their jobs owing to trade liberalization are apt to lose income, which may be offset by severance and welfare payments to which they are entitled. But as we have seen, unemployment also induces a range of other harms that undermine the well-being of those who are unemployed and their families. Unemployment generates social isolation and exclusion, deepens social divisions and inequalities, and increases morbidity and mortality. Bracketing momentarily the question whether such harms are in principle reparable, we should take note of their magnitude. Is it really the case that displaced workers who suffer them will be made whole through government checks and the lower prices now available at Walmart for the imported goods they once produced?

Grand economic reform projects, like economy-wide institutional redesign, and large-scale infrastructure projects that uproot communities, like megadam construction that floods valleys and requires relocation of thousands of people, are prone to causing harms that can be massive relative to the flow of benefits that Paretian defenders of Kaldor-Hicks presume will eventually compensate the losers.[57] So are smaller interventions that economists routinely endorse. Gentrification of low-income urban neighborhoods, for instance, involves "exclusionary displacement" and eviction of low-income residents and businesses with damaging effects on mental and physical health, poverty, and political disenfranchisement (Chapple et al. 2017, 33).[58] Harms on this scale can be life-shattering, dwarfing any benefits that will ultimately flow to the project's victims.

One can of course defend reform involving massive harm with the claim that future generations will enjoy greater levels of prosperity than could have been achieved without the reform-induced suffering. This is McCloskey's "Win-Win . . . Lose" defense that justifies short-run harm by reference to intergenerational economic gains. But the defense is exceedingly dangerous. It can be harnessed in support of even the most irresponsible and devastating policy regimes. "Don't worry," it reassures the victims, "those who follow will be better off!" As Nozick (1974, 298) puts it wryly, "Utopia is where our grandchildren are to live." For our purposes what is most notable is that the Win-Win . . . Lose defense is off point. It turns its back on the Paretian promise and returns us squarely to Bentham since it accepts permanent policy-induced harms to some as the price to be paid for increased welfare for others.

Zero Welfare

Kaldor-Hicks attributes no special meaning to zero or negative welfare (see the discussion of figure 7.4). In contrast, and to their credit, some SWF theorists have used the concept of zero welfare to describe a deprived level of living that is "equally good as nonexistence." In this account, negative welfare implies "bad lives—lives not worth living" (Adler 2019, 239; see also Broome 1999, chap. 10). The concept of zero welfare is awkward for moral geometers, however, because Kaldor-Hicks/CBA and the SWF approach are geared toward comparative distinctions that allow ranking of alternative policies. Zero welfare involves a categorical judgment that is not comparative (Adler 2019, 239). An implication is that a jump from a welfare level with a positive value to another with a zero or negative value might entail a catastrophic welfare discontinuity. That idea undermines the prevailing conception of reparability and compensability of all harms upon which Kaldor-Hicks/CBA and SWFs depend. Moral geometry largely resolves the problem by simply assuming no absolute thresholds.

But the question of a zero-welfare threshold won't go away just because it is inconvenient for moral geometers. The possibility of catastrophic harms arises especially in cases when a policy threatens to reduce the welfare of relatively disadvantaged individuals for the benefit others who are better-off. Moral geometers accept that transfers from the relatively worse-off to the relatively better-off are legitimate provided the gains to the winners are sufficiently large. The case of low-paid textile workers producing intricate, expensive fabrics who lose their jobs owing to trade liberalization comes to mind. Under standard moral geometry their loss of welfare may be offset by some multiple by the gains to those who buy couture, even though the consumers for high fashion enjoy much higher levels of welfare than the displaced workers. If the gains are substantial enough, benefiting a sufficiently large number of consumers, say, even an economist employing a SWF that gives special attention to the welfare of the worst-off must endorse the policy change. We must then ask, is there *no* welfare threshold that the worse-off should not be expected to traverse on behalf of others? Should some special attention be paid (and somehow registered in the moral geometry) if the displaced workers experience a drop from positive to negative welfare? This is not a contrived example. Losses from actual economic policy, such as the trade liberalization, shock therapy, and austerity examined in previous chapters, can ramify in ways that reduce the value of a life to one not worth living, leading to deaths of despair (Case and Deaton 2020). The analytical clarity of moral geometry would be undermined by a zero-welfare threshold when policy shunted the worst-off below the zero-welfare threshold. Moral geometry typically excludes the concept of zero welfare to ensure the clarity needed to reach definitive policy assessment. *But catastrophic harms happen.* How can it be morally legitimate to exclude that fact from policy assessment?

Harm Distribution

Over the course of the past four decades we find dramatic evidence of an association between radical market liberalization and rising within-country inequality. In the US, investors and other high-income earners have benefited enormously from successive rounds of trade liberalization. In contrast, workers displaced by economic retrenchment have generally faced declining wages in the industries to which they have migrated (Bivens 2008, 3; Arestis, Charles, and Fontana 2013; OECD 2005, 46–47; Scott 2003; 2013; Senate Committee on Finance 2002; Weidenbaum 2001, 17). But investors and high-income earners have also been the principal beneficiaries of other market fundamentalist policies. Financial liberalization, the destruction of labor unions, successive rounds of tax cuts on capital gains and high salaries, and the restructuring of public services like education have served the privileged at the expense of the vulnerable. The result is a historically unprecedented and sustained surge in income and wealth inequality in the US with economic stagnation and decline for the majority of households. Moreover, recent evidence establishes that trade and financial liberalization during the 1980s and 1990s has had similar effects across the developing world (Goldberg and Pavcnik 2007; Grabel 2015). These trends provide prima facie evidence that the benefits and harms of successive rounds of liberalization have been serially correlated. When harms are serially correlated the Paretian promise collapses.

REPARABILITY, COMPENSABILITY, ACKNOWLEDGMENT

We can now approach what is perhaps the most significant error that follows from the welfarist approach to harm. The empirical question whether all agents can expect to be compensated in the long run for any harms they suffer along the way comes one step too late in the argument. *The question presumes, after all, that all harms are in fact reparable through compensation.* Reparability through compensation implies that a harmed individual can be rendered whole through the substitution of goods; that there are no lexicographic preference orderings. It assumes that individuals who have been harmed can always be restored to their previous level of welfare following the goods transfer that effects the repair.

Are all harms reparable, and are all reparable harms compensable? The consensus among legal scholars is that they are not. Many harms cannot be repaired in the sense of rendering the victim whole.[59] Appreciation of the scale and qualitative nature of harms that humans suffer as a consequence of economic arrangements sustains that conclusion. Sen's caustic comment on the Bengali famine reminds us that those who died in this catastrophe could not be made whole; the loss of life was simply irreparable. Economists make a fundamental error when they treat reparable harms as representative of all harms. Many physical, psychological, social, political, moral, and autonomy harms are irreparable. It is professionally irresponsible to presume otherwise. Those who are severely damaged physically or mentally; or whose loved ones are killed; or who are induced to suffer shame or the loss of self-respect, the capacity for inventiveness, or access to irreplaceable goods (to name just a few items in the harm taxonomy) might not be able to be repaired at all. Alternatively, the possible repair may be partial rather than full.

It is important in this connection to theorize repair properly—in terms of healing, coping, or restoring the ability to have a full human life—and not in the simplistic way of the economist, as restoration to one's previous level of welfare. Partial repair for catastrophic harms, if it comes at all, might therefore require time, hard work, luck, and substantial support. Compensation may not be central to the process of repair. Indeed, some categories of harm, such as being dishonored, are not amenable to repair through compensation. As McGowan puts it, "Once lost, honor is extraordinarily hard, if not impossible, to regain. . . . The very idea of [pricing honor] seems inconsistent with the concept" (McGowan 2010, 589–90).

The *causes* of harm bear on the *nature* of the harm suffered, including its reparability and compensability. Potential causes include atrocities, negligence, error, accident, coerced or voluntary risk-taking by individuals in pursuit of their own interests or in the service of others, etc. A broken arm suffered in a sporting competition may register to the injured person as a benign inconvenience. But the same injury resulting from an assault can be experienced as a trauma. The injured athlete may be healed in every sense within weeks. The assault victim may suffer cascading harms, including physical and psychological trauma that persists and even compounds over time. Contrary to moral geometry, it follows that the causes of harm also bear on the matter of the requisite response.

Acknowledgment, Not Compensation

Some forms of harm, such as reversible damage to property from negligence or misfortune, are typically resolved through compensation, just as economists claim. But other forms of harm require something qualitatively different and much more difficult to achieve: *acknowledgment*. Acknowledgment takes diverse forms, reflecting the particular causes and nature of the harm in a given case. Acknowledgment can involve public *apology* or expressions of *sympathy* for, or *recognition* of, one's loss, as often occurs in the context of post-atrocity truth commissions. Here, the admission by perpetrators of their culpability, combined with apology in the context of public sympathy, might provide the victim a degree of solace and a chance at recovery that explicit monetary compensation would trivialize (Bouris 2007). Acknowledgment can also take the form of the expression of *gratitude* or *respect*, and the bestowal of public *honors*. These are the appropriate forms for those individuals whose harm is a consequence of risk-taking and sacrifice on behalf of others, such as those who put themselves in harm's way to ensure the safety of their communities.

Table 8.1 revisits our earlier examination of moral geometry's approach to reparability and compensability. Under moral geometry all harms appear in the northwest cell: all are deemed reparable through compensation. But the present discussion points to the failure of that characterization.

If not all goods are welfare commensurable, and if some goods are not substitutable, then the harm associated with the loss of these goods may be irreparable. And if a harm is irreparable, then it is by implication noncompensable. Such harms reside in the southeast cell in the matrix. But we've now seen that even some reparable harms—those that are wholly or just partially reparable—may not not be repaired through compensation. These harms reside in the southwest cell. Their repair depends on noncompensatory measures of acknowledgment that do not fit into any sort of moral geometry.

TABLE 8.1. Compensable vs. noncompensable, reparable vs. irreparable harm: An alternative perspective

	Reparable harm	*Irreparable harm*
Commensurable, substitutable goods	Compensable harms	Undefined
Incommensurable, nonsubstitutable goods	Noncompensable harms Acknowledgment: apology, sympathy, recognition, gratitude, respect, honor	Noncompensable harms Remedial measures unavailable

If some goods are not welfare commensurable and substitutable, then some harms will be irreparable, and even some reparable harms will be noncompensable. Irreparable and noncompensable reparable harms require appropriate forms of acknowledgment.

Acknowledgment and Monetary Transfers

Sometimes, monetary transfer accompanies public acknowledgment. This fact leads to confusion among economists who are trained to see all transfers as an exchange of values—as compensation. But in cases involving the violation of rights or the loss of irreplaceable goods, *monetary transfers serve purposes other than compensation that renders the harmed victim whole.* The "sorry money" that is paid in New Guinea, as exemplified in a story recounted by Jared Diamond (2012), is illustrative: in the wake of a traffic accident that killed a child but where the truck driver was exonerated of any wrongdoing, the truck company owner gave money to the parents and said to them, "This money is nothing compared to your son's life, but I give it to show how sorry we are." The simple example highlights the necessity of deciphering the social function of monetary transfers in instances of harm. It is an elementary mistake to presume, with the economist, that all transfers represent monetary compensation that has the capacity to render the harmed agent whole.

Monetary transfers in response to atrocities can signal the genuineness, depth, and honesty of acknowledgment of wrongdoing. Speaking of the reparations from the German government to the survivors of the Holocaust, Martha Nussbaum puts it this way: "Indeed, we might say that the main importance of reparations, too, is *expressive* . . . its primary significance [may be] a public expression of wrongdoing and the determination to do things differently in the future" (Nussbaum 2001, 173; emphasis added). To view reparations simply as compensation that renders victims whole is to trivialize the atrocities that led to the harm, and the harm itself.

In her examination of bourgeois virtues, McCloskey recounts Diamond's analysis of sorry money. McCloskey discusses approvingly a historical trend in the Germanic north of Europe to commercialize disputes over injury or harm that might otherwise generate social conflict and disrupt economic progress. In place of honor-based, eye-for-eye justice, "Germanic law codes of early times encourage *cash* compensation for dishonor. . . . The savages of the northern forests . . . were making delicate calculations of monetary equivalences" (McCloskey 2016c, 444–45). Payment for wrongs in the form of "*wergelt*," which became the norm in northern Europe, helped to curtail costly feuds that otherwise might have disrupted commerce. In contrast, in the supposedly more advanced and mercantile south, "a more primitive and anticommercial code of honor" survived through the centuries. "From Homer to El Cid to *The Godfather*, one's honor is absolute. . . . They would not accept money for murder."

A distinction needs to be drawn between the bourgeois view that McCloskey recommends and the modern neoclassical view. Commercialization of harms does not presume that all harms are reparable and compensable. The virtue of payment for harms resides in its *instrumental effects*—keeping the peace, sustaining beneficial commerce, and incentivizing precaution by those in position to do harm. These transfers are not to be understood as compensation. The idea that those who harm must make amends in ways that are consistent with the social interest bears no likeness at all to the naive, modern economic treatment of all harms as reparable and, indeed, compensable. They are not: just ask the parents who are awarded damages for the wrongful death of a child whether they are indifferent between having their child and having the money.

Does Everything Have Its Price?

In *A Tale of Two Cities* Charles Dickens illustrates the central point that some harms are not compensable. The carriage of Monsieur the Marquis, "one of the great lords in the power of the Court," careens recklessly through a town square without regard for the safety of others. "At last, swooping at a street corner by a fountain, one of its wheels came to a sickening little jolt, and there was a loud cry from a number of voices, and the horses reared and plunged. . . ." A crowd assembles around the carriage and the distraught father of a child who has been trampled by the horses:

> "What has gone wrong?" said Monsieur, calmly looking out.
>
> A tall man in a nightcap had caught up a bundle from among the feet of the horses, and had laid it on the basement of the fountain, and was down in the mud and wet, howling over it like a wild animal.
>
> "Pardon, Monsieur the Marquis!" said a ragged and submissive man, "it is a child."
>
> "Why does he make that abominable noise? Is it his child?"
>
> "Excuse me, Monsieur the Marquis—it is a pity—yes."

The Marquis is disgusted:

> "It is extraordinary to me," said he, "that you people cannot take care of yourselves and your children. One or the other of you is for ever in the way. How do I know what injury you have done my horses. See! Give him that."
>
> He threw out a gold coin for the valet to pick up, and all the heads craned forward that all the eyes might look down at it as it fell. The tall man called out again with a most unearthly cry, "Dead!" . . .
>
> The Marquis leaned back in his seat, and was just being driven away with the air of a gentleman who had accidentally broke some common thing, and had paid for it, and could afford to pay for it; when his ease was suddenly disturbed by a coin flying into his carriage, and ringing on its floor.
>
> "Hold!" said Monsieur the Marquis. "Hold the horses! Who threw that? . . . You dogs! . . . I would ride over any of you very willingly, and exterminate you from the earth. If I knew which rascal threw at the carriage, and if that brigand were sufficiently near it, he should be crushed under the wheels."

The Marquis offends us, economists no less than the rest of us, for his cruelty and brazen indifference toward the extraordinary damage he has caused. But notice: the Marquis's calculations are consistent with standard moral geometry. A harm has been caused, and compensation has been provided. But the recipient of the payment will not accept it. The coin is flung back at the Marquis not because the amount is too little. Were that the case, the father would instead have held up the carriage to negotiate a better price. The father is repulsed by the payment. It is a grossly inappropriate response to the atrocity that took his child's life.

THE CASE OF THE LDN CONFEDERACY

We can now begin to make sense of the LDN's rejection of monetary compensation for the lands taken from the tribes in violation of the Treaty of Fort Laramie. The refusal illuminates the failure of moral geometry. Like Dickens's grieving father, the LDN tribes have been deprived of a "good" through a barbarous act. In return they have been offered monetary compensation. They have rejected the monetary award not because it is insufficient in magnitude, and not because they have any recourse to secure a better deal. They have rejected the compensation because it is an inappropriate response to the egregious violation of their rights and assault on their way of life.

The case of the LDN's refusal to accept compensation reveals the economist's egregious error of subsuming all instances of transfer under the category of *compensation*, and of believing that once compensation has been paid, all harm is fully repaired. Breaking the economist's conflation of monetary transfer and compensation, we might be able to recognize a wide range of social functions that transfers can serve. One is to reduce the social tension that might otherwise persist in the wake of a harm: *wergelt*. Under tort law the expectation that harming another will require monetary transfer also serves as an incentive for those in position to harm to act responsibly, taking measures to reduce the risk of harming (Kornhauser 2015). What monetary transfer can't always do is restore harm victims "to their previous level of enjoyment," to borrow Kaldor's evocative phrasing (1939, 551), or restore their previous level of freedom, rights, or well-being.

The standard economic view has difficulty making sense of cases such as the LDN. Or of cases in which promised monetary compensation to communities for public projects that threaten harm to them, such as the siting of hazardous waste facilities near residential areas, *reduces* support for the projects (Frey, Oberholzer-Gee, and Eichenberger 1996). Counterintuitively, communities in the crosshairs of policy makers are sometimes willing to accept projects that risk harming them when offered *nonmonetary amenities* in the form of public goods, such as schools, firehouses, or even walking paths, rather than monetary compensation. Mansfield, Van Houtven, and Huber (2002) attribute this finding to what they identify as the bribery effect, the crowding out of public-spirited altruism and feelings of moral responsibility. Equally important, "public goods may be viewed as a way to effectively mitigate the psychic harms associated with local public harms" (Mansfield, Van Houtven, and Huber 2002, 368). The appropriate inference, one that is obscured by the economic convention of referring to all harm remediation as "compensation," is that the provision of public goods is sometimes not regarded (or not *just* regarded) by the harmed parties as compensation. It is regarded as sorry money that expresses acknowledgment of the sacrifice that the community is asked to bear for the good of society. It may very well serve the function of *acknowledging* rather than *compensating* those who face the risk of being harmed for the greater good. The act of honoring may not just repair but also reduce the harm associated with the project by treating those who will be harmed with due respect.[60]

When does monetary transfer represent compensation, and when does it represent something else? One test is this: When all that matters is the magnitude of the transfer, we should infer that the transfer serves the purpose of compensation just as the economist conceives it. When instead the conditions surrounding the transfer, not just its magnitude, matter—when it matters from whom the payment is received, under what conditions the transfer is made, and what sentiments are conveyed with the transfer—then we have good reason to infer that the transfer is conveying acknowledgment and not compensation. To the economist that may seem a distinction without a difference. To those who have been harmed, however, the distinction may determine whether the transfer facilitates repair from egregious harms.

CANADA'S FIRST NATIONS PEOPLES

It is instructive to compare US and Canadian cases concerning recognition and rectification of past injustices toward indigenous people. Canada's First Nations peoples have suffered the same injustices as Native American tribes in the US. One particularly notable example involves the Catholic and Protestant residential schools where First Nations children were sequestered to "civilize" them by indoctrinating them in Canadian and Christian values. The schools operated for over a century, from 1883 to 1996. Children were abducted, and families were tricked and pressured into giving up their children to the schools. The effect is now recognized by the Canadian government as "cultural genocide." As of this writing (July 2021), thousands of children's bodies have been exhumed from unmarked mass graves on the grounds of several schools (Austin and Bilefsky 2021).

The Canadian government has responded in ways that seek to acknowledge the horrors suffered by the First Nations peoples. In 2008 it established the Truth and Reconciliation Commission of Canada to investigate the residential schools. The commission issued a massive report (Truth and Reconciliation Commission of Canada 2015) chronicling the injustices associated with the schools. The commission has called for an apology by the Pope. The Pope has not complied, but the Archbishop of Vancouver apologized on behalf of the archdiocese, as did the leader of the United Church of Canada, the country's largest Protestant denomination. The Canadian Prime Minister formally apologized and committed to provide resources to support indigenous communities and further research into the atrocities. In 2019 the provincial government of British Columbia became the world's first to adopt into law UN guidelines for heightened indigenous sovereignty. In June 2021 Canada's Parliament passed legislation extending those measures nationwide.

The leaders of the First Nations peoples have mobilized for over fifty years to reverse colonialism by achieving indigenous sovereignty. According to John Burrows, a prominent legal scholar and a member of the Chippewa of the Nawash Unceded First Nation, their recent achievements were once unthinkable. Nonetheless, the leaders believe that the government must do much more to meet its commitments and to rectify past injustices. Difficult challenges remain, such as achieving First Nations sovereignty regarding resources on indigenous lands (Fisher 2021). That said, the First Nations peoples' successes are now serving as a model for indigenous movements around the world seeking historical reckonings. Acknowledgment is key. Substantial monetary transfers are warranted, too. But those transfers represent something very different from and far more important than compensation.

EXPECTED UTILITY AND IRREPARABLE IGNORANCE

Predicting policy effects, which is central to all consequentialist moral geometry, presumes that economists can know the range of policy outcomes and the probability distribution of those outcomes. That kind of knowledge depends on our knowing the causal relationships that drive events through time. We must know how natural, political, and economic causal systems interact, and with what effects. We must also know the external, contingent circumstances under which those causal relationships operate, the ways in which people will respond to the changing world they confront, and how those responses will affect the course of future developments. Accurate predictions also require the economist to anticipate the factors that will disrupt the "normal" flow of events. All of this is required if we are to treat our knowledge of policy outcomes like our knowledge of the outcome of throwing dice. Without all this knowledge, the economist cannot know how many faces are on the relevant dice or what value is stamped on each one. The longer the likely effects of a policy choice, the greater the epistemic demands facing the social welfare accountant.

Irreparable ignorance makes a mockery of policy predictions, such as E(U) calculations. In a non-ergodic world of Knightian uncertainty (see chaps. 5 and 6), the presumption that we can know the full range of potential policy outcomes and their relative probabilities is exceedingly reckless. It should not be surprising, then, that "when estimates [of CBA studies] are checked by being reestimated by independent methods or by being audited in the light of history, it is entirely usual for discrepancies of 200% or 300% or even an order of magnitude to be disclosed" (Dorfman 1993, 319). Grappling with the problem of uncertainty a leading authority on CBA concludes that "the problem of how to make decisions in any situation where the past affords little if any guidance is not one that can be satisfactorily resolved either by logic or empiricism, *and what rules have been formulated are either of limited application or of no practical value*" (Mishan 1975, 337, emphasis added).[61] And yet, the apparent ability to calculate expected values, such as E(U), gives economists substantial influence in the policy arena that they would not be likely to achieve otherwise. Deference to economists is fully unwarranted when it is secured by an *illusion* that the economist can know the unknowable. That path undermines decision makers' preparedness for surprising future states of the world, when policy choices yield outcomes that were not among those taken account of in the policy assessment exercise.

In chapter 11 we will explore a powerful approach to policy assessment that explicitly rejects predicting the future. For now, it should be clear that recognition of irreparable ignorance puts the lie to moral geometry. The prevalence of moral geometry in economic practice today indicates a continuing professional convention to repress the severe epistemic constraints that economists confront in pursuit of professional authority and influence. That convention serves the economics profession very nicely. It is a stretch to claim it also serves society.

DISCOUNTING THE FUTURE

Moral geometry requires taking a position on the appropriate discount rate when assessing policy with long-term benefits and harms, like climate change policy. In chapter 7 we explored one rationale for discounting, pure time preference. People themselves place higher value on current costs and benefits than on future ones of the same magnitudes. Higher discount rates induce a strong bias in policy assessment in favor of the current generation over future generations. Lower discount rates reduce but do not eliminate the bias. What, then, is the *right* discount rate? Without it, moral geometry is capricious just when we need it to be most dependable.

Unfortunately, there is no right discount rate. Speaking of the Stern-Nordhaus controversy, Hal Varian (2006) asks, "Should the social discount rate be 0.1 percent, as Sir Nicholas Stern, who led the study, would have it, or 3 percent as Mr. Nordhaus prefers?" Varian rightly concludes that "there is no definitive answer to this question because it is inherently an ethical judgment that requires comparing the well-being of different people: those alive today and those alive in 50 or 100 years."

Moral geometers like Nordhaus have sought technical grounding for their choices of discount rates. One alternative is the real return on (or the opportunity cost of) capital, that is, the rate of return that is available on capital investment (Nordhaus 2007). If investors can earn 6% per annum on today's investments (after taxes and corrected for inflation), then $1.00 today is the equivalent of $1.06 a year from now (since we can invest today's dollar and receive back $1.06 next year). Going in the other direction, the present discounted value of $1.06 a year from now is $1.00. In his critique of the *Stern Review*, Nordhaus emphasizes its failure to adopt a discount rate grounded in the opportunity cost of capital (or some other theoretically warranted rate).

Typically, using the opportunity cost of capital yields a different discount rate than using pure time preference. So should the discount rate be based on pure time preference, the opportunity cost of capital, or some other variable? Or should we adopt the view of Roy Harrod that *any* discounting in public policy is a "polite expression for rapacity" (cited in NOAA n.d.)? Should we then follow Stern (2007) and use an effective discount rate of zero to ensure that we give due consideration to future generations? US federal agencies don't think so. Currently, the federal Office of Management and Budget recommends the very high rate of 7% for the analysis of federal programs. That rate is predicated on a theoretical proposition that is widely contested today: that federal spending necessarily crowds out private investment and consumption. But agencies like the National Oceanic and Atmospheric Administration, which monitors climate change and promotes ecological sustainability, use 3% instead (NOAA n.d.). A gap that large has enormous effects on the assessment of policy with long-term effects.

Ultimately, choosing a discount rate based on some technical principle involves an objectionable strategy that appears throughout moral geometry. Moral geometry requires a sleight of hand that makes the intractable, tractable. It requires reducing extraordinarily complex ethical problems to math problems. Discounting permits elegant policy judgments, and that is its appeal. But the procedure obscures the ethical element in policy assessment. Returning to the example in chapter 7, once we choose a discount rate we can determine whether a project that costs $1 billion today and is expected to generate $3 billion in benefits thirty years from now is "worth it." But this is also moral geometry's fundamental weakness. Complex, ethically fraught questions cannot be tackled formulaically. "Mattering does not inhere in a number," McCloskey (2005, 23) warns. Simple math won't do when the lives and livelihoods of billions are at stake.

Conclusion

Fortunately, scholars beyond economics have adopted more adequate notions of harm and harming. The setback-to-interest approach in legal philosophy embraces the complexities of harm. The social-harm approach, encompassing structural violence, expands the domain of harm further still. And in economics, the capabilities approach to human flourishing provides a much more compelling and ethically viable framework for theorizing economic and econogenic harm. We turn now to these perspectives.

9

Beyond Moral Geometry: Interests, Social Harm, Capabilities

> The general formula behind structural violence is inequality, above all in the distribution of power.
>
> —JOHAN GALTUNG (1969, 175)

Kerala, India, and COVID-19

The state of Kerala, India, has been in the news during the COVID-19 pandemic. Kerala's response to the pandemic has been recognized internationally as a model for other Indian states and other countries. It was the first Indian state to mobilize a response, establishing a coordination center and initiating communications with medical staff in Wuhan, China, four days before Kerala's first documented case. Kerala took an *all government, whole society* approach, involving all relevant agencies to ensure coordination and consistency in actions and communications. It created fourteen district war rooms, initiated contact tracing, and disseminated "route maps" of infected individuals so that others could ascertain whether they were at risk. Civic institutions organized their members into mass cleaning groups, targeting buses, bus stations, and other public spaces, while providing support for quarantined workers. The cleaning campaigns served to educate Keralans about the crisis and the need to "break the chain" of virus transmission. The government converted abandoned buildings to quarantine care centers. Eleven hundred health professionals, including mental health workers, were assigned to support those in quarantine and the most vulnerable in the community, targeting in particular those living in crowded dwellings. The government provided a relief package of $270 million comprising loans to families through a women's cooperative, funding for an employment guarantee initiative, pension payments to the elderly, food, and subsidies to restaurants to provide low-cost meals. By the end of March 2020, twelve hundred community kitchens had provided 8.6 million meals. Kudumbashree, a grassroots network of organizations including women's self-help groups, produced two million masks and five thousand liters of hand sanitizer in the first month of the national lockdown (Tharoor 2020). These activities relied on extensive participation of volunteer support groups that had been formed in response to floods in 2018 (Subin and Prashad 2020; Chowdhury and Jomo KS 2020; Tharoor 2020; Bhagat 2021).

Kerala faced a surge in infections owing in large part to the return of migrants—over 6% of Kerala's population—who had been working abroad. Yet it managed the pandemic much better than other Indian states. As of early May 2020, it had a very low mortality rate even though it has the highest elderly population in India, and it had managed to limit the spread of the virus (Shankar 2021). Its performance exceeded by far that of other countries with substantially higher per capita income.

India was devastated by a second wave of the pandemic in early 2021. Transmission and death rates soared across the country, overwhelming hospitals, personnel, and medical supplies. Kerala again excelled in its management of the crisis. Anticipating an acute need for oxygen, public-health officials in 2020 had ordered suppliers to increase oxygen production. Daily production had grown from 149 to 197 metric tons prior to the second wave. As of May 2021, supplies of oxygen and hospital beds remained adequate to meet demand. War-room personnel triaged patients. They imposed at-home quarantine and coordinated care for those patients who did not need hospital services, while transporting those who needed acute care to facilities with excess capacity. By May 2021 Kerala had also achieved a vaccination rate nearly double the national average. Though the statistics on COVID-19 deaths in Kerala and throughout India are undependable, it is noteworthy that Kerala's reported death rate is less than .4%, one of the lowest in India (Bhagat 2021; see also Shankar 2021).

Western readers, perhaps especially in the US, might worry that the Kerala model involves excessive state intervention that compromises personal liberties. But is that the only or even the best way to make sense of the Keralan situation? Could it be that in fact Keralans enjoy greater autonomy and freedoms than many in societies that purport to privilege personal liberty?

*

We have seen that welfarism oversimplifies harm for the sake of tractability. All goods are taken to be welfare commensurable and substitutable, and all harms are then treated as reparable through compensation. That strategy leads to an egregious trivialization of harm. It fails to accord respect to those whose lives are upended by economic arrangements that economists advocate.

Members of other professions, and those economists who can tolerate moral aperture, do far better in grappling with the complexity of harm. In the field of criminal law, legal philosopher Joel Feinberg has advanced the "interest" approach to harm and harming. Feinberg's approach represents an important corrective to welfarism. But his focus on criminal law limits its applicability for theorizing and managing econogenic harm, where violations of law are not typically at issue. The social-harm approach, zemiology, does better. Zemiology emerged as a critique of the narrow focus of the criminal law on direct harm. In economics, the capabilities approach to human flourishing provides a particularly rich, nuanced framework for theorizing economic and econogenic harm.

Wrongful Setback to Interests

Feinberg (1984) begins his magisterial, four-volume investigation of harm with this question: in a liberal society predicated on personal liberty, what actions should the state proscribe and penalize under criminal law? On its face the question may seem irrelevant to the study of economic and econogenic harm. But in fact, Feinberg's approach illuminates central aspects of harm and harming while clarifying central deficiencies of the welfare approach.

Feinberg argues that a liberal state committed to personal liberty is right to criminalize behaviors that represent "wrongful setbacks" to the interests of others. What amounts to "wrongful" is a complicated matter that Feinberg examines over several hundred pages. For him, wrongfulness is a key determination since the state has no business criminalizing actions citizens pursue that might induce harm to others through no fault of their own. If we all drive to work tomorrow, we all contribute to the traffic congestion that harms many if not all of us, but that fact provides no grounds for criminalizing driving. Fortunately, Feinberg's question of what is "wrongful" harming is one we can largely sidestep since our focus is not on which actions should be criminalized but instead on how to theorize responsible conduct when professional practice causes harm.

The key concept for our purposes is Feinberg's notion of harm as a "setback to interests." Interests span the broad range of states, conditions, and rights that people value. People have an interest in something if they have a stake in it, if how their lives go depends on the achievement of the interest. Good health represents an interest, for instance, since it is central to the quality of individuals' lives and to the achievement of their life plans. When health is significantly undermined, interests are thwarted. Freedom from arbitrary constraint or coercion, physical security from threats of violence, security in shelter and other property, physical mobility, and many other conditions and rights represent interests, setbacks to which entail harm.

SETBACK TO INTERESTS VS. MORAL GEOMETRY

Feinberg advances several arguments that are directly relevant to the investigation of economic harm. We've encountered many of these throughout earlier chapters. It is helpful to pull them together here and to investigate their relevance for theorizing economic harm (see table 9.1)

Interests are not equivalent to welfare. Being deflected from a career as a concert pianist by a permanent injury represents a setback to interests even if the pianist herself comes to find equal enjoyment from watching hockey on TV (Rachels and Rachels 2015, chap. 8). An interest can be thwarted without any psychic response, as we saw in the case of adaptive preferences. But the rejection of welfare reductionism does not imply that the approach ignores welfare. *Welfare interests* matter deeply here. Feinberg defines welfare interests in terms of needs, like adequate nutrition and shelter, not in terms of preference satisfaction. Welfare interests are foundational since their fulfillment is necessary for securing higher-order interests. One cannot become a concert pianist if one suffers serious and persistent insecurity or homelessness.

An important claim of the interest approach is that the frustration of preferences does not automatically qualify as harm. Whether a defeated preference entails a thwarted interest depends on the nature of the preference, its centrality to a person's life plans, the extent of the frustration, the condition of the person suffering the frustration, and other factors. A wealthy gourmand who, owing to a trade embargo, is deprived of the caviar he would prefer to the oysters he consumes instead suffers disappointment, maybe even deep disappointment, but not a setback to interests. On the other hand, a parent who cannot satisfy her desire for shelter for her family does suffer a thwarting of interest—indeed, a particularly important interest.

Moral geometry does not typically recognize welfare thresholds that apply to all individuals. Under moral geometry, an individual is harmed if she suffers any diminution in preference satisfaction. Feinberg adopts two thresholds that separate those interest setbacks that rise to the level of harm from those that do not. One threshold entails how well-off is the person suffering the loss. The thwarting of an interest enjoyed by the privileged is not to be treated like the thwarting of an interest of those in dire circumstances. A second threshold is the magnitude of the loss. Trivial reductions in well-being do not rise to the level of harm. The distinction helps us to make sense of Hicks's

TABLE 9.1. Relevant features of setback-to-interest approach to harm

- Rejection of welfare reductionism . . .
- . . . but welfare interests matter
- Preference frustration does not equate to harm
- Interest thresholds
- Diversity of interests, diversity of harms
- Reparable vs. irreparable, compensable vs. noncompensable harm
- Cascading setbacks—harmful conditions
- Distinction between not benefiting and harming

error of overidentifying harm, seeing harm in virtually every policy innovation. In the interest approach, setbacks that are trivial relative to fundamental life plans do not rise to the level of harm regardless of how irritating such setbacks are to the person who suffers them.

The interest approach recognizes the broad diversity of interests that people have, which leads to recognition of the broad diversity of harms that they suffer. Many of the harms listed in the taxonomy of table 3.1 can be theorized in terms of thwarted interests. In this account, however, the diversity of harms is not reducible to some underlying common element. Instead, Feinberg recognizes the nonfungibility of diverse goods: one must secure adequate levels of all important goods to avoid setbacks to interests. Obstacles to accessing one good, then, cannot be overcome with an abundance of other goods. The approach therefore recognizes a distinction between reparable and irreparable harm and between compensable and noncompensable harm. Legal practitioners have taken an expansive view of irreparable, noncompensable harm. A standard definition of irreparable harm, under which plaintiffs can seek a restraining order against someone who threatens to cause the harm, gives "cutting down shade trees" as a leading example of irreparable harm, right alongside "not giving a child needed medication" (USLegal.com n.d.). In sharp contrast, and as we have seen, economists operating within the standard welfarist approach do not even treat blocked access to medication as irreparable.

Feinberg offers a conceptual distinction that separates harms that are self-correcting from those that cascade and compound. A *harmed* condition is one in which a person faces a setback to her interests. In contrast, a *harmful* condition is one that induces further setbacks to interests beyond the immediate harmed condition. Chronic pain from an injury can induce depression and a range of economic and social harms while compromising autonomy; it is to be recognized as a harmful and not just a harmed condition. But what is harmful for one person may not be harmful for another. For an aspiring concert pianist the loss of a fingertip may thwart her life plans, while for an academic the same physical injury may be easily surmountable (Feinberg 1984, 31).

HARMING VS. NOT BENEFITING

The setback-to-interest approach provides means to distinguish harming from not benefiting. Recall that standard moral geometry conflates the two. Under that approach the decision to preserve the status quo rather than adopt a policy that would confer benefits is deemed harmful to anyone who would have received the benefits. Feinberg's treatment of the issue is nuanced, introducing morally relevant baselines to the analysis. The first baseline is given by individuals' current quality of life, defined in terms of nonthwarted interests, that is, interests they are not precluded from pursuing. Policy that prevents individuals from experiencing a deterioration in their quality of life so defined is understood as preventing harm. An example is unemployment insurance that allows the unemployed to pay their rent rather than be rendered homeless. The same is true of policy that restores individuals who have suffered deterioration to their previous quality of life. An example is retraining programs to supply the unemployed with new skills that will promote their employability. *Not implementing the preventive or restorative policy amounts to imposing harm.*

In contrast, policy that advances individuals to a quality of life that is above their current quality of life is theorized as mere benefiting. It generates "pure benefits" (Shiffrin 2012). An example is an income tax cut. *Not implementing the policy is theorized not as harming but simply as not benefiting them.*

Figure 9.1 captures the argument. Not enacting a policy that would prevent Jamal from slipping from x to y harms him. If the policy is not enacted, he slides from x to y, as indicated by the lower arrow. If he has slipped to y, not enacting a policy that would restore him to x also harms him. Failure to introduce restorative policy is indicated by the upper arrow, where his return to his original position is blocked. But not enacting a policy that would shift Maria from x' to y' does not harm her; it merely fails to benefit her.

That argument is, however, incomplete. Feinberg argues we also should consider the condition in which Jamal and Maria find themselves prior to an intervention. In criminal law, not rescuing a drowning child when it is safe to do so is theorized *not* as not benefiting but as harming the child because the child is in desperate straits. The approach depends on a threshold between those who are in a harmed condition and those who are not (Shiffrin 2012). Bad Samaritan laws recognize the harming/not benefiting distinction, punishing those who cause harm to others by failing to pursue easy rescue.

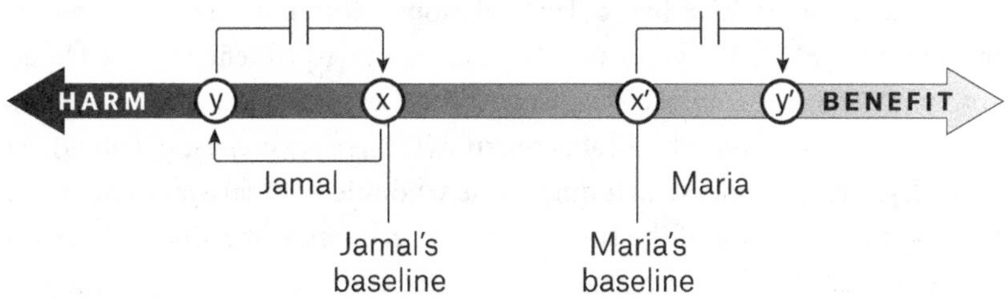

FIGURE 9.1. Not benefiting vs. harming

Not enacting a policy that would block Jamal's fall from *x* to *y*, or not enacting a policy that would restore him to *x* following a fall to *y*, represents harming. In contrast, not enacting a policy that would propel Maria from *x'* to *y'* represents not benefiting her.

In the economic context, the setback-to-interest approach would have us recognize that not pursuing an available policy that would assist those living in a harmed condition, below a certain threshold, amounts to harming. Examples include policies that would mitigate poverty, provide medical care in cases of severe illness, or eliminate other forms of suffering. In contrast, not implementing policy that would benefit those living above the threshold does not count as harm (see figure 9.2).

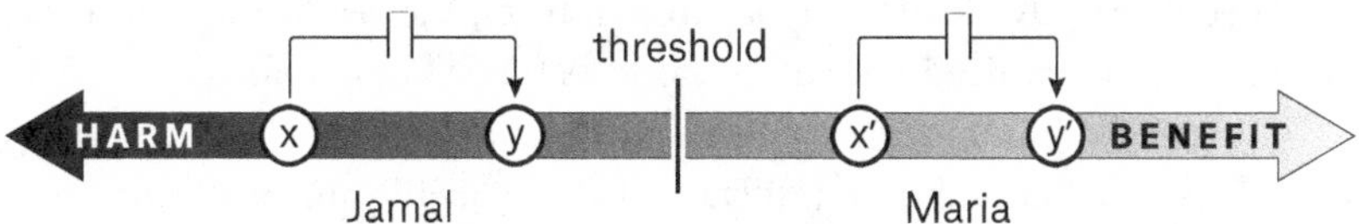

FIGURE 9.2. Harmed condition threshold

Failure to benefit Jamal entails harming him since he exists in a harmed condition. Not benefiting Maria does not entail harming.

Where does this review of the setback-to-interest approach leave us in our pursuit of a better conception of harm for economics? The chief virtue of the interest approach is that it reveals and resolves many of the significant weaknesses and conceptual failures of the welfarism that informs economics. For instance, the interest approach corrects the economist's simplistic treatment of harms as commensurable with benefits. But it also reveals the price of doing so. When adjudicating harm, the legal profession relies on statute and precedent. The legal procedure can be messy and inconsistent owing to the wide variety in circumstances, consequences, and identities of those involved in legal disputes, and to the range of interpretations that officers of the court bring to the litigation of individual cases. Perhaps as a consequence, some legal practitioners long for the clarity of economic moral geometry. This is particularly true of those in the "law and economics" movement that emerged in the 1960s in the US and came to influence jurisprudence in the US and abroad. Advocates embrace the disposition of cases based on standard decision rules of neoclassical moral geometry (Posner 1973; Geistfeld 2008). But many legal practitioners, including those who reject welfarism, dissent from the tradition. In place of the tractable moral geometry of economics we find in the setback-to-interest framework nuance and the need for careful judgment, which complicate greatly assessments of harm and harming.

Social Harm, Structural Violence

Since the late 1990s a critical perspective has challenged criminology's approach to harm. Critics allege that criminology restricts attention to "direct" harm in which an identifiable perpetrator with a guilty mind (mens rea) pursues a specific course of action that harms an identifiable victim. Only harms that fit this pattern are deemed illicit. Think of the 9/11 attacks in which three thousand people were killed. As a consequence of its limitation to direct harm, the approach overlooks the broad, structural systems that shape social interactions and outcomes, which arguably induce more extensive harm than do individual criminals targeting victims. Today approximately twenty-five thousand people worldwide die each day from hunger. Viewed through the lens of criminology, those deaths are understood as tragic but not illicit.

Critics of criminology established a new field of inquiry, "zemiology," that focuses on "social harm" (Hillyard et al. 2004; Hillyard and Tombs 2017). Social harm refers to harms that are brought about by social arrangements. Insights from this field are particularly relevant for economics given its focus on the assessment and design of social institutions and policies.

Economic arrangements can induce widespread, deep harms even if no one intends or is directly responsible for them. Economic arrangements generate widespread poverty, morbidity, mortality, and ecological destruction, all of which induce cascading and compounding harms. Economic arrangements can also induce subtler harms such as excess "winter deaths" brought about by inadequate housing and insufficient income to heat dwellings, as well as occupational injuries and illnesses (Hillyard and Tombs 2017). Economic arrangements can deprive many of society's members of opportunities for meaningful participation, concentrate that deprivation within disadvantaged groups, and then incarcerate substantial numbers of those affected by the deprivation. In these kinds of cases of social harm no perpetrator violates the law or contravenes prevalent rules, conventions, or norms. There typically is no mens rea and no targeted victim. Consequently, criminal law overlooks the harms no matter how widespread and deep they may be. Social harm is the result of the operation of formal institutions and informal social arrangements that structure social intercourse and provide roles that members of society play as they go about their lives. Employer/employee, teacher/student, professional/layperson, police officer/policed—these roles structure social interactions and generate social effects. For the zemiologists, they often also induce irreparable, indefensible harm.

Several concepts that inform the social-harm approach—most importantly, structural violence—can help rescue the notion of economic and econogenic harm from the narrow and distorting field of welfare economics.

STRUCTURAL VIOLENCE

The conceptual groundwork for the field of zemiology has been laid by social critics from political economy, sociology, political science, theology, ecology, and beyond. The critics demonstrate the ways in which what are widely taken to be legitimate institutions and social arrangements often generate extensive harms. Karl Marx exemplifies this tradition. Marx ([1867] 1977) famously explored how the capitalist mode of production damages lives. While eighteenth- and nineteenth-century liberal political economists had sought to dismiss the harms of poverty, unemployment, and short life spans as the consequence of natural forces (such as the laws of population) and personal failures, Marx targeted the operation of the economic system. Marx argued that capitalists were driven by the imperative to accumulate wealth to exploit workers at an increasing rate. He claimed that a system that appears to embody "Freedom, Equality, Property and Bentham" (Marx [1867] 1977, 280), wherein all economic actors appear in the market as equally free, pursuing their own self-interests, in fact depends on coercive force that ensures that workers face deprivation and unfreedom. For Marx it is not capitalist greed but the *social system* sanctified by the existing legal framework and moral codes that protect property rights and free contracting that generate harm. Socially produced, the harms are neither natural nor inevitable. In Marx's view they could be overcome by social transformation that displaced the capitalist mode of production.

The focus on the damage wrought by institutions and social systems came to inform the influential contribution of Johan Galtung (1969) to the study of violence. For Galtung (1969, 168), "violence is present when human beings are being influenced so that their actual somatic and mental realizations are below their potential realizations." Violence in this account is defined explicitly in counterfactual terms. Violence is "the cause of the difference between the potential and the actual, between what could have been and what is. Violence is that which increases the distance between the potential and the actual, and that which impedes the decrease of this distance" (Galtung 1969, 168).

Galtung's approach opens the concept of violence to considerations of the diverse impediments obstructing human capacities. Galtung argues that in the contemporary world, direct violence has been eclipsed in scope and reach by what he calls "structural violence." He encourages us to examine situations where resources that could promote well-being are diverted into uses that either do not promote or that interfere with human flourishing. "If insight and/or resources are monopolized by a group or class or are used for other purposes, then the actual level [of human flourishing] falls below the potential level, and violence is present in the system" (1969, 169).

A surprising and yet compelling argument appears in Galtung concerning the nature of influence. We intuitively distinguish negative from positive forms of influence, and we tend to think of just the former as illicit. Coercion is the culprit here: violence and threats of violence that compel behavior are on their face unjust. When instead behavior is influenced by positive inducements, such as monetary incentives, we tend to treat the influence as benign. Galtung disagrees. For him, monetary incentives that undermine human flourishing are just as illicit as coercive threats (cf. Grant 2011).

Galtung locates the source of structural violence in inequality, as indicated by the epigraph to this chapter. Most important is inequality in "the power to decide over the distribution of resources" (Galtung 1969, 171), which structures inequality in other areas, such as education and health. Inequality complicates the assessment of positive inducements, such as when a desperate individual is offered money to take on dangerous or degrading work. Inequality transforms legitimate bargains among equals into illicit bribes that hamper human development.

Direct violence typically "shows." In stable societies, Galtung writes, direct violence is visible "not only as ripples on waves, but waves on otherwise tranquil waters" (1969, 173). A homicide or burglary is readily apparent and attracts attention because it disturbs the normal course of events. Structural violence, on the other hand, is typically obscured, or "silent": "it is static; it is the tranquil waters." Galtung concludes on this basis that "personal [i.e., direct] violence is more easily noticed, even though the 'tranquil waters' of structural violence may contain much more violence" (1969, 173–74).

Direct and structural violence coexist, sustain each other, and reinforce each other's pernicious effects. When structural violence is challenged by concerted action, such as civil disobedience, those who benefit from the unjust social arrangements may resort to direct violence to stabilize the social system. The social movement opposing racialized, militarized policing following the George Floyd murder in May 2020 was met with police violence across the US. Police forces used chemical and other "nonlethal" weapons on peaceful protestors to assert control. President Trump threatened to deploy the military to restore "law and order." An important implication follows. An adequate account of harm's causes and effects requires analysis of both direct and structural violence and how they operate in concert in ways that amplify social harm.

Galtung vs. Friedman

Galtung's approach breaks sharply with neoclassical thinking on harm. Consider what Chicago School economist Milton Friedman had to say about the harm associated with racial discrimination. Writing sixty years prior to the protests of the George Floyd murder, at another time of social mobilization against racist injustice, Friedman famously ridiculed the advocates of the Fair Employment Protection Commission (FEPC). The FEPC was created to root out racial discrimination in labor markets. Friedman (1962, 112) argued that the case for the FEPC "involves a serious confusion between two very different kinds of harm."

> One kind is the *positive* harm that one individual does another by physical force, or by forcing him to enter into a contract without his consent. An obvious example is the man who hits another over the head with a blackjack. . . . The second kind is the *negative* harm that occurs when two individuals are unable to find mutually acceptable contracts, as when I am unwilling to buy something that someone wants to sell me and therefore make him worse off than he would be if I bought the item. [emphasis added]

Here Friedman anticipates the distinction between direct and structural harm Galtung would examine just a few years later. But Friedman argues that only positive harm is morally indictable. In his critique of the FEPC Friedman theorizes racial discrimination as a mere matter of *preferences*. In his view, some people simply prefer to associate exclusively with those of their own race. A consequence of this preference might be reduced opportunities for members of particular racial groups. Reasoning in this way allows Friedman to equate discrimination against Black workers with discrimination against opera singers in a community that prefers the blues:

> If the community at large has a preference for blues singers rather than for opera singers, they are certainly increasing the economic well-being of the

> first relative to the second. If a potential blues singer can find employment and a potential opera singer cannot, this simply means that the blues singer is rendering services which the community regards as worth paying for whereas the potential opera singer is not. The potential opera singer is "harmed" by the community's taste. . . ." (Friedman 1962, 113)

The harm to the opera singer may be regrettable, but surely she has no claim on government to fix the problem. So it is, Friedman argues, with racial minorities facing difficulties in the labor market. "There is a strong case for using government to prevent one person from imposing positive harm, which is to say, to prevent coercion. There is no case whatsoever for using government to avoid the negative kind of 'harm.' On the contrary, such government intervention reduces freedom and limits voluntary co-operation" (Friedman 1962, 112–13).

Friedman's strategy of dismissing the import of negative harm is central to the standard economic defense of market outcomes. In this account, market outcomes are unimpeachable provided all parties are free to contract with whom they will. And so even if it is the case (as in fact it is) that workers in US meatpacking and poultry plants face extraordinary risks of on-the-job disabling injuries and death (McConnell 2019), and even if those workers are disproportionately from groups with the fewest economic opportunities and with no influence over workplace safety standards—44% are Latinx, and 25% are Black (Fremstad, Rho, and Brown 2020)—their taking the jobs offered by the industry indicates that they accept the health risks voluntarily. In the standard economic view, then, their injuries and deaths are regrettable but not indictable.

This is precisely the one-sided logic that, in Galtung's view, distorts our perceptions of acute social harms. Friedman's moral geometry makes no room for structural violence. Friedman does not probe the presence of or effects of inequality in the power to control resources as a driver of structural violence. He does not recognize the silent forces that prevent many individuals from achieving a quality of life that is routinely available to others, and he does not consider how direct violence operates in racist societies to shore up structural violence against those who are targeted with discrimination even though during his life the Ku Klux Klan terrorized Black communities. Galtung corrects these errors. He urges us to inquire, for instance, whether employers who consider breaking with established racist norms by hiring a Black worker anticipate not just a loss of business but also threats of physical violence against their person and property; and whether Black workers who seek employment to do "white" work will be subject to threats of physical injury and even murder at the hands of white supremacists. Far from being a simple matter of preference, racist ideologies and practices are inscribed in social systems that structure differential opportunities and outcomes for white and nonwhite members of the economy and society. They impose deep "relational" harm in the form of "misrecognition" that bears on all aspects of individuals' existence (Pemberton 2015, 30).

Negative vs. Positive Freedom

In the text quoted here, *Capitalism and Freedom*, Friedman privileges freedom over all other values. And yet he trivializes the concept. For Friedman, effective freedom exists provided there is a market system that ensures individuals can choose when, with whom, and on what terms to form contracts. The key determinant of freedom in this context is "law and order to prevent physical coercion of one individual by another and to enforce contracts voluntarily entered into" (Friedman 1962, 14). A secondary determinant is the absence of monopoly. Approached in this way, effective freedom obtains even when the market generates substantial inequality in income, wealth, control over productive resources, and opportunities. Friedman recognizes only what is generally called "negative" freedom—freedom from physical coercion by the state or other parties. For Friedman, the free-market economy ensures that a poor individual with low income and few choices as a consequence of racial discrimination will be just as free as a wealthy individual with unlimited choices. Neither has a gun to the head when deciding how to allocate their eforts or their budgets.

Those who explore social harm adopt "positive" freedom as a centrally important basis for social assessment. Positive freedom captures what a person can actually *be*, *do*, or *become*. An individual's positive freedom is shaped by many aspects of her situation, including, for instance, her personal attributes, her access to resources, and the nature of the existing institutions and norms. If she is Black in a racialized society, she will face diminished positive freedom despite her intellect and effort. In this account the poor and the wealthy in a market society enjoy radically different levels of freedom, even if both have extensive latitude in deciding how to allocate their efforts and incomes. In a market economy marked by discrimination, the conditions for negative freedom of the disadvantaged might obtain, but the conditions for their positive freedom will not. Those who face economic discrimination will enjoy substantially lower levels of positive freedom than they would in a social order free of racial bias. They therefore face structural violence. The social-harm approach registers this harm as profoundly consequential and deeply indictable. In this context, exclusive focus on direct harm at the expense of social harm "leads to a neglect of much more damaging and dangerous forms of harm" (Hillyard et al. 2004, 2).

Recognition of positive freedom points toward an approach to harm that focuses on the social resources required to meet human needs (Hillyard and Tombs 2017, 300). The approach requires a theory of human needs to ascertain which needs should be deemed salient in harm assessment. Zemiologists see harm wherever "human flourishing is demonstrably compromised." Contributors to the field categorize harms in various ways, such as "physical/mental harms, autonomy harms, and relational harms." What makes harms "social" is the fact that they are "socially mediated" and are therefore taken to be preventable "insofar as they are either 'foreseeable' events or the result of 'alterable' social conditions" (Pemberton 2015, 9–10). Pulling all this together, Simon Pemberton (2015, 24) usefully defines social harm as "a shorthand to reflect the relations, processes, flows, practices, discourse, actions and inactions that constitute the fabric of our societies which serve to compromise the fulfillment of human needs and in so doing result in identifiable harms."[62]

SOCIAL DISTANCE AND MORAL INDIFFERENCE

One factor that serves to render social harm invisible is social distance. In complex social systems there is often a substantial gap between those acting in ways that generate harm, and those who will suffer its effects. In the era of economic globalization, for instance, we find long contracting chains linking far-flung intermediaries that separate economic actors from each other, such that "individuals do not experience the consequences of their actions" (Pemberton 2004, 78). Consumers typically do not know the conditions under which the goods they buy were produced. They cannot see the sweat, blood, and deprivation of exploited workers whose labor provides them with their purchases (Pemberton 2004; McIntyre 2008; Sen 2009). Likewise, economists will never meet most of the people who will be affected by their professional practice. That gap can be geographic, temporal, and/or social. Moreover, social harms arise from the coordinated and uncoordinated actions of dispersed actors (Hillyard and Tombs 2017, 300–301). Economists produce reports that policy makers will utilize as they see fit, the consequences of which will depend on how any resulting policy measures are implemented and enforced. In this kind of context, involving "many hands" (Adams and Balfour 1998), responsibility falls from view and with it, too often, the harms themselves.

The hidden nature of social harm presents a risk for professions like economics that seek to promote social betterment. Since social harms lack identifiable perpetrators harming particular victims, we are tempted to treat them as unavoidable by-products of the nature of things. Doing so takes us off the hook, with the effect that we display "moral indifference" toward those facing devastating harms (Pemberton 2004, 72; Opotow 1990). We are induced to look for ways to unburden ourselves of our duties to confront the harms. This is Friedman's approach. It is enabled by a professional convention to theorize harm via a moral geometry that takes no account of social harm.

STRUCTURED PATTERNS OF HARM

The social-harm approach illuminates a fact that is largely missed by those who focus exclusively on personal or direct harm. A restricted focus on direct harm leads to a view of harms as a series of disconnected events: one person is just as apt as another, it might seem, to be victimized by assault, theft, or other direct acts of violence. Appreciation of social harm grounded in structural inequality leads us to see instead that violence is patterned, driven by underlying social processes. Certain groups suffer its damaging effects while others remain largely insulated from them (cf. Hillyard and Tombs 2017, 291). We encountered this issue in chapter 8, where we found that reliance on Kaldor-Hicks as a decision rule achieves just outcomes only if the harms of successive policy decisions are serially uncorrelated. But in the presence of structural violence, harms will necessarily be serially correlated. Being harmed from today's policy decisions will predispose the same individuals to suffer harm again tomorrow. The greater the inequality in power, the greater the bias in policy-induced harms. The social-harm approach encourages us, then, to explore "harms across the life course": to appreciate the depth and cascading effects of a series of harms individuals face over time as a consequence of social arrangements (Hillyard et al. 2004, 7).

ARE HARMFUL ARRANGEMENTS INEVITABLE?

A challenge arises in this context to ascertain which harms are socially mediated and eliminable, and which are not. Judgments of that sort are sometimes driven by theoretical frameworks that tell us that only certain kinds of social arrangements will work or be sustainable, given the nature of human beings and social relationships. Neoclassical theory embraces this way of thinking. In that account, only policy that is consistent with human self-interest will succeed; expecting individuals to act against their own narrow self-interest "strains and damages moral muscles" (Yeager 1976, 566). Any harms that result from well-crafted policy are taken as morally benign.

Social-harm theorists push back against the claim that social harms are inevitable. Pemberton (2015) explores the diverse forms of capitalist systems that exist across many countries and finds that there is wide variance among them in the harms they generate. He concludes that the harms economists so often treat as inevitable are instead grounded in *alterable* social arrangements that can be reformed through policy choices. The claim that social harms are ineradicable, he argues, typically reflects self-interest of the privileged and a profound lack of imagination among professional practitioners. A consequence of resignation to the necessity of harm is moral indifference to a wide range of social harms that destroy the lives of very large numbers of people (Pemberton 2004). "The reasons why world leaders and policy-makers are indifferent to the death and suffering of the 'poor,'" Hillyard et al. (2004, 9) write, "is that they are an indirect consequence of the capitalist global economic system. Since no one intended all these children to die young their deaths are seen as unfortunate but not unjust."

Economists in the tradition of Milton Friedman are certainly not indifferent to mass privation that occurs in market economies. Their error, and it is a grave one, is to view privation as unfortunate rather than unjust.

The Capabilities Account of Human Flourishing and Harm

Over the past several decades leading economists and philosophers have advanced a critique of welfarism's conception of well-being and harm that parallels zemiology in important respects, including its focus on human needs. The dissenters, including most notably economist Amartya Sen and philosopher Martha Nussbaum, have advanced what has come to be called the "capabilities" approach to human development. The capabilities approach provides a viable alternative to the moral poverty of moral geometry. The capabilities approach is by now well-known within and beyond economics, especially in the field of economic development, and so this summary will be brief (see DeMartino 2000).

CAPABILITIES: CENTRAL FEATURES AND IMPLICATIONS

The capabilities approach emerged in opposition to the predominant approach to economic development during the latter half of the twentieth century. That approach embraced welfarism. As a consequence, it defined development simplistically in terms of incomes and sought to promote rising incomes in poorer countries.

Sen, Nussbaum, and other advocates of the capabilities approach objected to the income approach to development on multiple grounds. First, they took issue with welfarism. Sen emphasized the error of reducing all goods to welfare and treating them as substitutable. He objected equally to equating human development exclusively with improving welfare (Sen 1992; 1999). He argued that a good human life entails far more than the achievement of high levels of welfare. In place of that standard he advocated for the expansion of human freedom, defined in terms of the "capability to achieve functionings." *Functionings* refers to the beings and doings that people have reason to value. Being well nourished, avoiding preventable morbidity or premature mortality, and having access to adequate shelter are obvious conditions that are central to a good life—a life of freedom. But so are more subtle states and abilities, such as "appearing in public without shame," political efficacy, self-respect, and the respect of others in one's community. The list of potential valued functionings is a long one that includes a diverse range of beings and doings. *Capabilities* refers to the ability to achieve these valued functionings. The greater a person's capability set, the greater is her substantive freedom to live a valued life. Emphasis here, then, is on positive freedom which depends on but reaches beyond negative freedom defined as the absence of physical coercion.

The capabilities framework involves insights that sharpen our understanding of economic harm. First, a good life requires the achievement of many distinct, nonfungible functionings. Good nutrition cannot compensate for the harms associated with physical immobility. Second, the framework helps us to understand why distinct harms cascade. Any individual functioning failure may induce a range of others. Being homeless can induce diminished self-respect, social exclusion, political inefficacy, diminished autonomy, and other functioning failures. These functioning failures in turn interfere with the pursuit of individuals' most important life plans. Third, the capabilities framework takes a needs-based approach to human development and harm, with emphasis placed on interpersonal differences. Distinct individuals will require distinct bundles of resources, such as health care and income, to achieve the same level of substantive freedom (and to avoid capabilities failure). Those inhabiting a malaria-infested region will require greater levels of resources for health care than those who inhabit more hospitable regions; pregnant individuals will require greater nutrition than many who are not pregnant.

Capabilities Inequality

Under standard moral geometry, individuals' levels of well-being depend exclusively on their absolute levels of consumption. Inequality is taken to have no impact on well-being. In contrast, the capabilities approach, like zemiology, draws our attention to the harms associated with inequality. Being relatively low-income, for instance, triggers a range of relative functioning failures. Relative functioning failures, in turn, induce absolute functioning failures, such as avoidable morbidity. The US again demonstrates the connection. Those with relatively low ability to achieve income also face the greatest risk of physical harm at work, least income security, least ability to respond to unanticipated hardships (such as the illness of a child), least political efficacy, greatest frequency of victimization by violence, and highest mortality rate. This would not be the case if each good were distributed based on principles appropriate to it (Walzer 1983). In that case, health care would be allocated based on medical need and honors would be distributed according to merit. But in our world unequal achievement in one or more functionings distorts the achievement of other functionings, undermining the positive freedom of the most vulnerable.

These insights bear on the cascading harms faced by marginalized groups in society. When inequality stems from social misrecognition in the form of dehumanization tied to race, gender, and other social divisions, its effects are particularly pronounced. In the US, for instance, racial inequalities manifest as inequalities in every important economic measure, including income, wealth, employment, security, and opportunity. Accumulated wealth from savings or inheritance provides a wide range of benefits, permitting investments in housing, financial assets, and human capital. In 2016, the median white family had about $170,000 in wealth, ten times more than the median Black family holding of just $17,000 (McIntosh et al. 2020). Racial income disparities were equally notable. In 2018 the annual median household income for white families was $70,000; for Hispanic families, $51,000; and for Black families, $41,000. In that year the official child poverty rate for whites was about 8%, for Hispanics, about 18%, and for Blacks, almost 21% (Wilson and Williams 2019). During the COVID-19 pandemic, racial disparities in unemployment, incomes, and savings widened, leaving Black families in dire straits (Weller and Roberts 2021). In the twelve months ending in February 2021, net job losses were greatest for Black and Latinx workers. At the end of that period the jobless rate stood at 9.9% for Black workers, 8.5% for Latinx workers, and 5.6% for white workers (Bahn and Sanchez Cumming 2021).

Race-based inequality is reflected in many other functioning failures, including exposure to financial predation; reduced access to housing, education, and other public services; diminished life expectancy; increased rates of unemployment; incarceration (and harsher court sentencing outcomes); violent death; childbirth-related complications and deaths; and increased exposure to climate-related crises. For instance, in the US between 2001 and 2004, "the gap in life expectancy between the richest 1% and the poorest 1% of individuals was 14.6 years . . . for men, and 10.1 years . . . for women" (Chetty et al. 2016). In 2020, life expectancy for white inhabitants was 78.6 years; for Black inhabitants, 75.0 years (Burd-Sharps and Lewis 2015). To put those figures in context, life expectancy for white Americans would place them in fiftieth place in the world tables (compared with all countries), while Black Americans would place ninety-sixth. The figure for white Americans is not good, given the enormous resources available in the US to promote good health. But the figure for Black Americans is appalling. It is at a level between those of Jordan and Jamaica even though the US is substantially richer than both those countries (United Nations Population Division 2020).

The capabilities approach illuminates the fact that relative inequality can impair the ability of the disadvantaged to achieve the full range of vital functionings. Sen (1992) may in fact be right when he argues that it is more damaging to be relatively poor in a wealthy society than to be equally poor in a lower-income society. In a wealthy society the relatively poor suffer particular functioning failures, such as an inability to achieve self-esteem, social standing, and physical health, that undermine their capabilities freedom. For instance, inequality in functionings achievement in advance of a crisis place those worst-off at higher risk of suffering harm from the crisis. This has been borne out by COVID-19. A study of twenty-two thousand deaths in New York City through the early months of the pandemic found that having low income had the greatest impact on deaths, followed by being sixty-five years or older, having been born in Latin America, living 1.5 persons to a room, and being Black. While many well-to-do Americans have been able to work safely from their spacious homes, low-income white, Latinx, and Black workers have been put in positions where they face much higher risks of contracting and dying from the virus (Leopold 2020).

Capabilities Harms

The capabilities approach opens up alternative ways to theorize economic and econogenic harm. *Ways, not way*: there is no uniquely correct path to elaborate the capabilities framework in regard to harm and harming. *The approach does not provide an alternative moral geometry to replace welfarist decision rules*. Instead, the approach is explicitly open ended. It forces us to engage difficult moral and practical questions that resist formulaic resolution. And as a consequence of that fact, it challenges the status of the economist as the ultimate harm accountant. It points toward the need to incorporate as chief decision makers the communities that risk being harmed by economic arrangements and policy innovations (see chap. 11).

One promising way to theorize harm within the capabilities framework is to follow Nussbaum (1992) in acknowledging distinct levels of living defined in terms of limits and capabilities. Nussbaum offers what she calls a "thick, vague conception of the good" that is derived from a survey of the judgments about human well-being that have emerged in distinct cultures throughout human history. She emphasizes that the conception of the good is always open to further refinement as thinking about human existence continues to evolve.

Nussbaum presents two distinct thresholds: a "minimally human life" and a "good human life." Living a minimally human life requires many things. Nussbaum's list includes, inter alia, requirements imposed by the fact that humans inhabit bodies that need food and shelter. Individuals must understand mortality and view it as "an occasion for grief and/or fear"; achieve sufficient nutrition, shelter, and mobility; have the capacity to experience pleasure and pain; enjoy certain cognitive abilities, including the capacities for perceiving, imagining, and thinking; and achieve the capacity for practical reason, affiliation with other human beings, and the capacity for humor and play (Nussbaum 1992, 216–21). A life lacking one or more of these attributes and abilities is impoverished in terms of the most basic human freedoms.

Living a good human life encompasses targets that societies should seek for all their citizens. It includes a wider range of capabilities, including, for instance, "being able to live to the end of a complete human life, as far as is possible"; achieving good health and having opportunities for sexual satisfaction and physical mobility; being able to avoid unnecessary and nonbeneficial pain and to have pleasurable experiences; being able "to imagine, to think, and to reason"; "being able to live for and with others"; and "being able to live one's own life and nobody else's." In Nussbaum's view, two of the capabilities on the list, "practical reason and affiliation," are "architectonic, holding the whole enterprise together and making it human" (Nussbaum 1992, 221–22).

The elements on both lists encompass separate, nonfungible components. "We cannot satisfy the need for one of them by giving a larger amount of another one." The implication for moral geometry is profound. Nonsubstitutability "limits the trade-offs that it will be reasonable to make, and thus limits the applicability of quantitative cost-benefit analysis" (Nussbaum 1992, 222).

Nussbaum's thresholds provide guidance for theorizing economic and econogenic harm. Individuals living in conditions that place them below the first threshold are in an acutely harmed condition. Failure to pursue available strategies to lift them from this level of abject misery is harmful. We harm them—*and not just fail to benefit them*—by maintaining the status quo. Individuals living below the second threshold experience a higher level of existence, but the moral obligation for those who can intervene is much the same. These individuals, too, are surviving in a harmed condition, and their situation demands of policy makers and the economists who advise them rectification in the form of an improvement in the quality of their lives. Their situation demands priority over those who enjoy good human lives.

KERALA—A CAPABILITIES PERSPECTIVE

How might the capabilities approach help us make sense of Kerala's relative success in stemming the COVID-19 pandemic?

In 2019 Kerala had a per capita income of about $11,000. That places it in the top third of Indian states, though it has a much lower per capita income than the leading states. Incomes earned locally in Kerala are supplemented with remittances sent home by the many Keralans who work elsewhere. But income in Kerala is extremely low relative to incomes of advanced economies. And yet, the state outperformed most richer jurisdictions in confronting COVID-19.

Sen (1999) has pointed to Kerala for its extraordinary performance in promoting human capabilities relative to its per capita income, and for having achieved a high degree of capabilities equality. Over the past forty years the communist leadership of Kerala has prioritized public health, for instance, spending six times the national average on health care. It has also supported nongovernmental institutions that promote solidarity and social inclusion, such as trade unions, worker co-ops, and youth groups (Chowdhury and Jomo KS 2020). As a consequence of these and other measures, Kerala outperforms many richer states in important indicators of human well-being, such as infant mortality, life expectancy and other aspects of health, and economic stability. It also boasts the highest literacy rate in all of India. And its physician-to-population ratio of twenty-five per ten thousand is about equal to that of Canada (Shankar 2021).

As has become clear during the pandemic, Kerala has succeeded where so many others have not in promoting freedom defined in terms of the ability of its residents to live valued lives. In the present case, that means nothing less than the ability to preserve life. Kerala was able to implement an effective COVID-19 response when many jurisdictions in India and abroad stumbled; to secure the trust necessary to mobilize their citizens to take preventive measures when much wealthier jurisdictions were confronted with uncooperative, distrusting citizens; to ensure adequate resources when other jurisdictions faced shortages of hospital beds, supplies, and personnel; and to utilize efficiently those resources when others could not manage to direct available resources to where they were most needed. A long-term emphasis on the promotion of human capabilities in Kerala helped the government minimize the harm from what has proven to be a very difficult medical crisis.

Conclusion

The capabilities approach poses a challenge to professionals whose authority depends on moral geometry. The capabilities approach calls on economists to widen their conceptions of the forms of and interconnections between distinct harms; to prioritize the harms to those who suffer capabilities deprivation; to forgo moral geometry in public-policy matters, especially when some individuals exist in harmed conditions; and to take full account of the diverse and deep harms that are associated with inequality. The capabilities approach asks a lot of the profession—no doubt much more than many economists are willing to tolerate.

How might the profession proceed differently were it to engage seriously the complexity of harm that we have now explored at some length in this and previous chapters? What would it mean to pursue "harm-centric economics"? And how can a profession that faces irreparable ignorance ameliorate harm when so many of its interventions are apt to generate unforeseeable consequences, many of which might be harmful to those the profession seeks to serve? We explore these questions in part IV of the book. Chapter 10 presents a harm-centric approach to economic practice. Chapter 11 explores how economists can proceed responsibly in a world they cannot ever fully know or even begin to control.

PART IV

Confronting Econogenic Harm Responsibly

10

Economic Harm Profile Analysis

> Indeed, the fact that some societies have lower incidences of harm than others would suggest that harm is not inevitable, but rather a product of the way we choose to organise the societies in which we live.
>
> —SIMON PEMBERTON (2015, 8)

High Per Capita Income, Not Enough

Twentieth-century economists might be forgiven for having thought that rising per capita income would mitigate the most important economic harms. Poor health and high mortality, low literacy, extreme inequality, inadequate housing, and economic insecurity can be tied to poverty. Wealthy countries should be expected to outperform lower-income countries in these and other important harm metrics.

Do the data support that reasoning? At first glance they seem to. For example, the sixty or so countries with the worst performance in life expectancy are among the world's poorest, while the world's wealthiest countries dominate the top of the rankings.The US in 2020 enjoys a median life expectancy of 79.11 years. That places it far ahead of many low-income countries, such as Cameroon at 60.32 years, Somalia at 58.34 years, and Chad at 55.17 years.

But now consider this. According to the IMF, the US is the eighth-richest country in the world. In terms of life expectancy, however, it is ranked forty-sixth. Many countries with substantially lower income outperform the US in life expectancy. Greece is in nineteenth place, with a longevity of 82.8 years, though its income is just 30% of US income. Costa Rica, the territory of the US Virgin Islands, Guam, Chile, and the Commonwealth of Puerto Rico also have higher life expectancy than the US (United Nations Population Division 2020). And Cuba is one place above the US in the longevity tables even though its income per capita is just 14% of US income.

The same kinds of anomalies appear in other indicators of well-being and harm. The US has a much higher homicide rate than other wealthy countries and many mid- to low-income countries even though its incarceration rate is much higher than those of other countries. The US today has 737 prisoners per 100,000 residents; in comparison, Russia has 615 and China 118 (BBC News n.d.). The US infant mortality rate of 5.22 deaths per 1,000 live births is worse than those of over fifty other countries. The US is far behind Cuba at 4.19 deaths per 1,000 live births, Italy and Spain at 3.14, and Slovenia at 1.53 (CIA 2017). The US also faces an obesity rate about twice those of Italy, Denmark, and Switzerland (CIA 2016). Deficient performance in the US in these measures is not the result of low spending. The US spends a higher share of its total GDP on health care but achieves lower measures of health than many other countries, such as South Korea, Norway, Finland, Sweden, and Ireland (Pemberton 2015). Equally troubling, the US has a very high share of its population living below the poverty line. One measure of the poverty rate is the share of individuals living in households with incomes that are half the median household income. By that standard about 18% of the US population lived in poverty between 2016 and 2019. Among members of the Organisation for Economic Co-operation and Development (OECD), only Costa Rica and Colombia had worse poverty rates. In contrast, sixteen OECD countries had poverty rates of 10% or less (OECD 2020). The US has an extraordinarily high share of children living in poverty. Its rate was 18%, third worst in the OECD, compared to Canada's rate of 12% and Denmark's rate of just under 5% (OECD 2020).

Fifty years ago development economists typically theorized the relationship between economic growth and inequality as an inverted U-shaped curve, called the Kuznets curve. Poor societies initially become more unequal as they develop, it was thought, but soon reach a turning point after which increasing per capita income promotes income equality. During the middle decades of the twentieth century the pattern held. Even today the countries with the greatest levels of income inequality are in fact low- to middle-income. The country with the fifty-first-worst distribution, however, is the US. It is characterized by much greater inequality than eastern, central, and western European countries and even many low- to middle-income countries (World Bank 2019). Today we find substantial variation in the extent of inequality across high- and low-income countries. Moreover, over the past several decades inequality in many countries has deepened with rising per capita income. With deepening inequality comes all the harms we examined earlier.

We now know that many economic harms are not correlated neatly with per capita income. Countries at similar levels of income exhibit wide variation in the economic and other harms to which their inhabitants are exposed. The good news is that this suggests existing harms may be eradicable through institutional reform. But doing that requires placing harm at the center of economic analysis.

*

Most economists in the public arena are tinkerers, working to make marginal changes in policies with limited reach. But in the aggregate, economists' practice adds up to something much more substantial. The economics profession aspires to social engineering. It aspires to influence an economy's design and the practices of individuals and institutions, and, via these pathways, to alter economic outcomes.

Economies differ in their economic institutions, rules, and practices. The differences bear on the harms that proliferate in these economies. Distinct economies are characterized by what I will call distinct "harm profiles." *Economic harm profile analysis* examines those harm profiles. It takes a harm-centric view of economic performance. It entails investigating the harms that proliferate under distinct economic arrangements, including those arrangements that economists advocate.

Economic harm profile analysis represents an opportunity for economists. To the degree that economists can influence economic institutions and practices, they have an opportunity to improve an economy's harm profile by eliminating gratuitous harms while preparing for and ameliorating inescapable harms. Economic harm profile analysis requires a serious engagement with harm's complexity that acknowledges competing judgments concerning which harms it is legitimate to impose on society's members and outsiders in pursuit of valued goods.

Here we explore the concept of economic harm profile analysis in some detail, while nonetheless passing quickly over the myriad issues that a full-blown economic harm profile analysis would entail. The purpose here is to demonstrate how economic analysis might be reoriented were the profession to take a harm-centric approach to its work.

Economic Harm Profile Analysis

An economy's harm profile comprises five principal categories, each of which encompasses multiple subcategories (see table 10.1). They are the (1) *nature* of prevalent, averted, and covered harms; (2) *productivity* of harms; (3) *distribution* of harms; (4) *mechanisms* of harm generation and distribution; and (5) *consent* and *coercion* that are associated with harm-generative and distributive mechanisms. The five features are complex and traverse each other's boundaries. Moreover, they necessarily entail positive and normative elements, a consequence of the inherently normative nature of the concept of harm.

In what follows I primarily discuss *economic systems* even though I am primarily interested in the harm profiles of *economies*. The distinction is important. Any actual economy comprises one or more economic systems,

TABLE 10.1. Elements of economic harm profile

1. Nature of prevalent, averted, and covered harms	1a. Prevalence, depth, and risk of –*reparable* versus *irreparable* harms –*compensable* versus *noncompensable* harms –*foreseeable* versus *unforeseeable* harms –*avoidable* versus *unavoidable* harms
	1b. Nature of harms *averted or diminished* in frequency/severity
	1c. Nature of *uncovered* harms versus nature of harms *insured against* or otherwise *ameliorated*
2. Productivity of harms	2a. *Necessary* versus *unnecessary* harms
	2b. *Ethically benign* versus *indictable* harms
3. Distribution of harms	3a. Distribution of winners and losers in each period and over the course of successive periods
	3b. Relative stakes, winning and losing
4. Mechanisms of harm generation and distribution	4a. Direct versus indirect harm
	4b. Direct versus structural harm
	4c. Fairness of harm-generative arrangements
	4d. Ability of those causing harm to escape consequences
	4e. Fragility versus antifragility of economic arrangements
5. Consent and coercion	5a. Extent and intensity of coercion within each particular contest within the economic system
	5b. Extent and intensity of coercion to participate in any particular contest
	5c. Extent and intensity of coercion to participate in any particular class of contests
	5d. Extent and intensity of coercion to participate in any particular economic system

defined as *alternative arrangements of economic provisioning*. The distinction will emerge as salient when we consider the last element of the harm profile analysis, consent and coercion.

1. THE NATURE OF PREVALENT, AVERTED, AND COVERED HARMS

The first element of an economic harm profile concerns the nature of the harms that the economic system generates, averts, and ameliorates.

1a. Prevalence, depth, and risk of . . .

. . . *reparable versus irreparable harms*. A central problem with the standard welfarist approach to harm is that it treats all harms as reparable through compensation (see chap. 8). The approach fails to recognize harm's complexity. It mocks rather than respects those who experience a loss of vitally important goods by presuming that their loss can be fully offset by the provision of alternative goods. As I type these words there are economists instructing introductory economics students that the diminution in preference satisfaction a consumer suffers from the loss of an apple can be fully offset by gaining access to oranges, where the amount of oranges necessary to do the job is determined by a person's willingness to trade one good for another. After the substitution the individual is just as well-off as she was before. A naive student might ask, "Can we infer then that a father who loses a daughter owing to his inability to afford essential medical care will be just as well-off after her death provided he receives a lump sum payment in the requisite amount? Are the two states 'with the child but without the money' and 'without the child but with the money' really just two points on the same indifference curve?" The economist *qua* economist will find little help in standard moral geometry in crafting a compelling reply. The reason, to reiterate the point, is that the standard view presumes that all goods are welfare commensurable and substitutable. There is no lexicographic ordering of preferences here. In this view there is always some amount of money that can render the grieving father whole.

Other professions recognize the distinction between reparable and irreparable harm as meaningful and normatively salient. Normative economics should do the same. An economy characterized by greater risk of irreparable harms to some for the benefit of others is deficient in this regard relative to an alternative economy with less risk of irreparable harms.

. . . compensable versus noncompensable harms. Moral geometry is inadequate to address the problem of noncompensable harm. Its assumptions and conceptual framework are designed to eliminate the problem: it simply takes all harms to be compensable. Some harms, of course, are compensable, such as the loss of a good with no nonpecuniary value. But as we have seen, all irreparable harms and even some reparable harms are noncompensable in the sense that monetary transfer cannot make the harmed agent whole (see chap. 8).

Unlike moral geometry, harm profile analysis distinguishes between compensable and noncompensable harms. An economy characterized by greater risk of noncompensable harms is deficient in this regard relative to one with less risk of noncompensable harms.

. . . foreseeable versus unforeseeable harms; avoidable versus unavoidable harms. Economic systems diverge regarding which harms are foreseeable and which

are unforeseeable. Monitoring systems ranging from weather to market forecasting are intended to transform unforeseeable to foreseeable harms. Institutions play a key role in this regard. Institutions seek to gather information and extend their control over their environments to transform unforeseeable adverse events into foreseeable events in the hope of increasing their ability to prepare for and ameliorate the effects. Up against an inherently unknowable future, however, institutional control faces insuperable limits (Taleb 2010).

Economic systems also diverge regarding which harms are avoidable and which are unavoidable. A privatized medical care system provides immediate treatment for people with health insurance by way of their employment status, say. But under a privatized system it may be unavoidable that some individuals lacking adequate medical insurance will be unable to secure care or will be bankrupted by the costs of care. In contrast, a system of universal health care funded by taxation might eliminate the risk of financial hardship for patients but might induce harms associated with long waits for medical procedures.

Many harms that arise in the context of professional practice are avoidable. This is the case, for instance, with harms that result from professional incompetence, hubris, ethical failure or malfeasance, or negligence. It is not always easy to discern which harms are in fact the outcome of these professional failures. Some cases are clear, such as when economists take on policy work for which they are clearly unqualified or where they have conflicts of interest. Other cases are more difficult to evaluate. The case of gratuitous harms, to which we will turn momentarily, is particularly difficult to assess.

1b. Nature of harms averted or diminished in frequency/severity

The inverse of the harms that prevail in an economic system are the harms that are averted or diminished in frequency or severity. No system can avert all harms. Some harms, like those resulting from natural events, can't be entirely eliminated, but they can be reduced in intensity and ameliorated. Appropriate building codes or zoning regulations, for instance, can substantially diminish a region's vulnerability to the high winds and flooding associated with hurricanes.

One reason why not all harms can be averted is that some strategies designed to avert particular harms might impair the ability of the system to avert others. For instance, liberalized, "liquid" financial systems exist when assets like stocks and bonds can be bought and sold instantaneously with low transactions costs and little government oversight. Advocates claim that such systems eliminate the harms associated with credit shortages that obstruct beneficial economic activity. But Keynes (1936) pointed out that such systems are also prone to unpredictable financial bubbles and crises. In liquid financial systems individual investors can often protect themselves from losses by selling off assets that they think might fall in value. But that strategy fails when many investors try to dump the same asset at the same time. The combined effect of their individually rational behavior can be to induce a financial panic that destroys their portfolios.

Economic systems exist not just to avert harm but to generate valued goods whose achievement necessarily entails the risk of harm. Were we to be able to design a harm-proof economic system, it would not likely be one that most of us would choose to inhabit. That said, distinct economic systems will be more or less defensible according to which kinds of harms they avert or diminish, and how they achieve harm diminution. Not all harms are equal, and neither are all harm-reducing arrangements. Economic harm profile analysis directs economists to examine and open to public scrutiny the harms that they believe *can* be averted and, when choices have to be made, *should* be averted even when doing so would interfere with access to other socially valued goods.

1c. Nature of uncovered harms versus nature of harms insured against or otherwise ameliorated

Economic systems vary according to their performance in hedging against adverse, unpreventable events. Insurance provides one form of protection. But distinct forms of insurance cover distinct adverse events while leaving others uncovered. Government stockpiling of agricultural surpluses in good years may prevent food shortages during a drought, though it leaves farmers whose crops are destroyed by the drought vulnerable to financial ruin. In contrast, private crop insurance and agricultural commodity futures markets may protect against income shortages among farmers (but see Breger Bush 2012) but can leave uncovered a shortfall in food supplies owing to a drought. Absent stockpiles, food shortages may be averted only if the appropriate markets and distribution systems exist, external sources of food are readily available, and nonfarmers have sufficient income to pay higher prices for food. These conditions are not always met (see Griffiths 2003). The point is that no scheme can insure against all disruptions.

2. PRODUCTIVITY OF HARMS

It is uncomfortable to contemplate that some serious harms are "productive," but that is surely the case. Harm profile analysis must investigate which harms that arise in an economy are and are not productive.

2a. Necessary versus unnecessary harms

Necessary, or productive, harms are those whose risk is vital to generating widely shared, highly valued goods. For instance, neoclassical theory holds that the risk of harm associated with market competition, including business failures that put people out of work, is essential to the achievement of economic efficiency. Unnecessary, or gratuitous, harms are those that do not produce widely shared, highly valued goods, though they may generate advantage for particular individuals. Economic systems that are alike in other important respects may nonetheless vary in the degree to which they generate or tolerate gratuitous harms. One economic system may encompass measures to eliminate gratuitous harms, while another may demonstrate broad tolerance for them, owing to factors such as indifference, concerns about the cost of regulation, and judgments about the significance of the harm.

In harm profile analysis, productive harms are to be accorded a higher moral status than harms for which the connection to valued goods is remote or absent. *Danger lurks, however, whenever a theoretical account purports to demonstrate a necessary connection between a good and a harm.* That path, on full display in neoclassical theory, inures economists to harm. The ethically appropriate attitude is to resist the presumption of the necessity of harm until one has definitive proof of the necessity, not just an appealing argument. Avoiding catastrophic error in this regard requires a strong commitment to theoretical pluralism and open-mindedness in the profession that prevents a rush to judgment concerning harm's necessity.

Unequivocal evidence of the productivity of harm, shared by diverse theoretical accounts, concludes one line of inquiry but opens another. A virtue of the economic harm profile approach is that it problematizes the perception that what is, must be. The finding that a harm is necessary to achieve a good under *prevailing social arrangements* cannot be taken as proof that the harm is necessary under *all viable alternative arrangements*. The point is fundamental: the *necessity* of harm may be and often is *contextually contingent*—necessary only under established economic arrangements. A finding of obligatory harm to achieve a good entails a "tragic choice." It should trigger in the minds of the professional what Nussbaum (2001, 187) identifies as the "Hegelian question": "How can we bring it about that citizens do not face such tragic choices all the time?"

Economic harm profile analysis would be of service to a profession that rises to the Hegelian challenge. Comparison of alternative economic arrangements helps to eliminate incorrect inferences about the universality of any particular tragic choice. Comparisons can help to distinguish those harms that arise under most if not all economic arrangements from those that arise under some but not other economic arrangements. Opportunities might exist to pursue what Wiener (1998, 64) calls "risk superior innovations," innovations that can eliminate tragic choices by "reducing multiple risks in concert." Appreciation of a range of economic harm profiles undermines the status quo bias in which we take existing arrangements to be invariant and the associated tragic choices to be ineliminable. It is better to recognize that "the arrangements that we observe in operation today, varied as they are, themselves constitute a subset of the full range of potential institutional possibilities" (Rodrik 2001, 12). Reforms that eliminate tragic choices—that break the link of dependence between particular goods and harms—serve to generate a more benign economic harm profile.

2b. Ethically benign versus indictable harms

The preceding discussion implies that economic systems vary in the ethical status of the harms they induce. Not all serious harms are ethically indictable, but neither are all legally permitted harms ethically benign. The first point follows from the nature of any reasonably complex society. We harm each other as a routine feature of living with others. We often seek the same pecuniary and nonpecuniary goods, positions, partners, rankings, and honors under circumstances where the success of one person necessarily involves loss to others. Two people competing for the same job can't both win it, and the harm to the loser might be deep and enduring. Her life plans might be altered for the worse for the duration of her life. And yet, we would not be apt to condemn the victor for her success, provided the contest was fair in salient respects. The harm suffered in this case, even if severe, is ethically benign. The harm might call for compassion for the loser, perhaps, but not outrage.[63] Alternatively, legal systems may permit ethically illegitimate harm. The legacy admission system at elite universities in the US is a case in point (Kahlenberg 2010). When making admissions decisions, private universities typically reserve a significant percentage of places in the entering class for children of alumni. The harm this practice does to more qualified applicants from less privileged families who are thereby excluded from admission is illegitimate on the basis of the most basic and relatively uncontested justice criteria.

Cases such as these demonstrate that it is not enough to show that one economic system generates fewer or less severe harms than another. Numbers count, to be sure. But in drawing up an economic harm profile we are forced to distinguish between harms that are and are not ethically worrisome.

That determination may depend on the mechanisms that generate harms—a matter to which we will turn presently.

3. DISTRIBUTION OF HARMS

Economic arrangements vary in terms of the distribution of rewards and harms. Economic harm profile analysis would take account of the principal features of harm-distributive patterns.

3a. Distribution of winners and losers in each period and over the course of successive periods

The risks of harm that an economic system generates in one time period will be distributed across society's members in some way or other. The distribution can be fairly egalitarian. Alternatively, the risks can be concentrated among a majority, to the benefit of a risk-insulated minority; or among a minority, to the benefit of an insulated majority. An assessment of the justice of the economic system ought to concern itself inter alia with harm-distributive patterns in each particular time period. The imperative to do so is amplified by the degree to which some harms are irreparable or noncompensable.

Eclipsing the importance of the distribution of the risk of harm in any one period, however, is the distribution of harms over successive periods. An economic system in which being harmed today predisposes individuals to being harmed in the future is morally indictable. Serial correlation of harms implies that those who are worst-off suffer compounding harms. Any proposed defense of the serial correlation of harms needs to clear a very high bar before that feature of the system can be judged to be ethically legitimate. The productivity justification for harm is particularly hard to sustain in this context.

Economic systems characterized by extensive structural violence are prone to serial correlation of harms that defeats the Paretian promise. Wherever economic elites enjoy outsize political influence we should anticipate that policy choices will reflect their interests at the expense of the relatively disenfranchised. Assessing an economy's harm profile, then, requires attention not just to economic but to political institutions and practices as well, informed by normative criteria that focus on the distribution of harms across individuals with disparate levels of capabilities. A plausible case can be made for what might be called "harm prioritarianism": all else equal, a distribution in which harms are absorbed disproportionately by those with greater capabilities is to be preferred morally over one in which harms are concentrated among the capabilities deprived (see Arneson 2013 and the critique in Hansson 2013, 28).

3b. Relative stakes, winning and losing

Economic harm profile analysis must take account of the stakes associated with winning and losing in the competitive contests the economic system comprises. For the past several decades the US economy has gravitated to what can be called a "conquistador economy" in which the victors enjoy the lion's share of the goods that arise as a consequence of economic activity while the losers face irreparable threats to their capabilities. In contrast, one can imagine tempered competitive arenas where the stakes for winning and losing are substantially diminished, where even the losers receive an adequate share of the goods the system generates. Between the two poles lies a broad range of economic arrangements that involve relatively greater or lesser stakes associated with winning and losing. Economic harm profile analysis would direct economists to search for institutional arrangements that yield highly valued goods with lower rather than higher stakes of winning and losing.

4. MECHANISMS OF HARM GENERATION AND DISTRIBUTION

Many kinds of mechanisms generate and distribute harm. Economic harm profile analysis requires investigating these mechanisms to discover which can be eliminated altogether or amended to lessen the severity of the harms they generate.

4a. Direct versus indirect harm

Harm may figure into a pattern of events in diverse ways. One important distinction in the philosophical literature is between "direct" and "indirect" harm. Direct harm occurs when the harming act is the *means* to achieve a valued good (McIntyre 2019). Examples of direct harm in the ethics literature are typically evocative: is it ethically appropriate to push a large man with a heavy backpack from an overpass, killing him, if that is the only way to stop an oncoming trolley that will otherwise kill several people who are stuck on the tracks? More realistically, a monopoly might have to be broken up to promote industry vitality. Indirect harm occurs as the *unintended but often likely adverse consequences* of an action taken to achieve a good (Cushman, Young, and Hauser 2006). An example is the loss of industry viability and employment following trade liberalization. Here, the harm to the industry and its employees is not the means to the end; it is instead an indirect, unintended by-product of the pursuit of the goal of improved economic performance (Spranca, Minsk, and Baron 1991; Howard-Snyder 2008).

Neoclassical economists and utilitarian philosophers tend not to concern themselves with the distinction between direct and indirect harm. Economists are in the minority in this regard. Other professionals, nonutilitarian moral philosophers, and laypeople wrestle with the moral distinction. Recent experimental studies reveal the presence of an "indirect harm bias" among research subjects. Unintended but foreseeable harmful effects of an act are treated as less ethically troublesome than harms that are the means to the end being pursued. The bias is also in evidence in many professions, such as medicine (Cushman, Young, and Hauser 2006).[64] Given the normative salience that the distinction between direct and indirect harm has to laypeople and to practitioners in other professions, economic harm profile analysis ought to be sensitive to the moral relevance of the distinction even if such analysis is not necessarily decisive when assessing harms.

4b. Direct versus structural harm

Structural harm (what Galtung calls "structural violence") is by far more relevant than direct harm for economic policy assessment (see chap. 9). Individuals and communities suffer harm from economic arrangements that threaten their livelihoods and otherwise reduce their capabilities. With Galtung (1969) we have reason to conclude that economic structural violence often operates silently, but it is no less forceful for that. The university legacy admissions system just discussed is but one of innumerable practices that together constitute structural violence against the disadvantaged. While affirmative action programs in the US that respond to overt discrimination against historically disadvantaged groups are politically controversial, affirmative action practices that benefit the most privileged escape ethical scrutiny by economists and others. Economic harm profile analysis would undertake to discover and expose the pernicious effects of arrangements, such as legacy admissions, that induce structural violence.

4c. Fairness of harm-generative arrangements

Economic systems typically encompass a wide range of competitive contests and cooperative arrangements that generate and distribute valued goods and harms. Harm-distributive arrangements of diverse economic systems are apt to vary in regard to fairness. Arrangements that distribute harms fairly are morally preferred to those that distribute harms unfairly. Any ranking of economic systems on these grounds would be subject to dispute owing to distinct, plausible conceptions of fairness and justice. But certain features of harm-distributive mechanisms are apt to draw similar judgments under diverse normative approaches. For instance, the competitive contests that distribute rewards and punishments should not be biased in favor of some contestants over others.[65] The more consequential the contest, the more vital it is that the contest not be rigged and that all contestants have genuine opportunities to prevail and to secure reasonable returns from their participation. A contest that benefits individuals by virtue of their group affiliations or prior privileges not enjoyed by other contestants and that involves large stakes is on these grounds normatively objectionable. The practice of legacy admissions fails this ethical test, too. Moreover, the contest should be fairly played and fairly judged. A contest that rewards violations of the rules or permits the changing of rules midstream by privileged actors to their benefit is to be regarded as unjust. Finally, the distinct contests that bear on the distribution of rewards and harms should be independent, in the sense that an individual's success in one arena ought not give her a leg up in other arenas. Earning more money than others by virtue of having prevailed in the contest over income, or having political influence by virtue of having prevailed in a political contest, should not bear on the distribution of medical care, the grounds for which should be need rather than economic wealth or political power (see Walzer 1983). An economic system in which losing one kind of contest predisposes the victor to lose in others is ethically suspect.

4d. Ability of those causing harm to escape consequences

In all economic systems individuals take and generate risks. But systems differ in terms of who is imperiled by those risks. Under one set of arrangements actors may pursue strategies from which they stand to benefit substantially if all goes well, but also stand to be harmed if things go badly. The actors have what Nassim Taleb (2012; 2018) aptly calls "skin in the game." Under alternative arrangements actors may benefit from the upside of their risky behavior but be insulated from the downside. A prominent example involves investment bankers who profit from risky investing, knowing they can count on public bailouts when their behaviors generate systemic instability. Another example involves legislators who vote in support of sending troops to war when they know their own children will not be among them. An influential actor lacking skin in the game gambles with the livelihoods and the lives of others.

Advocates of diverse political and moral philosophies are apt to converge on the matter of harm shifting. An economic system that permits agents to offload risk onto others while remaining insulated from their imprudence is, in this respect, fundamentally unjust.

4e. Fragility versus antifragility of economic arrangements

Taleb (2012) draws an important distinction between fragile and antifragile systems that bear on the matter of an economic harm profile. Fragile systems are those in which instability in one area ramifies and compounds throughout the system. A large bank failure can touch off a general banking crisis owing to the interconnections in the system that leave each institution dependent on the viability of others. Systems of this sort are prone to unpredictable but inevitable disruptions that cause substantial harm to those who cannot insulate themselves from risk. In contrast, antifragile systems are those that don't just survive but actually thrive in response to disruption. The airline industry has antifragile properties. Each airline disaster provides learning and opportunities for new procedures that yield safer air transport.

Skin in the game relates to the matter of fragility. "Moral hazard" exists when influential individuals who are held harmless in the event of their errors tend toward riskier behaviors in search of greater private returns. In such cases imprudence is rewarded, caution is punished, and learning about how to avoid crisis is short-circuited. A banking system that features institutions deemed "too big to fail" is fragile. As banks grow larger, governments become less willing to let them fail, and the financial system as a whole grows more fragile. The harms that are offloaded onto others rise disproportionately.[66]

Economic harm profile analysis would assess the fragility of the institutions and networks that constitute the economic system. Fragility metrics might assist harm-sensitive economists to discover institutional reform that requires risk-takers to have skin in the game as a matter of basic fairness and as a matter of prudent economic regulation. A fragile economic system is one that exhibits gratuitous harm. It is more dangerous than it needs to be to generate the goods that people value.

5. CONSENT AND COERCION

Economic systems vary according to the extent to which they embody consent as opposed to coercion. The distinction between consent and coercion is normatively relevant for most moral, legal, and political philosophers, as well as economists. There is good reason to distinguish between the risks of harm that agents consent to and the risks that are imposed upon them. The standard argument holds that harm that follows from consensual behavior is ethically benign.[67]

But what is meant by coercion, and by consent? Is the presence of coercion obvious, always? Imagine an individual who is challenged to a duel by someone with a real or imagined grievance. Dueling involves a contest with pistols that is apt to leave one of the combatants dead. Under the "code duello," the challenged party can refuse to participate. In the standard economic perspective, as we'll see momentarily, the right of refusal suffices to make the decision to participate voluntary. But is that account adequate? Feinberg (1994, 221) argues that it is not. He holds that the institution of the duel is coercive since the challenge imposes a choice between the loss of honor and the risk of death.

> A single voluntary act of one person (the challenger) imposes an inescapable dilemma on the other: either kill-or-be-killed or be disgraced. The acceptance of the challenge under such circumstances could hardly be described as a fully voluntary assumption of risk, free of coercive pressures. The social practice of the duel is illegitimate precisely because it forces persons into dreadful risks in circumstances that make genuine consent usually impossible, and at best, always suspect.

Political theorist Ruth Grant (2012, 57) amplifies the point, emphasizing that freedom requires more than having choices; it requires genuine autonomy, defined as "the capacity to set one's own ends or purposes." Grant views many economic choices, such as taking on hazardous work, as compromising rather than extending freedom. Like Galtung, Grant finds that even economic incentives, which many economists take to be the hallmark of voluntarism, can instead reduce autonomy by manipulating individuals into behaviors that violate their values and obstruct their life plans.[68]

Economic harm profile analysis requires a more complex account of coercion, consistent with Feinberg's, Galtung's, and Grant's insights. Many forces can coerce, and some coercive forces are subltle. A commitment to genuine freedom should be attentive to all of them. Moreover, individuals can face coercive constraints at various levels of decision making. At one pole, individuals may face coercion within a particular economic contest. At the other, they may be coerced to participate in certain economic systems. Economies are typically complex, and it may therefore be the case that voluntarism at one level of decision making co-resides with and is normatively canceled by coercion at another. The point requires elaboration.

5a. Coercion within each particular contest

A complex economic system encompasses many distinct competitive arenas, or contests, that yield rewards and punishments. Ascertaining the degree to which the overall system entails coercive harm requires as a first step an investigation of each contest to discern whether *within that contest* participants enjoy extensive voluntarism or whether, instead, they are coerced in their conduct.

Economic liberals who value personal liberty over all other values, such as Hayek and Friedman most famously, argue that a competitive market uniquely features consent rather than coercion. But of the myriad coercive factors that diminish "effective freedom," the liberal view restricts its attention to just one, the threat of "physical coercion of one individual by another" (Friedman 1962, 14; see also Nozick 1974, 33). Provided the state prevents this form of coercion while protecting property rights, market exchange will be a site of voluntarism. In Hayek's ([1944] 2007, 86) view,

> Economic liberalism . . . regards competition as superior not only because it is in most circumstances the most efficient method known but even more because it is the only method by which our activities can be adjusted to each other without coercive or arbitrary intervention of authority.

Because the harms that result from market transactions are grounded in consent, they are treated by liberal economists as ethically benign.

The liberal defense of the market as coercion-free has been rejected consistently by critical economists. Marx ([1887] 1977) ridiculed the idea that workers in a capitalist system enjoy effective freedom. He argued that the mirage of equality in the labor market obscures fundamental asymmetries that coerce labor to serve capital. John R. Commons and other "original" institutionalist economists of the early twentieth century also emphasized that workers typically face coercion owing to constrained opportunities in the labor market (Ramstad 1987). Working in this tradition, legal scholar Robert Hale (1923) argued more broadly that market exchange, far from excising coercion, is a site of reciprocal coercion where transactors exact concessions from those who need what they have to offer (Fried 1998). What liberal economists view as an arena free from coercion, then, critics identify as a complex of coercive pressures. The goal for Marxists is to eliminate coercion altogether, while for institutionalists the goal is to establish laws and regulations that decrease coercive imbalances, with a view toward expanding substantive freedoms.

Constructing an economic harm profile requires attention to the presence and degree of coercion within each of the harm-generating arenas that constitute the economic system. For market economies that requires assessing the degree to which each market, such as the labor market and the markets for housing, medical care, and finance, embodies consent as opposed to coercion. A system that comprises individual arenas that are internally consensual, and/or that balance the coercive force of the participants, is morally superior in this regard to one where the arenas are characterized by coercive mechanisms, or where the coercive force is deeply unbalanced.

5b. Coercion to participate in any particular contest

Economic contests that feature voluntarism, affording the participants extensive latitude within the contest to decide which strategies to pursue, might yet be indictable if the participants are effectively coerced into participating. One way to frame the matter is in terms of "exit" and "voice" (Hirschman [1970] 2013). An arrangement where participants can exit a particular economic contest that threatens their well-being, and/or where they enjoy sufficient voice to alter the most egregious terms of the contest, is to be preferred, morally, over one that denies exit or voice. Genuine exit options and genuine, equal opportunities for participation in setting and amending the rules of the contest are central to harm profile analysis since they bear directly on agents' effective freedoms.

Friedman (1962) takes the existence of many alternative markets and the ability to remove oneself from the market altogether as evidence of the exit option, which is, for him, a guarantor of freedom (cf. Anderson 1990). Provided there is a sufficiently large number of firms confronting a sufficiently large number of consumers, suppliers, and laborers, any transaction that occurs within the market should be deemed voluntary since buyers and sellers have many others with whom to contract. And yet Friedman presumes rather than investigates the presence of exit options. He begins his discussion of the matter in *Capitalism and Freedom* with a description of a simple stylized economy in which "independent households" produce for themselves and exchange output with others. Here, "since the household always has the alternative of producing directly for itself, it need not enter into any exchange unless it benefits from it" (Friedman 1962, 13). A paragraph later he applies the same logic to the modern economy. He claims without evidence that workers who are unwilling to supply labor at the going market rate can withdraw from the labor market and produce independently. He fails to acknowledge that the disappearance of the household enterprise that possesses the means of production undermines the condition that he himself requires for effective freedom. It is hard to avoid the conclusion that he simply assumes that the exit option exists because his defense of the voluntarism of the market requires it. But harm-sensitive economists cannot assume what needs to be shown. The absence of exit options for those lacking resources may explain why so many individuals participate in economic contests, like the labor market, for which they are so poorly suited, and in which they are destined to suffer serious, compounding harms. On this issue Polanyi (1944) and Marx ([1867] 1977) serve as far more dependable guides. Both emphasized dispossession of the means of production as a coercive force driving vulnerable workers into the labor market.

To recognize the harms suffered within a particular contest as consensual we need to know not only that the contest's mechanisms afford all participants substantial "freedom to choose" (Friedman and Friedman 1980) within the contest. We must also ascertain that the participants freely choose to participate in it.

5c. Coercion to participate in any particular class of contests

In assessing consent and coercion we need to investigate whether there are alternative *classes* of economic contests wherein each class is characterized by reward- and harm-generative arrangements that are sufficiently diverse that individuals can avoid contests that comprise hazards they seek to escape. It does someone no good to exit one harm-inducing contest only to find that all the other available options include similar harm-generating mechanisms. In that case, the exit option is formal rather than substantive, and consent to play the contest is illusory.

Ascertaining the presence of genuine consent can be difficult, even in the presence of apparent exit options. Pressures to participate in harmful activities can be subtler than the physical aggression that defines coercion in neoclassical economics, as Feinberg's discussion of the duel illuminates. The analysis must probe the background conditions against which people appear to be making self-defeating choices to ascertain whether coercion lurks there in some form or other. Absent adequate information on such determinants, we might take as a proxy for coercion in an economic system the degree to which existing economic contests generate outcomes that are significantly hazardous, patently unequal, or serially correlated. The failure of those who are serially harmed to withdraw from contests in which they fare poorly provides at least prima facie evidence that the harmed actors participate under coercion.

5d. Coercion to participate in any particular economic system

So far I have treated an economic *system* as synonymous with an *economy*. But in assessing consent and coercion that simplification is misleading. A national or local economy might comprise homogeneous arrangements of economic provisioning, one economic *system*. That kind of economy is characterized by an economic monoculture that covers the entire landscape. Social scientists are trained to think that this is the norm; that a capitalist economy, say, is one in which capitalist production and exchange crowd out all other forms of economic provisioning. But recent research, especially by economic geographers, suggests that this view is incorrect. In fact, many economies feature the coexistence of a range of heterogeneous economic arrangements; the economic equivalent of biodiversity (Gibson-Graham 1996; 2006). Distinct economic arrangements arise and sometimes thrive side by side in complex, evolving, kaleidoscopic constellations. In some economies the proliferation of alternative economic systems is well developed and the diverse economic forms are easily legible. Some economies feature extensive opportunities for self-employment, for instance, in both the informal and formal sectors. In others, worker co-ops proliferate. A case in point is Spain's Mondragon Corporation, located in the Basque region, which houses the world's largest and most complex worker co-op network side by side with capitalist enterprises. Worker co-ops are now forming in advanced and emerging economies, from the US to Korea, Argentina, and beyond (Ji 2018). In some economies alternative economic systems are less developed and more difficult to locate. The research suggests that where *systemic monopolies* exist—where just one kind of economic system predominates and precludes the proliferation of alternatives—the predominant system is sustained by legal sanctions, privileges, and theoretical and policy biases that support one set of economic institutions and practices and obstruct viable alternatives.[69]

The extent of systemic diversity bears directly on the matter of coercion. Where one economic system crowds out alternative arrangements of economic provisioning, the exit option is diminished and the degree of coercion increases.[70] Where, instead, alternative systems flourish across the economic landscape, individuals have greater effective freedom to opt out of economic arrangements they find to be excessively hazardous.[71] Economic harm profile analysis would map the range of economic systems that constitute the economy and their accessibility, especially to those least advantaged. And harm-sensitive economists who aspire to reduce coercive and gratuitous harms would advocate for policy that creates the conditions for the proliferation of a diverse economic ecosystem that sustains alternative economic arrangements—not for the sake of efficiency but for the sake of expanding individuals' genuine freedom to choose the nature of the risks of harm that they are willing to accept (DeMartino 2013b).

Harm Regime Types

Simon Pemberton has compared what I am calling "economic harm profiles" across capitalist countries. Pemberton finds substantial variance in economic harms even among countries at the same level of per capita income. Pemberton proposes and tests a "harm regime hypothesis," which holds that countries grouped by economic regime types differ significantly in their harm profiles. Neoliberal regimes characterized by market fundamentalism lie at one pole of his regime continuum. Neoliberal regimes exist in various forms in states such as the US, Britain, Mexico, Chile, and Russia. They are characterized by extensive commodification of goods and services that are vital to well-being, as well as a strong bias against government intervention to protect individuals from hardship, on grounds that public protections would undermine market incentives. During the worst moments of the COVID-19 pandemic, for instance, many political leaders in the US opposed the extension of unemployment compensation for those who had lost their jobs, on grounds that "excessive" benefits were discouraging a return to work. At the opposite pole lie the social democratic regimes like those of Sweden, Finland, Denmark, and Norway that are marked by substantial degrees of decommodification, where individuals' well-being is far more dependent on social welfare protections and less dependent on the individuals' market success. Pemberton identifies other regimes lying at various distances from these two poles, such as the corporatist model that prevails in Germany, France, and other European countries.

Pemberton constructs three broad categories of harm: physical and mental health, autonomy, and relational harms. Pemberton finds that the neoliberal regime features a particularly dangerous harm profile. Commodification of valued goods and opportunities means that doing poorly in the market—say, being unemployed—places individuals in peril of cascading harms. Citizens fare much worse under this regime in terms of a wide range of harms than under social democratic regimes in which capitalism's damaging effects are tempered by government interventions that include extensive social safety nets and other supports for autonomy and social inclusion for those facing economic dislocation.

Pemberton's chief findings sustain the insight that *many economic harms originate in social arrangements*. Social harms result in part from long chains of institutional and policy decisions. As a consequence, they can be eliminated or at least ameliorated through institutional and policy reform. To the degree that they are eliminable, their persistence is morally suspect.

Pemberton is pointing the way forward for economists who recognize the moral urgency of economic and econogenic harm. In confrontation with dangerous economic harm profiles, economists have an opportunity to promote social betterment through designing and advocating reforms of economic arrangements that stand a chance of eliminating gratuitous harms and, whenever possible, the tragic choices that impose serious harms in pursuit of valued goods.

Conclusion

Economic harm profile analysis is intended to complement and not displace other normative criteria for assessing economic arrangements. Harm profile analysis emphasizes that the harms economies generate are as normatively significant to social assessment as the goods they promote.

In place of moral geometry, economists have an opportunity to probe the myriad factors that define and generate economic harm profiles. Sacrificing some tractability is the price to be paid for richer, more nuanced accounts of harm that begin to do justice to the complex harms individuals suffer—not with the unachievable goal of eliminating all risks of harm but with the achievable goal of promoting social betterment through means that entail more benign economic harm profiles.

11

Decision Making under Deep Uncertainty

> If we are up against mystery, then we dare act only on the most modest assumptions. The modern scientific program has held that we must act on the basis of knowledge, which, because its effects are so manifestly large, we have assumed to be ample. But if we are up against mystery, then knowledge is relatively small, and the ancient program is the right one: Act on the basis of ignorance.
>
> —WENDELL BERRY, in 1982 letter to Wes Jackson (2005, 14)

The Colorado River: Lifeline of the West

In the expansive Rocky Mountain and Southwest regions of the United States, water, not petroleum or minerals, now represents the critical resource on which the region's future depends. The region is extremely arid. It nonetheless comprises extensive agricultural land and is experiencing dramatic population growth. Today it faces uncertainty about factors that bear on the adequacy of its water resources. Key drivers of the region's water supply include rising temperatures, diminished snow and rainfall, the rate and timing of snow melt, and rates of evaporation and aquifer recharging. On the demand side it faces rapid in-migration, economic development, and industrial transition. There is ample evidence today that historical water supply and demand patterns provide inadequate guidance regarding future trends.

The Colorado River is the largest water source in the region. It provides water for approximately forty million people and irrigates 4.5 million acres (18,210 square km) of agricultural land across seven "basin" US states, twenty-two Native American tribes, and a portion of northwest Mexico. It also supplies water to seven national wildlife refuges, four national recreation areas, and eleven national parks (Bureau of Reclamation 2015; 2012a). Every drop of Colorado River water is claimed under existing treaties and agreements that hypermanage water flows to ensure that the river's myriad claimants receive their allocated shares. Twelve major dams and hundreds of smaller dams on the main river and tributaries create reservoirs along the way. Some of the compounds are massive. These include Lake Mead and Lake Powell.

Over the past century, water flows have been allocated according to the 1922 Colorado River Compact, which apportions fifteen million acre-feet. A 1944 treaty allocates an additional 1.5 million acre-feet to Mexico. The US

Bureau of Reclamation works with the basin states, Native American tribes, and Mexico to manage the relevant agreements and resolve disputes.

It is now apparent that the 1922 compact was negotiated in the context of two decades of significantly above-average rainfall and river flows, leading to overallocation. Today there is wide recognition that in the absence of appropriate reform, climate change and increasing demand will induce severe water shortages. The risk is imminent. A drought from 2000 to 2007 reduced water storage in the major basin reservoirs from nearly full (equivalent to four years of usage) to 55% of capacity (two years of usage; Groves et al. 2013). Dry conditions continue throughout the region. By late October of 2021 Lake Mead water levels had fallen to 34% of capacity and Lake Powell water levels to 30%. In just the past year, from October 2020 to October 2021, the total water storage in the system of reservoirs has fallen from 48% of capacity to 38% (Bureau of Reclamation 2021). The flow of water entering the reservoirs in 2021 is so low that the reservoirs may soon reach "dead pool" status, "where stored water is so low it can't spin the massive hydroelectric power generators buried in the dams." Those water levels would result in "large swaths of Arizona farmland going fallow" (Booth 2021). The near-term threat to many water users is, in a word, existential.

In 2010 the basin states and Reclamation initiated research to evaluate the ability of the Colorado River to meet water demands through 2060 and to identify strategies that could improve performance. Had Reclamation hired economists to pursue the standard methods, the procedure would have involved moral geometry. Economists would have likely treated future climate change, population growth, economic transition, and other key factors as probabilistically knowable. They would have used those projections to perform cost-benefit analysis (CBA), deriving the policy strategy that promised to maximize expected utility (E(U); see chaps. 7–8). The CBA would have laid out the optimal bureau strategy, which might have included, say, adding a certain amount of capacity to basin reservoirs and other initiatives that together promised to maximize net benefits.

All of which would have worked wonderfully . . . *provided the future unfolded just as the economists predicted.* And provided the various competing stakeholders shared the economists' values and objectives, and provided they accepted economists' predictions and the legitimacy of the distribution of benefits and harms induced by the recommended strategies. Absent any of these conditions, the economists' CBA would have failed to prepare water users for an unpredictable future. It most certainly would have generated intense controversy among stakeholders with competing visions and interests and, especially these days, created political paralysis.

Is there no better way?

Reclamation did not go this route. Instead, it worked with RAND Corporation analysts on a pilot study of alternative decision-making procedures. RAND pursued a relatively new method for addressing the uncertainties facing decision makers: "decision making under deep uncertainty" (DMDU). The analysis sought to explore the potential of "robust decision making." Robust strategies are those that are apt to do well under a very wide range of unpredictable circumstances. *What the researchers did not do was try to predict the future.* But how can effective strategies be discovered without knowing what the future will bring? Without prediction, what basis is there for rational decision making?

*

Irreparable ignorance is an inevitable cause of econogenic harm (see chaps. 5–6). If ignorance of a particular domain is irreparable, if the knowledge is simply inaccessible in the moment when the missing knowledge is needed to make a critical decision, then investing resources and energy trying to acquire the knowledge is misguided. And in this situation, basing policy decisions on E(U) calculations is dangerous. Economists who accept payment to generate ersatz knowledge and do E(U) assessments in the face of irreparable ignorance are guilty of professional malpractice.

In recent years a small but growing number of policy analysts have taken up the challenge of exploring what responsible policy design and assessment entail in contexts of irreparable ignorance. Experts in fields like climate change, international security, management of water systems and other infrastructure systems, and urban planning have embraced a new approach, DMDU. Though a handful of economists have been among the leading architects of DMDU, most economists continue to approach policy assessment with moral geometry. We explore DMDU here, focusing on its philosophical underpinnings and some of its methods of policy design.

Predict-Then-Act: The Economist Is in Charge

The standard economic approach, which relies on E(U) calculations to guide policy choice, is a "predict-then-act" model, where the value of the policy assessment exercise depends on the dependability of the forecasts of policy effects. A few features of the model not already examined in previous chapters deserve attention. One is that the model is *static*. The economist, operating at a particular moment in time, projects policy impacts well into the future when calculating the E(U) for each policy option. The knowledge and expertise to do the job are presumed to be available at the time of the economist's intervention. The approach is one-off. For example, an economic consultant might be hired by a municipal government to perform calculations and make a recommendation on a policy matter, such as an infrastructure project with long-run effects. The expert "provides completed results to decisionmakers" (Groves et al. 2016, 2), at which point the expert-client relationship is typically severed. If the client subsequently decides that it again needs this kind of expertise, it puts the new work out to bid and again hires an expert (perhaps the same one, but just as likely not) who performs another round of analysis de novo.

Economic moral geometry places the analysis of policy options strictly in the hands of economists. The economist's relationship with the client is notably arms length. Ensuring objectivity requires economists to maintain independence from the client since a closer relationship with clients could threaten to bias economists' work (see DeMartino 2011).

The arms-length relationship between economists and stakeholders implies that *economists'* normative framework typically guides the policy assessment. The criterion will almost certainly be welfarist, typically proxied by monetary measures. Economists rely on welfarist decision rules even when the community that will bear the policy's effects hold to other normative criteria, like equality. The approach is paternalistic. Economists are to be recognized as *knowing best*—not just about how to assess policy effects but also about what criterion of social betterment to apply.

The standard approach typically precludes meaningful post hoc analysis and assessment to see whether the predictions were realized and the policy induced the promised outcomes. Neither economists nor clients have incentive to expend resources for assessment studies that might reveal that they made bad decisions. Unfortunately, the absence of assessment blocks learning, leading to repetition of even grave mistakes. The assessment of economists' work is also complicated by cognitive errors like hindsight bias and by the fact that the effects of economic interventions are typically indirect, diffuse, and deferred. As a consequence, economists are typically insulated from even extreme policy failure (Ravallion 2009; Angner 2006).

Economic analysis is just as apt to generate conflict as consensus. This was the case in the controversy over the TPP (see chap. 6). The standard approach requires that stakeholders "agree on assumptions" that ground the model's assessments, including the causal relationships and background conditions about the world that are inputs to the model (Lempert 2019). But stakeholders with diverse understandings of how the world works and interests and values that they hope to protect are unlikely to reach agreement on these facets of the model. Those who might be harmed by a proposed policy can be expected to reject it. Even if an economist's recommendations are implemented, they are apt to lack legitimacy in the eyes of many stakeholders who will bear their harmful effects.

The "agree on assumptions" approach asks too much of those affected by economic policy. The proliferation of plausible assumptions provides grounds for amplifying rather than managing reasonably the differences in understandings and values that diverse stakeholders bring to policy matters. Like arms dealers who provide weapons to both sides of a conflict, the economics profession supplies science-based ammunition to all policy combatants. Moral geometry amplifies ideological divisions concerning pressing policy issues and undermines the usefulness of economic expertise rather than promoting productive dialogue among stakeholders with conflicting values.

When Prediction Is Perilous: Deep Uncertainty and Policy Making

Is this unflattering picture of economic policy analysis unfair? It would be if there were no viable alternatives. But alternatives are emerging that correct for the most egregious ethical and epistemic failures of the standard approach. One is DMDU.[72]

DMDU practice foregrounds irreparable ignorance. Practitioners refuse to treat the world as ergodic, where the future is just as probabilistically knowable as a throw of dice. DMDU analysts recognize they do not have time-travel machines to see the future before it arrives. DMDU procedures are offered in cases where "prediction is perilous," where the effort to know the future can lead to overconfidence and blind spots that can generate disastrous decisions (Lempert 2019, 25). Where there is irreparable ignorance, efforts to predict generate *negative returns* by inducing a false sense of confidence. The challenge is to discover good decisions without prediction.

In a rapidly evolving, complex, and deeply interconnected world, decision makers often face "wicked problems," like climate change (Rittel and Webber 1973; Crowley and Head 2017). A wicked problem "is not well bounded, is framed differently by various groups and individuals, involves large scientific to existential uncertainties, and tends not to be well understood until after the formulation of a solution" (Lempert 2014, 488). Wicked problems entail nonlinear dynamics and unpredictable breaks (tipping points) in trends that are not identifiable in advance. Wicked problems render useless standard predict-then-act decision-making strategies. In confrontation with wicked problems the effects of any model errors in assumptions or causal pathways can compound, yielding "an explosion of uncertainty" (Dessai et al. 2009, 111).[73]

DMDU practitioners seek to "help people manage wicked problems by facilitating participatory processes and interactions among analysts and decision makers" (Lempert 2014, 491). Instead of the misguided effort to know the unknowable in pursuit of the optimal decision, DMDU procedures "transform the age-old question 'what will the future bring?' into the more answerable one—'what can we do today to better shape the future to our liking?'" (Lempert et al. 2009, 120).

SOURCES OF DEEP UNCERTAINTY

DMDU analysts emphasize several sources of deep uncertainty. First, experts and other stakeholders may not know or may not agree upon the broader *external context* within which systems operate. External context refers to the forces outside the system that bear on the system's inputs. In the case of regional water management systems where the problem to be addressed is ensuring adequate water supplies well into the future, external forces determine the rate of climate change (temperature and rainfall patterns) that will be inputs into the water system model. Even a perfectly theorized water management system model will generate undependable predictions if it incorporates incorrect forecasts of input variable values.

Second, experts and stakeholders may not know the *causal features* of the system at issue. Causal models are always imperfect. There is typically deep uncertainty about the mathematical equations that make up the model and about how those equations will need to change over time to reflect changes in the system being modeled.

Third, there may be uncertainty concerning stakeholder *outcomes of interest*. Outcomes of interest concern the objectives that stakeholders value most. Only rarely do all stakeholders rank outcomes identically. Moreover, stakeholders' objectives are apt to change unpredictably as the world evolves. Fourth, there is uncertainty about *how people will adjust their behaviors* in response to unpredictable future events. If we cannot know in advance how behaviors will change, then we cannot know how those adjusted behaviors will affect policy outcomes (see chap. 5; Haasnoot et al. 2013; Marchau et al. 2019, 2). It is important to keep in mind in this context Douglas North's (1999) warning that well-developed economic theory is static, while the world we seek to understand is invariably dynamic.[74]

Wicked problems that arise in the policy world, such as those involving interactions among natural, economic, political, and other social systems, are apt to feature all four sources of uncertainty. This is certainly true of the Colorado River basin water management challenge. Sufficient supply of water throughout the southwestern US and northern Mexico depends on how changes in climate, hydrologic systems, regional economies, technologies, political processes and decisions, and the values and actions of tens of millions of water users affect the balance between supply and demand. There are deep uncertainties within each of the systems, and those uncertainties are significantly amplified by the complex and changing interactions among them.

DMDU practitioners emphasize that "we cannot know what is not yet discovered, such as tomorrow's news or fads and fashions, or future scientific theories or technological inventions" (Ben-Haim 2010, 4). Decision makers cannot know "what needs to be known in order to attain a favorable policy outcome" (Ben-Haim 2010, 4). In the face of irreparable ignorance, DMDU holds that implementing what appears to be the optimal outcome is far too dangerous. *Optimal outcomes are fragile.* They are realized only under the tightly specified assumptions of the models that predict them.

In place of optimizing outcomes, DMDU seeks to *satisfice on outcomes* while *optimizing on robustness.* Robust decision making (RDM) searches for policy that performs *well enough* by stakeholders' lights under the widest range of possible futures. Neither the experts nor the stakeholders are pressed into impossible activities, such as divining the future or deriving the optimal policy. Instead, they are invited to apply their expertise to the challenge of identifying strategies that will perform adequately under diverse possible futures.

REGRET MINIMIZATION

If maximizing E(U) over policy outcomes might be appropriate for an ergodic world characterized by probabilistic risk and widely shared values and goals, what kinds of decision criteria are appropriate for a world marked by deep uncertainty? When adverse and even disastrous outcomes are possible, as they sometimes are in cases featuring irreparable ignorance, alternative criteria come to the fore. DMDU policy exercises seek to *minimize stakeholder regret,* where the regret associated with a policy strategy under a possible future scenario "is defined as the difference in performance of that option compared to the best option, for that scenario" (Espinet et al. 2018, 18). DMDU practices search for policies that appear to generate good outcomes under most possible futures, such as fixing leaking pipes in water management schemes (Hallegatte et al. 2012), and that seem to promise tolerable regret if the world that emerges is characterized by particularly adverse circumstances. But regret minimization is treated in DMDU practice as a *disposition, not an ironclad decision rule.* DMDU does not seek to replace the standard economic moral geometry of maximizing E(U) with another rule, minimax, that considers only the worst possible outcomes (Lempert and McKay 2011). Treated as an inviolable decision rule, regret minimization would overweight, always, worst possible scenarios even when the relevant experts and stakeholders had good reason to believe that the worst-case scenario is not credible (Espinet et al. 2018, 23; Hallegatte et al. 2012, 12–13; Lempert and McKay 2011, 244). It would prevent stakeholders who would bear a policy's effects from sacrificing some degree of robustness to pursue windfall opportunities (Ben-Haim 2019).

DMDU Procedures

There are several distinct DMDU methods, tailored to the different kinds of policy dilemmas that arise. Here I draw on several of the simplest strategies to illuminate DMDU decision support.

DECISION FRAMING

When DMDU is to be applied to a problem, the approach begins with "decision framing" that involves stakeholder consultation (see figure 11.1). The goal is to draw on stakeholder values to discover what outcomes would be satisfactory. DMDU refuses to force arbitrary consensus among stakeholders. In cases involving water management, for instance, river-dependent tourist businesses might emphasize consistent river flows; farmers might prioritize adequate irrigation during dry months; water system managers might prioritize avoiding inadequate water supplies that require drastic usage reductions; and conservationists might prioritize restoring natural stream flows year-round. Under DMDU there is no presumption that diverse values and goals can be reduced to one desideratum, like welfare. What policy outcomes would be deemed adequate for *each* principal stakeholder? In place of a single evaluative criterion, the approach requires "multi-objective" optimization informed by the diversity of stakeholder values (Lempert 2019).

The RDM approach works "backward." Stakeholder consultation at the initial step elicits one or more candidate policy options. Stakeholders then provide systemic knowledge about the relevant causal models that capture what are believed to be the most salient causal relationships between the relevant variables and estimates of model parameters. This step generates "quasi-causal models" (Hallegatte et al. 2012; Lempert, Scheffran, and Sprinz 2009). In a regional water system, for instance, engineers, climate scientists,

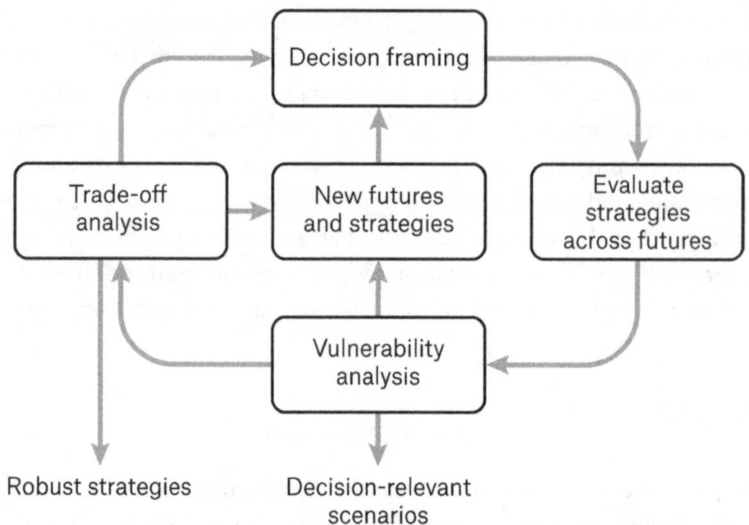

FIGURE 11.1. Iterative, participatory steps of DMDU robust decision making
Robust decision making entails an iterative approach in which strategies are sequentially stress-tested against many possible futures to ascertain their vulnerabilities; trade-offs across strategies are considered; a strategy is implemented; monitoring systems are introduced; and postadoption strategy adaptation occurs as new knowledge becomes available over time. Stakeholder input is vital to the exercise. Figure taken from Groves et al. (2021, open access).

biologists, demographers, urban planners, and economic development specialists have local knowledge about the relationships between rainfall and other weather patterns in the relevant watershed; riverine characteristics; reservoir design, capacity, and evaporation rates; population fluctuations; water usage patterns and policies; and local economic transformation (say, from agriculture to tourism), to name just some of the factors that bear on the adequacy of the region's water supply.

EVALUATE STRATEGIES: EXPLORATORY MODELING

In possession of fallible system knowledge and the goals provided by stakeholders, the second step of the exercise involves evaluating strategies through "exploratory modeling" (EM). EM is a computer-assisted stress-testing exercise. Strategies are tested against thousands of possible futures. EM involves running model simulations of the candidate policy alternative(s), each time adjusting the exogenous inputs into the model and the model's functional relationships between the causal variables, to see how these alterations affect the performance of each policy option. Each "run with a given model structure and a given parameterization of that structure . . . reveals how the real world would behave if the various hypotheses presented by the structure and the parameterization were correct" (Marchau et al. 2019, 15). How will each policy perform, say, if over the coming decade there is a 0.1°C increase in ground-level temperature, a 1% decrease in average rainfall, and a 3% increase in the region's population growth over baseline? What if, instead, the temperature increase is 0.3°C, the rainfall decrease is 4%, and population growth is 5%? EM permits the evaluation of policy effectiveness under a much wider range of potential futures than the unassisted human mind can possibly manage.

EXPLORATORY MODELING: CREATIVE COUNTERFACTUALIZING

EM is DMDU's technique for embracing the creative potential of counterfactualizing. It takes the form of "computer-guided exploration" of unknowable futures that is not intended to discover causality. DMDU employs counterfactualizing to help stakeholders "discover adaptive near-term strategies that are robust over large ensembles of plausible futures" (Lempert, Popper, and Bankes 2003, xiv). DMDU counterfactualizing serves as "a prosthesis for the imagination" when neither experts nor stakeholders are able to divine which of the innumerable possible futures is apt to emerge. "Narratives about the future, whether fictional or historical, are unmatched in their ability to help humans viscerally imagine a future different from the present" (Lempert, Popper, and Bankes 2003, xiii). DMDU scholars embrace the virtues of science fiction in "propelling people away from their familiar worlds" (Lempert, Scheffran, and Sprinz 2009, 107). The EM exercise permits investigation of the "load-bearing" assumptions, "the explicit and implicit assumptions made while developing that plan that, if wrong, would cause the plan to fail" (Lempert 2019, 28). EM therefore prepares stakeholders for unwelcome surprises while also allowing them to take advantage of unanticipated opportunities for gain (Ben-Haim 2019).

VULNERABILITY ANALYSIS: SCENARIO DISCOVERY

But what are the stakeholders to make of the tens of thousands of computer runs that generate these results? DMDU is a decision-support procedure that emphasizes the need to provide technical knowledge in ways that are most useful for stakeholders to support good decision making. The third step of the procedure, vulnerability analysis, involves "scenario discovery." It involves the application of computational algorithms to distinguish those clusters of variable values that appear to imperil a policy under consideration from those clusters that do not. Often, scenario discovery ascertains that just a few key variables affect most forcefully the fate of a policy, and that danger arises only when those variables reach critical levels (Parker et al. 2015). Data visualization provides stakeholders with relatively simple diagrams like heat maps that indicate the safe and perilous ranges of the key variables for each policy option, facilitating the ranking of options by their robustness.

TRADE-OFF ANALYSIS

The fourth step explores the relevant trade-offs between levels of robustness and performance. It is generally possible to attain higher performance in a system only by sacrificing some degree of robustness. An example is the economic efficiency achieved through international trade in which countries specialize in what they do relatively best. When all goes well, global supply chains produce goods efficiently, at very low cost. But as COVID has demonstrated, the international trading system is deeply vulnerable to shocks that break links in the chains. In the face of deep uncertainty, the highest possible level of achievable performance is not robust at all (Ben-Haim 2019). Decisions over trade-offs are to be made by those with skin in the game—the stakeholders and policy makers—not by the DMDU practitioner. The DMDU exercise is intended to inform reasoned deliberation and good judgments of this sort, not to substitute for them. As Yakov Ben-Haim (2010, 3) puts it, "models can help if we insist on retaining the pre-eminence of human judgment over the churning of our computers." A policy that is marginally less robust may promise a substantially higher level of performance than another when judged by various stakeholder-supplied metrics. In such a case stakeholders might conclude that it is appropriate to trade off some robustness for "opportuneness" (Ben-Haim 2010; see also Hallegatte et al. 2012).

NEW OPTIONS

In traditional economic practice a one-time policy assessment and recommendation typically terminate the exercise. But in DMDU, steps 1–4 represent just the beginning of the story. It is likely that the initial candidate policies will be found to be excessively fragile against alternative futures. That finding informs stakeholder deliberation over new options that are intended to counter the chief vulnerabilities identified by EM in the first iteration. The new options are then subjected to the same robustness analysis. The exercise also prompts stakeholders to envision *shaping* actions that alter the landscape in ways that make policy more robust, *hedging* strategies that are pursued in the event of policy failure, and *signposts* that will warn them when policy adjustments must be made (Lempert 2019, 28). Analysis with consultation continues, iteratively, until stakeholders are satisfied that a candidate policy promises adequate performance and is sufficiently robust.

MONITORING AND ADAPTING

Reaching a decision to implement a particular policy marks the end of just the first stage of DMDU deliberation. Imagine that a policy that satisfies stakeholders on grounds of performance and robustness is implemented. DMDU recognizes that the policy will be threatened if any important load-bearing assumptions are broken. Having identified those combinations of the salient variables that are apt to induce policy failure, the DMDU exercise requires careful *monitoring* of future events after policy implementation to ascertain which one of the innumerable possible worlds is actually coming into existence. That new knowledge informs adaptation. Dynamic adaptive planning (DAP) is wired into DMDU strategies. "DAP specifies the development of a monitoring program and responses when specific trigger values are reached. Hence, DAP makes adaptation over time explicit at the outset of plan formulation" (Marchau et al. 2019, 16; see also Walker, Rahman, and Cave 2001).

Most DMDU methods rely on DAP in one way or another. One method involves the construction of dynamic adaptive policy pathways (DAPP). The DAPP approach seeks to identify policy steps to be taken immediately, while at the same time generating a decision tree through time so that stakeholders and policy makers can anticipate and plan for policy adjustment in step with the state of the world that emerges (Haasnoot, Warren, and Kwakkel 2019). When *tripwires* are triggered, DAPP indicates which particular policy response is warranted.[75] In a water management context, a DAPP approach might indicate that the water management authority should adopt a set of water use restrictions immediately but augment them with recycling if rainfall, temperature, and population growth approach a critical threshold; and that it should impose more severe usage restrictions while investing in new water storage or desalination systems if the variables reach another critical threshold.

FLEXIBILITY, REVERSIBILITY

DMDU provides a flexible approach to decision support. It can range from computationally intensive simulations to simple heuristic frameworks (Lempert and Kalra 2011).[76] The appropriate level of complexity depends on the nature of the problem to be confronted, the resources available to the project, time constraints, the depth of stakeholder knowledge of the policy problem, and the receptivity of stakeholders to intensive quantitative analysis. The most important attribute of DMDU is the *orientation* it brings to policy analysis and planning. In place of an expectation among stakeholders that they need and that experts can supply accurate predictions before they can act responsibly, the DMDU approach urges stakeholders to foreground uncertainty and then to examine potential strategies against a broad range of unpredictable future states of the world. DMDU urges stakeholders to consider which possible futures could imperil their preferred strategies, what alternative strategies not yet considered might be more robust, and what steps can be taken now and in the future to adjust policy as new knowledge becomes available. Technical, computationally rich DMDU approaches systematize those steps, but that is not always necessary to bring about the salutary effects of designing policy with the goal of achieving robustness.

Emphasis on adaptability and dynamic planning privileges strategies that *are reversible and flexible, provide wide safety margins, and reduce decision-making time horizons* (Hallegatte et al. 2012, 16ff; Lempert and McKay 2011, 242). In a knowable world with shared stakeholder values these qualities would be superfluous. But in an uncertain world emphasis should be given to keeping options open, avoiding irreversible and inflexible commitments that lock in policy makers to strategies that work well only under a limited range of future states of the world. Inflexible policies are perilous. So are strategies characterized by narrow margins for error and long time horizons. The DMDU approach embraces the philosophy of the great environmentalist and essayist Wendell Berry (2005), who urges us in the epigraph to this chapter to "act on the basis of ignorance." Doing so entails, inter alia, preserving "exits" if policy decisions prove to be damaging.

What does reversibility look like in practice? Hallegatte et al. (2012) give the intuitive example of economic development in a region vulnerable to flooding owing to climate change, where planners have the option of authorizing the construction of infrastructure, dwellings, and businesses. The decision *not* to develop the area today entails immediate economic costs, the forgone benefits from increased economic activity, which could be substantial. But the decision not to develop is easily reversible if over time new knowledge indicates that the risk to the region is less severe than anticipated, or if other policy interventions somehow reduce the flood risk. In contrast, a decision to develop the area today might generate immediate economic benefits but be irreversible and extremely costly in the event of adverse climate change. In cases like this, regret-minimizing strategy might involve postponing a project until a better-informed assessment is possible.

Expert-Stakeholder Partnerships

DMDU transforms the relationship between experts and stakeholders. The success of DMDU policy exercises requires respect for the agency and autonomy of stakeholders and the cultivation of their competency in confronting wicked problems. Stakeholder agency manifests in the "coproduction of knowledge among information users and producers" (Marchau et al. 2019, 10). The approach depends on sustained "interaction between decisionmakers and the scientific analysis process: researchers do not simply pass data on to decsionmakers but instead support a deliberation-with-analysis engagement method" (Groves et al. 2016, 4). Under deliberation with analysis, the "parties to a decision deliberate on their objectives and options; analysts generate decision-relevant information using system models; and the parties to the decision revisit their objectives, options, and problem framing influenced by this quantitative information" (Lempert 2019, 30).

DMDU seeks to promote the evolution of stakeholder objectives "as they collaborate with others" (Lempert 2019, 30). The approach is consistent with Amartya Sen's framework of consultation that privileges "relational" as opposed to "transcendent" moral reasoning (Lempert 2019, 44ff). Transcendent reasoning imposes a central organizing principle to guide policy making, such as John Rawls's notion of equality of primary goods or the economist's notion of maximizing welfare. Sen argues that a world of uncertainty and "diversity of priorities, goals, and values" calls instead for deliberative procedures that provide space for negotiation, trial and error, and learning by doing. Lempert (2019, 45) writes,

> [Such] deliberations work best when they recognize the inescapable plurality of competing views; facilitate reexamination and iterative assessments; demand clear explication of reasoning and logic; and recognize an "open impartiality" that accepts the legitimacy and importance of the views of others, both inside and outside the community of interest to the immediate policy discussion.

Compared with the standard economic approach to policy assessment and design, DMDU places extraordinary emphasis on stakeholder participation and joint deliberation between stakeholders and DMDU practitioners. An imperfect but useful index of the expert-client inversion is the frequency of usage of key terms in the leading DMDU textbook (Marchau et al. 2019). In the text, some form of the term "stakeholder" appears 126 times; "consensus," 66 times; "community," 64 times; "learning," 63 times; "participation"/"participant," 58 times; "deliberate," 31 times; "collaborate," 24 times; and "democratic," 17 times. DMDU nevertheless establishes a prominent role for experts. Some form of the term "expert" appears 107 times. If anything, the role of the expert is expanded under DMDU strategies relative to the role of the expert in standard economic consulting. But the expanded role is associated with an explicit acknowledgment of severe limitations to expert epistemic abilities and authority.

The Colorado River Basin

In 2007, at a time of extended drought, the US Bureau of Reclamation (Reclamation) adopted the *Colorado River Interim Guidelines for Lower Basin Shortages and the Coordinated Operations for Lake Powell and Lake Mead.* The guidelines are to terminate in 2026, by which time a new plan for managing the river basin resources must be adopted. In 2010 Reclamation began work on the Colorado River Basin Water Supply and Demand Study (Basin Study), published in 2012 (Bureau of Reclamation 2012a). The report assessed the vulnerabilities of the water supplied by the Colorado River and considered preliminary strategies to respond to imbalances between water supply and demand.

The Basin Study was undertaken by Reclamation and RAND researchers in collaboration with the seven basin states and affected stakeholders who included "tribes, agricultural users, purveyors of municipal and industrial (M&I) water, power users, and conservation and recreation groups" (Bureau of Reclamation 2012b, 5). The partnership with RAND was intended to explore how RDM might inform long-term planning for the Colorado River (Marchau et al. 2019, 141). RAND's pilot study (presented to Reclamation in 2012, published as Groves et al. 2013) advocates substituting robustness and adaptiveness for optimality. It foregrounds deep uncertainty instead of the typical predict-then-act model of policy formation. Consistent with the recommendation, Reclamation decided to pursue a scenario-based planning alternative that did not attempt to predict which of the myriad possible futures would materialize (Bureau of Reclamation 2012a). Researchers constructed four supply and six demand scenarios in addition to a status quo baseline scenario. The scenarios permitted preliminary investigation of the ability of the Colorado River to meet stakeholder needs under a very wide range of conditions. The exercise suggested the design of strategies that decision makers should undertake in the short run and later on to prevent unacceptable performance.

Reclamation emphasized the methodological break that scenario-based planning represented. Speaking of the demand side of the problem, it noted that "historically, Reclamation has considered a single projection of future demands in long-term Basin planning studies. . . ." Reclamation recognized that the consideration of additional projections of demand, derived from a "scenario planning process," represented "a significant and important advancement in long-term water planning in the Basin" (Bureau of Reclamation 2012b, ES-3).

The Basin Study was exploratory. It was not intended to inform immediate policy decisions. Despite its preliminary status, the Basin Study was in fact quite sophisticated. Among its four supply scenarios is the "downscaled general circulation model (GCM)" projected scenario. Downscaled GCM modeling seeks to apply large-scale trends, like climate change effects at the national level, to the local level. The downscaled scenario projects the impacts of climate change on water supply in the Colorado River basin. It takes account of continued regional warming, reduced precipitation, increased evapotranspiration, decreased snowpack, and earlier seasonal melt of the snowpack. The GCM scenario uses an ensemble of 112 distinct future downscaled GCM projections. The goal in devising supply and demand scenarios was "to be sufficiently broad to capture the plausible range of uncertainty" (Bureau of Reclamation 2012b, 6). To this end, for instance, population growth predictions ranged from 9.3 million to 36.5 million people.

To construct a set of potential policy responses to future water imbalances, Reclamation solicited adaptive strategies from decision makers, stakeholders, and other interested parties through an open call. The call yielded 150 proposals to increase supply, diminish demand, modify system operations, and improve governance and implementation. Thirty of these were identified as representative and were assembled into four strategy "portfolios." Portfolio B included technically feasible options with long-term reliability, while portfolio C included ecologically sensitive strategies such as those that entailed low-energy intensity. Portfolio A included all the strategies in B or C, while portfolio D included just those that appeared in both B and C.

Elicitation from stakeholders generated a broad range of objectives that served as the basis for establishing metrics to evaluate policy options. For each objective, a level of "vulnerability" was identified. As it turned out, two overall indications of system vulnerability emerged as proxies for most others: a specified deficit in river flow at Lee's Ferry (between Lake Power and

Lake Mead) and a fall in Lake Mead elevation below a specified level (Bureau of Reclamation 2012b, 17).

Exploratory modeling undertaken by RAND and Reclamation subjected the baseline case and the four policy portfolios to stress-testing against twenty-three thousand simulations to identify the conditions under which each option would be expected to succeed and fail. The exercise generated the warning that "in the absence of timely action, there are likely to be significant shortfalls between projected water supplies and demands in coming decades." The shortfalls were anticipated to harm all water users from the source of the river in the Rocky Mountains to its termination in the Gulf of California. In the simulation, all of the policy portfolios performed substantially better than the status quo. Whereas under the status quo the Lake Mead vulnerability indicator was reached in 19% of the scenarios, that number was reduced to 3% under portfolios A and B. The Basin Study nonetheless emphasizes that none of the envisioned portfolios reduces the risk of water shortage to zero.

With these results in hand, researchers explored the matter of trade-offs. Analysts found that the four portfolios entailed trade-offs among various performance indicators and between performance and cost. The Basin Study refrains from choosing one optimal portfolio. It emphasizes instead the goal of providing stakeholders with the findings so that they can consider which trade-offs might be warranted. Finally, the report examines how each portfolio performs under worst-case future conditions, permitting considerations of regret minimization.

As a thought experiment the Basin Study was intended to serve as "a call to action" by decision makers and stakeholders. The next steps were taken in May 2013, when Reclamation and the basin states, "in collaboration with the Ten Tribes Partnership and conservation organizations, initiated the *Moving Forward* effort to build on future considerations and next steps in the Basin study" (Bureau of Reclamation 2015, 1). Consultation with diverse stakeholders elicited objectives ranging from water supply reliability for municipalities, industry, and agriculture to "hydropower production, ecosystem health, and recreation" (Marchau et al. 2019, 141). Phase I of Moving Forward established three work groups targeting (1) municipal and industrial water conservation and reuse; (2) agricultural water conservation, productivity, and transfers; and (3) environmental and recreational river flows. Each work group comprised wide representation of diverse stakeholder groups. The initial findings of the work groups were published in the phase I report in May 2015 (Bureau of Reclamation 2015). In it, several proposals are identified as low regret and high priority. These are strategies that generate benefit under most future states of the world. They include, for instance, increasing water use efficiency across diverse applications, reducing system losses (in distribution and storage systems), maximizing reuse, and enhancing environmental and recreational values by targeting areas where improved water management would have significant impacts.

Looking Ahead

Follow-up DMDU activities related to the Basin Study were paused in the wake of two particularly dry years in 2012 and 2013 (and persistent dry conditions since) that focused Reclamation's attention on actions needed to hedge against a severe drought. After concluding the phase I report the stakeholder groups stopped meeting as Reclamation shifted to more urgent tasks, including the drafting of emergency drought contingency plans for approval by the US Congress in 2019. But the RAND-Reclamation collaboration has had lasting effects on how Reclamation considers and conveys uncertainty. Reclamation initiated a series of decision-science research projects to continue to explore DMDU techniques in the context of designing Lake Mead operating policies. In an email exchange of June 2021, Reclamation civil engineer Rebecca Smith reported that "the second installment of this research thread will be completed by Fall 2021. Multiple staff with DMDU backgrounds have been hired to shepherd these projects and to bring DMDU perspectives into different studies and engagements with scientists and stakeholders." In the view of some experienced Reclamation engineers, one of the biggest challenges confronting integration of the DMDU approach at Reclamation, Smith explained, "is that coordinating agencies or decision makers who utilize our studies want 'one number.'" The engineers, unsurprisingly, identified economists in this context. "As such," said Smith, "I'd say the major obstacle for a single institution is that the 'one number' approach is part of a long history of coordinated analyses and decision making, and without relevant examples of how DMDU has been implemented by others, it is unclear how to move forward." Despite that, Smith cited multiple grounds for optimism, including growing awareness that climate change projections used in water resource impact studies must encompass a very wide range of plausible futures that should not be summarized probabilistically into one value of risk, and awareness that the science community will not be able to reduce the ranges of projections in the foreseeable future. In a follow-up email of November 2021, Smith also reported that Reclamation engineers are now beginning to incorporate DMDU strategies into study plans for upcoming Reclamation projects, and that in their reviews of proposals submitted to Reclamation for grants to fund case studies they are requiring that grantees document the limitations of their climate change data and explore ways to incorporate deep uncertainty concepts in their analyses.

The DMDU Challenge to Economic Practice

DMDU is not necessary or appropriate when uncertainty is shallow, that is, when system dynamics are well understood and ignorance is adequately characterized by known probability distributions. Under shallow uncertainty traditional approaches to policy making are often adequate (Hallegatte et al. 2012, 4). The urgent challenge facing policy makers and stakeholders is discerning which policy decisions are in fact marked by shallow uncertainty. The economics profession has operated for a century on the presumption that shallow uncertainty is the norm and wicked problems are the exception. Today there is ample evidence that the opposite is the case, especially as concerns our most grave threats. Economists and other experts have no business *presuming* shallow ignorance ex ante since the harmful consequences of improperly identifying a wicked problem as simple can be catastrophic.

The partnerships that emerge in DMDU projects represent a direct challenge to the paternalistic ethos and epistemic hubris that have prevailed in economics for well over a century. In their place we find a foregrounding of the values, knowledge, and agency of decision makers and stakeholders and those they represent. DMDU practice emphasizes the limitations to expert knowledge in the face of wicked problems. The approach cultivates learning and enhanced decision-making expertise among a diverse array of stakeholders. Under DMDU, stakeholders drive decision making in the sense of inputting their values and objectives, identifying the thresholds of performance that are satisfactory, engaging the trade-offs that inevitably arise in the policy exercise, and specifying the levels of risk of harm that they are willing to accept while building capacity for the surprises that the future will bring. DMDU accepts the legitimacy of diverse and even conflicting values, interests, and goals across stakeholders. Unlike the outputs of standard economic analysis, which are so readily weaponized in political forums, DMDU procedures seek to forge cooperation even among those with conflicting expectations and interests. The approach also diminishes the epistemic gap separating economic experts from those they hope to serve.

The alteration in economic practice that DMDU requires is radical. But it is necessary for a profession that seeks to promote social betterment in a world characterized by irreparable ignorance that it can certainly influence but never control.

12

Conclusion: From Reckless to Responsible Economics

Two archetypal economists have lurked in the background throughout this book. Twentieth-century "heroic" economists thought they could exert control, bringing about economic outcomes they knew to be best. They presumed that economies were simple enough systems, the mastery of which would allow them to determine the effects of public policy through blackboard exercises. They presumed that they occupied a position of epistemic privilege relative to other social scientists and laypeople, and that they and their science were up to the task of bringing about any result they chose, provided policy makers would listen and obey. Armed with their expertise, they set out to achieve heaven on earth, as *they* defined it. The heroic economists were prepared to tackle even the most complex challenges, like remaking national economies and even the world economy, brimming with confidence that their time-travel machines allowed them to know today the future effects of their projects. Their calling validated the imposition of whatever harms were necessary, even to the most vulnerable, to get the job done. They were unprepared to engage respectfully those who opposed them, dismissing them as economic innocents who could not begin to understand the economy. As for the victims of harm, moral geometry provided economists with the means to discount their harms by defining them as fully reparable through compensation. The expertise of the heroic economists gave them not just the right to direct human affairs, even over the objections of those put at risk, but the moral obligation to do so.

Heroic economists are reckless. Knowing best, they adopt a paternalistic ethos vis-à-vis those they purport to serve. They take far too many chances with the lives of others while having no skin in the game themselves. Their practice destroys communities without giving sufficient due to the countless victims of economic progress. They treat irreparable ignorance, which threatens their authority and influence, as calculable risk. "Economists, from Kenneth Arrow to Robert Lucas," North (1999, 2) reminds us, "have asserted that one cannot theorize in the face of pure uncertainty." For that reason alone, they cannot accept the possibility of irreparable ignorance.

For over a century heroic economists predominated in the profession. They won the most important prizes, monopolized positions at the most prominent universities, and directed the world's most important economic institutions. Their self-certainty and influence reached its zenith from the 1980s through the first decade of the twenty-first century. Heroic economists found themselves in position to engineer a global transformation toward a liberalized market economy defined by market fundamentalism, including the liberalization of trade, investment, and finance (Rodrik 2017). Their impact was immense.

Over the past century a second type of economist emerged to challenge the heroes. Let's call them the "self-aware, irreparably ignorant." These are the economists who have excoriated economic hubris, pointing out the limits to economic knowledge. They acknowledge not just what we don't know now but what we can't ever know. They emphasize the mistake of treating the world as ergodic. They highlight the fatal error of equating the growing influence of economists with growing control over the economy. And they urge the profession to tease out the practical and ethical implications of the tight epistemic constraints under which economists work.

Today hubris in the economics profession is tempered by a series of unwelcome surprises, including the stunning failure of market reform in Russia and other post-Soviet countries, a series of devastating financial crises (including the crisis of 2008), and existential crises associated with climate change. Each in its own way drove home the limits to economic expertise. Today some of the most influential economists on the right, center, and left are joining the self-aware, irreparably ignorant wing of the profession (see, e.g., Orszag, Rubin, and Stiglitz 2021). Increasingly the insights of the epistemic iconoclasts cited throughout the book are being acknowledged by a profession that, for well over a generation, repressed them. And not a moment too soon. The needless damage wrought by the heroic economists is now threatening the social fabric across the globe while undermining ecological sustainability.

Today we inhabit a world defined by wicked problems and deep conflicts over values. *There is no place in that kind of world for economic heroes.* In that kind of world, the heroes stand to do extraordinary damage by deluding themselves, and those whose lives they will affect, that they know what's best for society and know enough to achieve optimal outcomes while skirting danger. The more they succeed in inducing this belief, the greater the damage they cause.

If economists can contribute at all to social betterment in an environment marked by wicked problems, it will be the self-aware, irreparably ignorant economists who do it. The responsible approach for this brigade is simple to describe but very difficult to enact for a profession that has so long enjoyed privileges and authority owing to its presumed expertise. First, responsible economists should work to overturn the paternalistic ethos that has justified imposing even grave harms when, in the judgment of economists, those harms were warranted to promote social betterment. In place of paternalism, responsible economists must recognize the integrity and autonomy of laypersons—the right of those who will live with the beneficial and damaging consequences of policy interventions to participate, meaningfully, in the assessment of available strategies, risks, and trade-offs. Achieving that goal requires foregrounding the divergent aspirations and values of those stakeholders without imposing a simplistic framework for reducing them to some common desideratum, like welfare. Second, responsible economists must emphasize irreparable ignorance and push back against the view that economics provides the means for time travel. They can foreground how to promote social betterment in a world economists cannot ever know or control. Third, responsible economists can probe economic harm carefully, accepting its inherent complexity and exploring just what are the ethical entailments of the fact that the profession induces harm as it promotes social betterment.

Fortunately, we now have models of what responsible professional engagement entails in a world of irreparable ignorance and grave harm. Here we have explored just one such approach, DMDU, which at its best incorporates many of the necessary principles. Most importantly DMDU embraces irreparable ignorance, refusing to reduce future events to probability distributions. The approach depends on expertise that economists can provide, but it does not ask them to attempt the impossible—like predicting the unpredictable—while integrating them into ongoing collaborations with stakeholders as partners who share skin in the game.

If DMDU enacts some of the principles that should guide economists in managing harm, it is hardly a panacea that guarantees resolution of the most pressing public-policy problems. DMDU strategies do not solve the problem of structural violence stemming from the substantial inequalities in life circumstances and access to resources that characterize our world. Planning collaboratively for uncertain futures can help regional water system managers cope responsibly with the uncertainties of climate change. But if climate change goes unchecked, even the best local responses will fail to meet stakeholder needs or protect the most vulnerable from catastrophe. The profession can take the lead in a head-on confrontation with unwarranted privileges that stem from gross inequalities, such as those associated with income, wealth, race, gender, and nationality. An economics profession committed to harm-centric economic practice would embrace harm's complexity, explore economic harm profiles, and seek to interrupt the pathways by which diverse harms compound and cascade. That kind of profession would be on the lookout for institutional and policy reforms that might eliminate tragic choices and generate much more benign economic harm profiles.

*

Tragedies are ineliminable. Virtuous economists will continue to contribute to harm as they seek to do good. In the face of tragedy the profession faces a choice. It can proceed recklessly, repressing the tragedy so that economists can get on with their work, presuming that they know best just what social betterment is, how to achieve it, and what price is to be paid and by whom for the good of society. Or the profession can acknowledge the tragedy and explore with others its ethical implications in hopes of managing it with greater care and wisdom, and in ways that empower those who will bear its effects. I hope the right approach is by now clear. As concerns harm and harming, the economics profession can do much better than it has done until now. Given the stakes, it simply must.

Acknowledgments

I have benefited enormously while working on this book from conversations with colleagues and students at the Josef Korbel School of International Studies of the University of Denver, from wonderful research assistance, and from the feedback from audience members on many occasions when I presented ideas that now appear in this book. Thanks in particular to Matthew Adler, Kyan Aldrich, Matt Bloise, Abby Brown, Ted Burczak, Lauren Craig, Jack Donnelly, Joe Downes, Bert Garcia, Rob Garnett, Quentin Good, Amanda Hayden, Minsun Ji, Paul Kemp, Deirdre McCloskey, Logan Mooberry, Marco Nathan, Brian O'Neill, Paul Perasso, Tasia Poinsatte, Daniel Rinner, Zoe Sherman, Mark Silverman, Robert Wade, Mark White, and Hannah Wolf. Apologies to the students whom I subjected to the manuscript, whose reactions helped me clarify arguments. Special thanks to Claire Cooper, Holden Fitzgerald, Annee Lorentzen, and Sophia Gonzalez Mayagoitia for providing a critical student's-eye view of the book and pushing me to find ways to present the ideas intuitively and accessibly. Researchers in the Society for Decision Making under Deep Uncertainty have been very generous with their insights and time as I dove into their work. Thanks in particular to David Groves, Laurna Kaatz, Steven Popper, Julie Rozenberg, Matt Simpson, and Rebecca Smith. The members of the Societies for the History of Economics (SHOE) were extraordinarily helpful. Thanks to Spencer Banzhaf, David Colander, John Davis, Claude Diebolt, Max Ehrenfreund, Ramon Garcia Fernandez, Kevin Hoover, Roger Middleton, Mary Morgan, Hugh Rockoff, Menno Rol, Eric Schliesser, Brian Simboli, Nicky Tynan, Massimiliano Vatiero, Altug Yalcintas, and Adrian Yee.

I am grateful for the two anonymous referees for the University of Chicago Press who pushed me to sharpen the book's arguments and presentation.

Thanks to Chicago Executive Editor Chad Zimmerman for his guidance and support of the project, to Senior Production Editor Tamara Ghattas for taking extraoradinary care with the manuscript, and to illustrator Mike Brehm for his creativity in sorting out how to clarify arguments through visual representations. I so appreciate the support and encouragement of Amelia Cramer and Amy S. Cramer, Chiara Piovani, and Elizabeth Ramey. And the weekly respites from the book (and the world) provided by the lovely folks in the Friday Night Good Bad Movie Group. My deepest thanks, always, to Ilene Grabel for providing acute insights in her own work and in conversation, and for combing through multiple drafts, just as she has done throughout my career. I dedicate the book to her.

Notes

1. I borrow the felicitous phrase from philosopher Howard Radest (1997, 111), who offers it in his exploration of training in medical ethics. In economics moral *calculus* might be more precise, but I retain Radest's terminology throughout.

2. Zemiology (referring to Zema, the Greek god of harm) emerged as a new field only at the end of the twentieth century. It is traced to the 1998 annual conference of the European Group for the Study of Deviance and Social Control, which brought together scholars and practitioners in the fields of "criminal justice, development economics and development studies, geosciences, law, poverty studies, public health, social policy, and sociology" (Hillyard and Tombs 2017, 285). We explore this tradition in chapter 9.

3. Krugman's reversal appears in Krugman (2007), where he writes: "By all means, let's have strong labor standards in our pending trade agreements. . . ."

4. See the papers in the symposium "The Democratic Crisis and the Responsibility of Economics" in the *Forum for Social Economics* (47, no. 2 [2018]). Confronting the rise of illiberalism in 1930s Europe both Hayek ([1944] 2007) and Polanyi (1944) laid blame at the feet of the economics profession—though they certainly disagreed over the details.

5. Unless noted otherwise, the data reported here come from Stuckler and Basu (2013). On deaths following economic restructuring in the post-Soviet economies, see also Stuckler, King, and McKee (2009); and Angner (2006).

6. In 1976 Ivan Illich published the influential book *Medical Nemesis* in which he drew attention to physician-induced harms and popularized the term "iatrogenic harm."

7. This discussion draws on DeMartino (2011a).

8. The new professional economists emerged during the Progressive Era in the US that spanned the 1890s through the 1920s (Bernstein 2001). Progressivism was marked by a new sense of professional duty to serve society. Progressive philosophy viewed professionals as uniquely qualified to solve complex social problems through the application of expertise. Progressive idealism continues to inform economic thinking today. Robert Nelson, who served at high levels in US federal agencies during much of his career, speaks of the "missionary commitment" of economists to the goal of promoting human advancement. "Many—perhaps most—of them, I submit, have chosen to enter the profession of economics because they had a basic commitment to economic progress as the essential route of the common good" (Nelson 2004, 65). Nelson

(2004, 59) gives the example of William Baumol, who claimed to have become an economist because "I believe deeply with Shaw, that there are few crimes more heinous than poverty."

9. Apparently he failed to solicit the views of those who voted for Allende, or those whom Pinochet's regime imprisoned, tortured, or killed.

10. A barely more charitable interpretation is that they advocated the policy regime that they *knew* would succeed. In this interpretation epistemic hubris replaces wild adventurism.

11. Financial liberalization that facilitates international capital mobility, too, has uneven impacts that are if anything more dramatic than trade liberalization. Financial liberalization typically generates extraordinary gains to large investors while increasing the frequency of financial instability that devastates the most disadvantaged in countries that lack adequate social safety nets. See Grabel (2015).

12. The damaging effects of NAFTA were arguably worse for many agricultural communities in Mexico, where small producers faced intense competition from US agribusiness. NAFTA led to the destruction of businesses, massive outward migration of working-age men, and social dislocation (Otero 2011).

13. An important example of the dissenters are those economists who recognized the inequality-deepening effects of "green revolution" policy of the mid- to late twentieth century that upgraded agricultural inputs to improve productivity in low-income countries. The policies exacerbated existing inequality in rural areas, benefiting relatively well-off farmers at the expense of others who could not take advantage of the policies. See Boyce (1993) on the green revolution in the Philippines and on "immiserizing growth" more generally.

14. Beyond economics there has been a recent flourishing of sophisticated analyses of uncertainty and the limits to expertise. See in particular the contributions in Vitek and Jackson (2008); Katzenstein and Seybert (2018); and Scoones and Stirling (2020). A small sample of other valuable work includes Berry (2005); Taleb (2007; 2012); Mainelli and Harris (2011); Beckert (2016); Sloman and Fernbach (2017); Koppl (2018); and Kay and King (2020).

15. The concept "great moderation" was coined by Stock and Watson (2002), who explored reduced macroeconomic volatility since the mid-1980s. The final warning in the article is prescient: "But because most of the reduction seems to be due to good luck in the form of smaller economic disturbances, we are left with the unsettling conclusion that the quiescence of the past fifteen years could well be a hiatus before a return to more turbulent economic times." That warning was ignored by macroeconomists who sought to take credit for economic stability.

16. See also Resnick and Wolff (1987) and MacKenzie (2006) on the ways in which economic theory shapes rather than simply describes economic phenomena.

17. Rogoff's claim may be more hopeful than descriptively accurate, but it is true that there is greater appreciation today of the epistemic insights of Keynes and Knight than there was prior to the crisis of 2008. The work of Nassim Taleb (2007; 2012) ought to dampen economists' pretensions regarding prediction and control. Deirdre McCloskey (1990) has called the profession to task for peddling "snake-oil" in the form of confident predictions of future economic events. Friedrich Hayek ([1944] 2007) and the rightist Austrian economists deserve special recognition in this regard, even as they sometimes have lost sight of their own epistemic warnings in policy discussion. The ideologically elusive Albert O. Hirschman ([1970] 2013) did far better in both recognizing uncertainty and applying it consistently to push back against all overarching "isms" (see Grabel 2017). See also Resnick and Wolff (1987); Ruccio and Amariglio (2003); Nelson (2004), Bergeron (2004), and other leading feminists; Colander (2005a); Burczak (2006); and Crotty (2019) and other post-Keynesians.

18. The argument advanced here is developed further in DeMartino (2019) and DeMartino and Grabel (2020).

19. Shackle is speaking here of the ignorance facing individuals in the economy, but economists confront the same problem. Kenneth Rogoff (2018) writes, "It took economic historians seven decades to unpack the Great Depression. It is safe to assume that historians will have much more to say about the 2008 financial crisis in the years and decades to come." Maybe so, but the point remains that the knowledge often comes too late relative to when it is needed for decision making.

20. Not to quibble, but even this framing understates the problem. What we "know" at any moment is finite; what we don't know is infinite.

21. The new behavioral economics breaks with this approach by exploring how individuals actually behave and then deriving policy proposals from that knowledge. A chief finding is that individuals are irrational in ways that contradict the standard economic approach. But if it can be shown that individuals are "*predictably* irrational" (Ariely 2008), then the belief in economic time travel can be sustained because in that case economists can know in advance how individuals will respond to economic policy interventions. The new hope is to be able to "nudge" individuals toward better decision making by exploiting their cognitive patterns (Thaler and Sunstein 2008).

22. Nassim Taleb (2012, 329) presents a corrective. He argues that time is a powerful filter; the older a work that is still read today, the greater its merit, historical significance, or current relevance. But many other filters operate, including economic interests; professional status; gender, racial, and other biases; and so forth, and these factors filter out insightful work while also propelling the long-term flourishing of flawed work and methods. See, for instance, Ziliak and McCloskey (2008) on the continuing influence in the social sciences of the thinking of Ronald A. Fisher on statistical significance. On gender bias in citation practices see Pells (2018). On racial bias in economic research and publication see Mason, Myers, and Darity (2005).

23. Unfortunately, the history of economic thought no longer appears in the curriculum of most PhD programs. Students are forgiven for inferring that there is little to learn from earlier generations of economists. Colander and Freedman (2018, 210) have this to say about Chicago School economist George Stigler on the matter: "One of the rationales provided by Stigler for dropping History of Thought from graduate education was the danger of providing young minds with too many plausible alternatives. He required missionary soldiers, not ranks of puzzled philosophers."

24. Although much of the literature on the ethics of autonomous vehicles probes questions concerning whose lives should be imperiled and saved—for instance, see Lin (2016) and Awad et al. (2018)—it is not the case that AI today is at the level required to make these kinds of instantaneous judgments (Winfield et al. 2019). And so one might argue that it is incorrect to frame the ethical dilemma in this way. But the case is better understood as one that highlights the ethical complexities of new innovations, where different stages of technological advance pose unique ethical questions. We should not expect that the ethical controversies surrounding autonomous vehicles will ever be resolved once and for all. As the technology advances, the pertinent questions needing answers will change.

25. In fact, we'll find in the next chapter that unlike eating the berries, introducing the policy doesn't answer the question of its causal impact.

26. As concerns basic civil engineering I refer to certain of its mundane tasks, such as simple bridge building, and not adventurous projects like large-scale dam construction that involve much greater uncertainties and possibilities for unintended harm.

27. A notable exception is Fogel (1964).

28. See Cartwright (2004; 2007) for other forms of causal claims.

29. In addition to contributions explored here, see also Simon (1952); Abbott (1974); McCloskey (1987); Morgan and Winship (2014); Nathan (2017); and Mahoney and Barrenechea (2017).

30. Hicks (1980) explores Adam Smith's use of counterfactual reasoning in his analysis of the role of navigable waterways in economic development. Schliesser (2017, chap. 5) examines Smith's exploitation of counterfactualizing in his treatment of "perfect sympathy," "natural price," and optimal institutions.

31. It may be that the nonoccurrence of *X* requires, for the sake of plausibility, many other changes in the alternative world. But how are we to know what other changes must be made to accommodate the counterfactual antecedent? See the discussion of historical consistency, pp. 94–96.

32. Knight ([1921] 2014, 202) discusses the "two-fold inference" that predicting policy effects entails. "We must infer what the future situation would have been without our interference, and what change will be wrought in it by our action." He concludes that claims about future causality are terribly undependable. See Hicks's (1980, 10) related notion of "double vision" and Beckert's (2016, 10) concept of "doubling of reality" in the creation of fictitious expectations.

33. See Fischhoff and Beyth (1975) and the essays in Kahneman, Slovic, and Tversky (1982) and in Roese and Olson (1995).

34. See Hicks's (1980, 11) distinction between the "voluntarism" that shapes our perceptions of the future and the "determinism" that shapes our perception of the past. See also Hay's (2020) critique of Hobsbawm. Weber (1996, 275–276) provides a corrective: "I want to establish that when we say we have 'explained' an event in past time, it does not necessarily mean that we have also ruled out the possibility that things could have been radically different than they were."

35. Tetlock and Belkin (1996, 18ff) examine six widely used criteria for assessing counterfactuals. In addition to the two I discuss in the text, the list also includes cotenability, clarity, statistical consistency, and projectability.

36. Formally, "a counterfactual is nonvacuously true [if and only if] it takes less of a departure from actuality to make the consequent true along with the antecedent than it does to make the antecedent true without the consequent" (Lewis 1973, 560). The criterion also appears in the work of King, Keohane, and Verba (1994, 78); in Levy's (2015) "minimal re-write rule"; in the "plausible world" approach of Hawthorn (1991); and in the dynamic framework of Elster (1978, chap. 6).

37. Counterfactualizing is equally implicated in axiomatic-deductive modeling, agent-based modeling, randomized controlled trials, and other contemporary methods. Each method pursues distinct means for constructing "correct" counterfactuals. See DeMartino (2021).

38. We will return to this issue in chapter 10.

39. Hallegatte et al. (2012, 10) remind us of the dangers of thinking that existing models project the full range of possible future worlds. On climate models, they write, "There is no reason why existing models should represent the real uncertainty: they may all have the same flaw, since they are all based on the same incomplete and imperfect knowledge."

40. Thanks to Zoe Sherman for bringing this poem to my attention.

41. This assumption was upended by research in psychology and behavioral economics by the late twentieth century. People hold other regarding preferences, such as "social preferences" defined as "concern for the payoffs allocated to other relevant reference agents and the intentions that led to this payoff profile in addition to the concern for one's own payoff" (Carpenter 2018).

42. The interested reader should consult Adler (1998; 2012) and Boadway and Bruce (1984) for comprehensive accounts of welfarist assumptions.

43. More formally, a lexicographic preference ordering "assigns priority to a good *x* if a bundle with less of that good is non-preferred regardless of how much of the other goods it contains" (Boadway and Bruce 1984, 182n8).

44. See Hotelling (1938) and Buchanan (1959) for alternative perspectives.

45. There are technical discrepancies between Kaldor-Hicks and CBA (Boadway 1974; 2016; Boadway and Bruce 1984; Adler 2012). They nevertheless share the common normative framework explored here.

46. Any attempt to provide an accessible glimpse into CBA theory and practice risks oversimplification. A massive literature examines the approach, including alternative CBA methodologies, far more carefully than I can do here. Interested readers might start with Dorfman (1993), Adler and Posner (2006), Viscusi (2014), and Adler (2019).

47. "Willingness to pay" is a misnomer, suggesting that all that matters in the calculation is how strongly a person desires a particular outcome. In fact, it conjoins willingness with *ability* to pay. A low-income person may strongly prefer a policy and yet be severely constrained in her ability to pay to achieve it, yielding a low WTP.

48. I put aside in this example one important complicating factor—the question of discounting future costs and benefits. We explore this issue momentarily.

49. This section draws extensively on Adler (2019), which presents an extraordinarily lucid and balanced explication of the SWF approach.

50. More precisely, under the continuous prioritarian SWF, any pure gap-reducing, rank-preserving transfer of welfare from a better-off to a worse-off individual is taken to generate greater aggregate social welfare. One such SWF is derived by taking the square root of individual welfare levels before aggregation. As compared to aggregation of unadjusted welfare levels, the square root adjustment assigns a higher value to policies that generate greater welfare equality.

51. The relevant OMB document, "Circular A-4," has been in force since 2003. It reflects an antiregulation bias that was central to mainstream economic thinking during the late twentieth century. The Biden administration issued a memorandum in January 2021 insructing the director of the OMB and agency heads to modernize regulatory review. Specifically, the memorandum instructs them to develop recommendations on "how the regulatory review process can promote public health and safety, economic growth, social welfare, racial justice, environmental stewardship, human dignity, equity, and the interests of future generations." This initiative is significant. It reflects a renewed commitment to state intervention to bring about a wide range of goals that extend far beyond the standard economic concern with efficiency. It could mark a significant shift away from CBA in US federal regulatory review.

52. See Boardman et al. (2011, 167ff) for an intuitive exploration, which also presents "sensitivity analysis" to gauge the robustness of the projections of net benefits (anticipating the approach we will explore in chapter 11). For the sake of brevity I examine here just the "frequentist" approach to probabilities, leaving aside the Bayesian approach wherein probabilities reflect degrees of belief in future states of the world. Chapter 11 explores decision making under deep uncertainty. That approach shares certain features with the Bayesian approach, though it does not try to infer future probabilities. It emphasizes the need to monitor the world after policy implementation, update beliefs in light of new evidence, and adjust policy in light of the new knowledge.

53. In assessment that presumes probabilistic knowledge of policy effects, maximizing E(U) is one but by no means the only available decision criterion. One alternative strategy is to ignore

probabilities in policy selection and try to maximize the minimum possible value (maximin), while another seeks to maximize the possible gain (maximax). Both rules would endorse the second policy given in the text, with values given by the second die, since it has a higher minimum value (2) and a higher maximum value (7). See Mishan (1975, chaps. 50–52).

54. And to technical critique that I do not explore here. See Chipman and Moore (1978); Scitovsky (1941); Sen (1979); and Stringham (2001).

55. The argument is contractarian in the sense of Rawls (1971) and Harsanyi (1982). We are asked to presume that rational deliberators operating behind a veil of ignorance would consent to efficiency-promoting uncompensated harms provided they believed that all would be better-off from a long series of such policy innovations than they would be under any alternative policy rule (DeMartino 2016).

56. Polinsky (1972, 408) presents the case this way:

> By broadening the notion of compensation to include bundles of changes that have some effective randomness in distribution, it thereby becomes possible to leave particular individuals uncompensated and worse off for single changes, yet assure them that they can (mathematically) expect to be better off as a result of the entire bundle.

Interested readers should also consult Hotelling (1938); Hicks (1941); Buchanan and Tullock ([1962] 2004); Leibenstein (1965); Polinsky (1972); Posner (1980); Adler and Posner (1999); and White (2006).

57. On the massive harms attending dam construction, for instance, see Cernea (2003); Kanbur (2003); and Gasper (2016).

58. See the extensive citations to the literature on the harms of gentrification at https://urbandisplacement.org.

59. The distinction between reparable and irreparable harm is well established in the field of law, but it is specified in various ways and contested. See Kornhauser (2001); Rendleman (2002); Brooks and Schwartz (2005); Lichtman (2007); Grosskopf and Medina (2009); and McGowan (2010).

60. The distinction between compensation and acknowledgment arises also in cases such as reparations for slavery, where the injustice involves far more than economic damage. See Darity and Mullen (2020) for an important contribution to the literature.

61. Mishan (1975, part VI) provides a useful exposition and candid appraisal of the various means that are utilized in CBA to domesticate the problem of uncertainty.

62. Pemberton is drawing here on the needs-based account of harm of Doyal and Gough (1991). Doyal and Gough's approach to harm emphasizes "fundamental disablement in the pursuit of one's vision of the good" and "impediments to successful social participation" (1991, 50; cited in Pemberton 2015, 27).

63. One criterion for adjudicating between ethically benign and indictable harm is whether the behavior induces reciprocal risk in the pursuit or enactment of widely shared, highly valued goods, or the behavior entails nonreciprocal risk, such as when only some undertake actions that risk harming others without their consent. See Geistfeld (2008, 61–65). An example of reciprocal risk is the risk of accident that each driver imposes on others in a society where most people avail themselves of transportation by automobile in pursuit of the good of physical mobility.

64. The permissibility of indirect harm is sometimes defended on the basis of the "doctrine of double effect" (see McIntyre 2019).

65. The text passes over controversial issues here, such as just what is meant by bias, and what factors may and may not properly influence outcomes of fair contests. Merit-based contests are "biased" in favor of the talented, and we do not indict them on those grounds. But how differences in talent are acquired prior to the contest is normatively salient when judging the legitimacy of the contest.

66. I note in this connection an entropy argument in Hayek ([1944] 2007, 128–29). He claims that protections against economic risk enjoyed by the privileged concentrate and even amplify the risk of harm for those lacking privilege.

67. That view has been problematized by legal philosophers and philosophically minded economists. See Katz (2006 and the literature cited therein, especially in note 5); Hurd (1996); Grant (2012); Sen (1970); and Ellerman (1993). For Kantian perspectives see White (2009) and Lutz (1995). I will presume in what follows that the *absence* of consent in harm-generating arrangements is ethically worrisome, not that the presence of consent suffices to legitimate arrangements that generate harm.

68. Legal and moral philosophers generally do much better than economists in theorizing coercion. Wertheimer (1987) examines controversies in the fields of law and philosophy over this centrally important, contested concept. Feinberg (1986, chap. 17) explores limits to the *volenti non fit injuria* principle. White (2006, 240ff; 2009) examines the law and economics tradition that probes the matter of consent to harm. Grant (2012) identifies coercion as one of three forms of exercise of power, along with incentives and persuasion, and provides normative criteria for ascertaining when coercion is and is not legitimate. Hurd (1996) examines the "moral magic" of consent, which appears to transform what would otherwise be illicit into legitimate acts. See also Lukes (2005) and Boulding (1989).

69. See the work of the members of the Community Economies Research Network (https://www.communityeconomies.org/about/ce-research-network-cern).

70. An important strand in public choice literature (e.g., Ostrom, Tiebout, and Warren 1961) and libertarianism (see Nozick 1974, chap. 10) emphasizes local governance as a way of ensuring consent via the exit option. When local government enjoys policy autonomy, individuals can move to those jurisdictions that best align with their values. The discussion in the text makes a parallel point, emphasizing the normative salience of economic diversity within any particular jurisdiction as a means of expanding the opportunity for economic agency, consent, and freedom.

71. For an application of this idea to the global financial governance architecture, which extends the work of Albert O. Hirschman, see Grabel (2015; 2017).

72. See Marchau et al. (2019) for an accessible, comprehensive introduction to DMDU philosophy, methods, and applications.

73. Climate change may be thought of as a "super-wicked" problem for which there is too little time to figure out solutions (see Levin et al. 2012).

74. North (1999, 3) identifies three dimensions of uncertainty, which are consistent with the concept of deep uncertainty: "We do not know enough; we are dealing with a world of continuous change; and we do not have any dynamic theory to guide us when we attempt to get from one point to the next."

75. Though not an explicit contribution to DMDU literature, Grabel (2004) advocates the use of "tripwires" and "speed bumps" in the context of dangerous financial flows that can threaten national and even international financial stability. In this account, when financial flows approach danger zones, financial authorities are to enact capital controls and other protective

measures to tamp down systemic risk. In the years following the financial crisis of 2008, many national governments introduced and adjusted capital controls in this way (Grabel 2017).

76. DMDU can also be combined with other methods, including CBA. In the context of CBA, DMDU generates as outputs the robustness of net benefits of alternative policies across alternative unweighted future states of the world, and across diverse stakeholder values. See Espinet et al. (2018) and Lempert (2014).

References

Abbott, Barbara. 1974. "Some Problems in Giving an Adequate Model-Theoretic Account of Cause." In *Berkeley Studies in Syntax and Semantics*, volume I, edited by Charles Fillmore, George Lakoff, and Robin T. Lakoff, I-1–I-14. Berkeley: University of California.

Acemoglu, Daron, David H. Autor, David Dorn, Gordon H. Hanson, and Brendan Price. 2016. "Import Competition and the Great US Employment Sag of the 2000s." *Journal of Labor Economics* 34 (S1): S141–98. https://doi.org/10.1086/682384.

Acemoglu, Daron, Victor Chernozhukov, Iván Werning, and Michael D. Whinston. 2020. "Optimal Targeted Lockdowns in a Multi-group SIR Model." National Bureau of Economic Research Working Paper No. 27102.

Adams, Guy B., and Danny L. Balfour. 1998. *Unmasking Administrative Evil*. Thousand Oaks, CA: Sage.

Adler, Matthew D. 1998. "Incommensurability and Cost-Benefit Analysis." *University of Pennsylvania Law Review* 146 (5): 1371–1418. https://doi.org/10.2307/3312809.

———. 2012. *Well-Being and Fair Distribution: Beyond Cost-Benefit Analysis*. Oxford: Oxford University Press.

———. 2015. "Value and Cost-Benefit Analysis." In *Oxford Handbook of Value Theory*, edited by Iwao Hirose and Jonas Olson, 317–37. Oxford: Oxford University Press.

———. 2019. *Measuring Social Welfare: An Introduction*. Oxford: Oxford University Press.

———. 2020. "What Should We Spend to Save Lives in a Pandemic? A Critique of the Value of Statistical Life." Duke Law School Public Law & Legal Theory Series, No. 2020-40. https://doi.org/10.2139/ssrn.3636550.

Adler, Matthew D., and Eric Posner. 1999. "Rethinking Cost-Benefit Analysis." *Yale Law Journal* 109 (2), 165–247. https://doi.org/10.2307/797489.

———. 2006. *New Foundations of Cost-Benefit Analysis*. Cambridge: Harvard University Press.

Adler, Matthew D., and James Hammitt. 2020. "A Better Way to Grapple with Benefit-Cost Trade-offs in a Pandemic." *Hill*, April 13, 2020. https://thehill.com/opinion/healthcare/492437-a-better-way-to-grapple-with-benefit-cost-trade-offs-in-a-pandemic.

Alacevich, Michele, and Anna Soci. 2017. *Inequality: A Short History*. Washington, DC: Brookings Institution Press.

Anderson, Elizabeth. 1990. "The Ethical Limitations of the Market." *Economics and Philosophy* 6 (2): 179–205. https://doi.org/10.1017/S0266267100001218.

Angner, Erik. 2006. "Economists as Experts: Overconfidence in Theory and Practice." *Journal of Economic Methodology* 13 (1): 1–24. https://doi.org/10.1080/13501780600566271.

Arestis, Philip, Aurélie Charles, and Giuseppe Fontana. 2013. "Financialization, the Great Recession, and the Stratification of the US Labor Market." *Feminist Economics* 19 (3): 152–80. https://doi.org/10.1080/13545701.2013.795654.

Ariely, Dan. 2008. *Predictably Irrational: The Hidden Forces That Shape Our Decisions.* New York: Harper Collins.

Arneson, Richard. 2013. "Egalitarianism." In *The Stanford Encyclopedia of Philosophy*, edited by Edward Zalta. https://plato.stanford.edu/archives/sum2013/entries/egalitarianism/.

Atkinson, Tony. 2009. "Economics as a Moral Science." *Economica* 76 (suppl. 1): 791–804. https://doi.org/10.1111/j.1468-0335.2009.00788.x.

Austin, Ian, and Dan Bilefsky. 2021. "Hundreds More Unmarked Graves Found at Former Residential School in Canada." *New York Times*, June 24, 2021. https://www.nytimes.com/2021/06/24/world/canada/indigenous-children-graves-saskatchewan-canada.html.

Autor, David H., David Dorn, and Gordon H. Hanson. 2013. "The China Syndrome: Local Labor Market Effects of Import Competition in the United States." *American Economic Review* 103 (6): 2121–68.

———. 2016. "The China Shock: Learning from Labor-Market Adjustment to Large Changes in Trade." *Annual Review of Economics* 8 (1): 205–40. https://doi.org/10.1146/annurev-economics-080315-015041.

Avineri, Shlomo. 1968. *The Social and Political Thought of Karl Marx.* Cambridge: Cambridge University Press.

Bahn, Kate, and Carmen Sanchez Cumming. 2021. "Jobs Report: A Year into the Coronavirus Recession, Employment Losses Have Been Greatest for Black Women Workers and Latinx Workers." Washington Center for Equitable Growth, March 5, 2021. https://equitablegrowth.org/jobs-report-a-year-into-the-coronavirus-recession-employment-losses-have-been-greatest-for-black-women-workers-and-latinx-workers/.

Baker, Dean. 2009. "Creating Political Space for Effective Financial Regulation." *Dialogue on Globalization* 42:66–72.

Bazerman, Max, and Ann Tenbrunsel. 2011. *Blind Spots: Why We Fail to Do What's Right and What to Do About It.* Princeton: Princeton University Press.

BBC News. n.d. "World Prison Populations: UK and the Rest of the World." http://news.bbc.co.uk/2/shared/spl/hi/uk/06/prisons/html/nn2page1.stm.

Beckert, Jens. 2016. *Imagined Futures: Fictional Expectations and Capitalist Dynamics.* Cambridge, MA: Harvard University Press.

Ben-Haim, Yakov. 2010. *Info-Gap Economics: An Operational Introduction.* Heidelberg: Springer.

———. 2019. "Info-Gap Decision Theory (IG)." In *Decision Making under Deep Uncertainty: From Theory to Practice*, edited by Vincent A. W. J. Marchau, Warren E. Walker, Pieter J. T. M. Bloemen, and Steven W. Popper, 93–115. Heidelberg: Springer. https://doi.org/10.1007/978-3-030-05252-2_4.

Bentham, Jeremy. (1789) 1996. *An Introduction to the Principles of Morals and Legislation.* London: Payne. Reprint, Oxford: Clarendon.

———. 1830. *The Rationale of Reward.* London: Robert Heward.

Bergeron, Suzanne. 2004. *Fragments of Development*. Ann Arbor: University of Michigan Press.

Bergson, Abram. 1938. "A Reformulation of Certain Aspects of Welfare Economics." *Quarterly Journal of Economics* 52 (2): 310–34.

Bernanke, Ben. 2006a. "Basel II: Its Promise and Its Challenges." Transcript of speech delivered at the Federal Reserve Bank of Chicago's 42nd Annual Conference on Bank Structure and Competition, Chicago, May 18, 2006. http://www.federalreserve.gov/newsevents/speech/bernanke20060518a.htm.

———. 2006b. "Modern Risk Management and Banking Supervision." Transcript of speech delivered at the Stonier Graduate School of Banking, Washington, DC, June 12, 2006. http://www.federalreserve.gov/newsevents/speech/bernanke20060612a.htm.

———. 2006c. "Monetary Policy and the State of the Economy." Transcript of hearing before the Committee on Financial Services, House of Representatives, 109th Cong., 2nd sess., Washington, DC, July 20. Serial No. 109-10. https://www.govinfo.gov/content/pkg/CHRG-109hhrg31539/html/CHRG-109hhrg31539.htm.

Bernstein, Michael. 2001. *A Perilous Progress*. Princeton: Princeton University Press.

Berry, Wendell. 2005. *The Way of Ignorance: And Other Essays*. Washington, DC: Shoemaker & Hoard.

Bhagat, Shalini V. 2021. "As India Stumbles, One State Charts Its Own Covid Course." *New York Times*, May 23, 2021. https://www.nytimes.com/2021/05/23/world/asia/coronavirus-kerala.html.

Bhagwati, Jagdish. 1994. "Which Way? Free Trade or Protection?" *Challenge* 37 (1): 17–24. https://doi.org/10.1080/05775132.1994.11471713.

Bivens, Josh L. 2008. "Trade, Jobs, and Wages" Economic Policy Institute Issue Brief 244, May 6, 2008. https://www.epi.org/publication/ib244/.

Blyth, Mark. 2013. *Austerity: The History of a Dangerous Idea*. Oxford: Oxford University Press.

Boadway, Robin. 1974. "The Welfare Foundations of Cost-Benefit Analysis." *Economic Journal* 84 (336): 926–93. https://doi.org/10.2307/2230574.

———. 2016. "Cost-Benefit Analysis." In *Oxford Handbook of Well-Being and Public Policy*, edited by Matthew D. Adler and Marc Fleurbaey, 47–81. Oxford: Oxford University Press.

Boadway, Robin, and Neil Bruce. 1984. *Welfare Economics*. Oxford: Blackwell.

Boardman, Anthony E., David H. Greenberg, Aiden R. Vining, and David L. Weimer. 2011. *Cost-Benefit Analysis: Concepts and Practice*, 4th ed. Boston: Prentice Hall.

Booth, Michael. 2021. "The Colorado River Is Drying Up Faster Than Federal Officials Can Keep Track." *Colorado Sun*, July 13, 2021. https://coloradosun.com/2021/07/13/drought-drains-colorado-river-reservoirs-faster/.

Boulding, Kenneth. 1989. *Three Faces of Power*. Newbury Park, CA: Sage.

Bouris, Erica. 2007. *Complex Political Victims*. Bloomfield, CT: Kumarian.

Boushey, Heather. 2019. *Unbound: How Inequality Constricts Our Economy and What We Can Do about It*. Cambridge, MA: Harvard University Press.

Boyce, James K. 1993. *The Philippines: The Political Economy of Growth and Inequality in the Marcos Era*. Honolulu: University of Hawaii Press.

———. 2002. *The Political Economy of the Environment*. Cheltenham, UK: Edward Elgar.

———. 2018. "The Environmental Cost of Inequality." *Scientific American* 319 (5): 72–77. https://doi.org/10.1038/scientificamerican1118-72.

Breger Bush, Sasha. 2012. *Derivatives and Development: A Political Economy of Global Finance, Farming, and Poverty*. New York: Palgrave Macmillan.

Bricker, Jesse, Sarena Goodman, Kevin B. Moore, Alice Henriques Volz, and Dalton Ruh. 2020. "Wealth and Income Concentration in the SCF: 1989–2019." *FEDS Notes* No. 2020-09-28-1. https://doi.org/10.17016/2380-7172.2795.

Bronfenbrenner, Kate. 2000. "Uneasy Terrain: The Impact of Capital Mobility on Workers, Wages, and Union Organizing." United States Trade Deficit Review Commission. Ithaca, NY: Cornell University.

Brooks, Richard, and Warren Schwartz. 2005. "Legal Uncertainty, Economic Efficiency, and the Preliminary Injunction Doctrine." *Stanford Law Review* 58 (2): 381–410.

Broome, John. 1999. *Ethics out of Economics*. Cambridge: Cambridge University Press.

Buchanan, James. 1959. "Positive Economics, Welfare Economics, and Political Economy." *Journal of Law and Economics* 2:124–38.

Buchanan, James, and Gordon Tullock. 1962. *The Calculus of Consent: Logical Foundations of Constitutional Democracy*. Ann Arbor: University of Michigan Press.

Burczak, Theodore A. 2006. *Socialism After Hayek*. Ann Arbor: University of Michigan Press.

Burd-Sharps, Sarah, and Kristen Lewis. 2015. "Geographies of Opportunity." Press release, Measure of America of the Social Science Research Council, April 22, 2015. http://measureofamerica.org/congressional-districts-2015/.

Bureau of Labor Statistics. 2016. "Youth Unemployment Rate, 11.5 Percent; Employment–Population Ratio, 53.2 Percent in July 2016." *Economics Daily*, August 22, 2016. https://www.bls.gov/opub/ted/2016/youth-unemployment-rate-11-point-5-percent-employment-population-ratio-53-point-2-percent-in-july-2016.htm.

Bureau of Reclamation. 2012a. "Colorado River Basin Water Supply and Demand Study: Study Report." US Department of the Interior. http://www.usbr.gov/lc/region/programs/crbstudy/finalreport/Study Report/StudyReport_FINAL_Dec2012.pdf.

———. 2012b. "Colorado River Basin Water Supply and Demand Study: Executive Summary." US Department of the Interior. https://www.usbr.gov/lc/region/programs/crbstudy/Report1/ExecSumm.pdf.

———. 2015. "Colorado River Basin Stakeholders Moving Forward to Address Challenges Identified in the Colorado River Basin Water Supply and Demand Study, Phase 1 Report." US Department of the Interior. https://www.usbr.gov/lc/region/programs/crbstudy/MovingForward/Phase1Report.html.

———. 2021. "Lower Colorado Water Supply Report." US Department of the Interior. https://www.usbr.gov/lc/region/g4000/weekly.pdf.

Capaldo, Jeronim, Alex Izurieta, and Jomo Kwame Sundaram. 2016. "Trading Down: Unemployment, Inequality and other Risks of the Trans-Pacific Partnership Agreement." Global Development and Environment Institute Working Paper 16-01. Medford, MA: Tufts University.

Cárcamo-Huechante, Luis E. 2006. "Milton Friedman: Knowledge, Public Culture, and Market Economy in the Chile of Pinochet." *Public Culture* 18 (2): 413–35.

Carpenter, Jeffrey. 2018. "Social Preferences." In *The New Palgrave Dictionary of Economics*, 12615–19. London: Palgrave Macmillan UK.

Cartwright, Nancy. 1980. "The Truth Doesn't Explain Much." *American Philosophical Quarterly* 17 (2): 159–63.

———. 1983. *How the Laws of Physics Lie*. Oxford: Oxford University Press.

———. 2004. "Causation: One Word, Many Things." *Philosophy of Science* 71 (5): 805–19. https://doi.org/10.1086/426771.

———. 2007. *Hunting Causes and Using Them: Approaches in Philosophy and Economics*. Cambridge: Cambridge University Press.

Case, Anne, and Angus Deaton. 2020. *Deaths of Despair and the Future of Capitalism*. Princeton: Princeton University Press.

Cavero, Gonzalo, and Irene Martín Cortés. 2013. "The True Cost of Austerity and Inequality: Greece Case Study." Oxfam International. https://www-cdn.oxfam.org/s3fs-public/file_attachments/cs-true-cost-austerity-inequality-greece-120913-en_0.pdf

Cernea, Michael. 2003. "For a New Economics of Resettlement: A Sociological Critique of the Compensation Principle." *International Social Science Journal* 55 (175): 37–45.

Chapple, Karen, Daniel Chatman, Anastasia Loukaitou-Sideris, Paul Ong, and Paul Waddell. 2017. "Developing a New Methodology for Analyzing Potential Displacement." ARB Agreement No. 13-310. https://www.urbandisplacement.org/sites/default/files/images/arb_tod_report_13-310.pdf.

Chetty, Raj, Michael Stepner, Sarah Abraham, Shelby Lin, Benjamin Scuderi, Nicholas Turner, Augustin Bergeron, and David Cutler. 2016. "The Association between Income and Life Expectancy in the United States, 2001–2014." *Journal of the American Medical Association* 315 (16): 1750–66.

Chipman, John, and James Moore. 1978. "The New Welfare Economics 1939–1974." *International Economic Review* 19 (3): 547–84.

Chowdhury, Anis, and Jomo Kwame Sundaram. 2020. "Kerala Covid-19 Response Model for Emulation." Inter Press Service, April 9, 2020. http://www.ipsnews.net/2020/04/kerala-covid-19-response-model-emulation/.

CIA (Central Intelligence Agency). 2016. "The World Factbook—Obesity Adult Prevalence Rate." https://www.cia.gov/the-world-factbook/field/obesity-adult-prevalence-rate/.

———. 2017. "The World Factbook—Infant Mortality Rate." https://www.cia.gov/the-world-factbook/field/infant-mortality-rate/country-comparison.

Coats, Bob. 1960. "The First Two Decades of the American Economic Association." *American Economic Review* 50 (4): 555–74.

Colander, David. 2003. "Muddling through and Policy Analysis." *New Zealand Economic Papers* 37 (2): 197–215.

———. 2005a. "From Muddling through to the Economics of Control: Views of Applied Policy from J. N. Keynes to Abba Lerner." *History of Political Economy* 37 (suppl. 1): 277–91. https://doi.org/10.1215/00182702-37-Suppl_1-277.

———. 2005b. "What Economists Teach and What Economists Do." *Journal of Economic Education* 36 (3): 249–60.

———. 2009. "What Was 'It' That Robbins Was Defining?" *Journal of the History of Economic Thought* 31 (4): 437–48. https://doi.org/10.1017/S105383720999024.

Colander, David, and Craig Freedman. 2018. *Where Economics Went Wrong: Chicago's Abandonment of Classical Liberalism*. Princeton: Princeton University Press.

Cole, Cristie M. 2013. "Physician-Owned Hospitals and Self-Referral." *AMA Journal of Ethics* 15 (2): 150–55. https://doi.org/10.1001/virtualmentor.2013.15.2.hlaw1-1302.

Coleman, Jules. 1980. "Efficiency, Utility, and Wealth Maximization." *Hofstra Law Review* 8 (3): 509–51.

Community Economies Research Network. 2020. "CE Research Network (CERN)." https://www.communityeconomies.org/about/ce-research-network-cern.

Congressional Budget Office. 2019. "The Effects on Employment and Family Income of Increasing the Federal Minimum Wage." https://www.cbo.gov/system/files/2019-07/CBO-55410-MinimumWage2019.pdf.

Crotty, James. 2019. *Keynes against Capitalism*. New York: Routledge.

Crowley, Kate, and Brian Head. 2017. "The Enduring Challenge of 'Wicked Problems': Revisiting Rittel and Webber." *Policy Sciences* 50 (4): 539–47.

Crunden, Robert. 1982. *Ministers of Reform: The Progressives' Achievement in American Civilization, 1889–1920*. New York: Basic Books.

Cushman, Fiery, Liane Young, and Marc Hauser. 2006. "The Role of Conscious Reasoning and Intuition in Moral Judgment: Testing Three Principles of Harm." *Psychological Science* 17 (12): 1082–89.

Darity, William A., Jr., and Kirsten A. Mullen. 2020. *From Here to Equality: Reparations for Black Americans in the Twenty-First Century*. Chapel Hill: University of North Carolina Press.

Dasgupta, Partha. 2005. "What Do Economists Analyze and Why: Values or Facts?" *Economics and Philosophy* 21 (2): 221–78.

Dasgupta, Ajit Kumar, and David W. Pearce. 1972. *Cost-Benefit Analysis: Theory and Practice*. London: Macmillan International Higher Education.

DeMartino, George F. 2000. *Global Economy, Global Justice*. New York: Routledge.

———. 2011a. *The Economist's Oath: On the Need for and Content of Professional Economic Ethics*. Oxford: Oxford University Press.

———. 2011b. "The Economic Crisis and the Crisis in Economics." In *Consequences of Economic Downturn: Beyond the Usual Economics*, edited by Martha Starr, 25–44. New York: Palgrave Macmillan.

———. 2013a. "Epistemic Aspects of Economic Practice and the Need for Professional Economic Ethics." *Review of Social Economy* 71 (2): 166–86.

———. 2013b. "Ethical Engagement in a World Beyond Control." *Rethinking Marxism* 25 (4): 483–500.

———. 2015. "Harming Irreparably: On Neoliberalism, Kaldor-Hicks, and the Paretian Guarantee." *Review of Social Economy* 73 (4): 315–40.

———. 2016. "Econogenic Harm: On the Nature of and Responsibility for the Harm Economists Do as They Try to Do Good." In *The Oxford Handbook of Professional Economic Ethics*, edited by George F. DeMartino and Deirdre N. McCloskey, 71–97. Oxford: Oxford University Press.

———. 2018. "Editor's Introduction." In "The Democratic Crisis and the Responsibility of Economists," special issue, *Forum for Social Economics* 47 (2): 153–57.

———. 2019. "The Tragedy of Economics: On the Nature of Economic Harm and the Responsibilities of Economists." In *The Oxford Handbook of Ethics and Economics*, edited by Mark D. White, 474–93. Oxford: Oxford University Press.

———. 2021. "Should Economists Deceive? Prosocial Lying, Paternalism, and the 'Ben Bernanke Problem.'" Unpublished manuscript, University of Denver.

DeMartino, George F., and Ilene Grabel. 2020. "Irreparable Ignorance, Protean Power, and Economics." *International Theory* 12 (3): 435–48.

DeMartino, George F., and Deirdre N. McCloskey, eds. 2016. *The Oxford Handbook of Professional Economic Ethics*. Oxford: Oxford University Press.

Department of Health and Human Services. 2014. "New HHS Data Shows Major Strides Made in Patient Safety, Leading to Improved Care and Savings." US Department of Health and Human Services. May 7, 2014. http://innovation.cms.gov/Files/reports/patient-safety-results.pdf.

Derbyshire, James. 2020. "Answers to Questions on Uncertainty in Geography: Old Lessons and New Scenario Tools." *Environment and Planning A: Economy and Space* 52 (4): 710–27. http://eprints.mdx.ac.uk/27636/.

Desmond, Matthew. 2019. "Dollars on the Margins." *New York Times Magazine*, February 21, 2019. https://www.nytimes.com/interactive/2019/02/21/magazine/minimum-wage-saving-lives.html.

Dessai, Suraje, Mike Hulme, Robert Lempert, and Roger Pielke Jr. 2009. "Do We Need Better Predictions to Adapt to a Changing Climate?" *Eos* 90 (13): 111–12.

Diamond, Jared. 2012. *The World Until Yesterday: What Can We Learn from Traditional Societies?* New York: Viking.

Dorfman, Robert. 1993. "An Introduction to Benefit-Cost Analysis." In *Economics of the Environment: Selected Readings*, 3rd ed., edited by Robert Dorfman and Nancy S. Dorfman, 297–322. New York: W. W. Norton.

Doyal, Len, and Ian Gough. 1991. *A Theory of Human Need*. London: Palgrave Macmillan.

Drake, Celeste. 2016. "5 Reasons the Rosy Predictions about the TPP Are Wrong." AFL-CIO, February 3, 2016. https://aflcio.org/2016/2/3/5-reasons-rosy-predictions-about-tpp-are-wrong.

Easterly, William. 2013. *The Tyranny of Experts*. New York: Basic Books.

Economou, Charalampos, Daphne Kaitelidou, Alexander Kentikelenis, Anna Maresso, and Aris Sissouras. 2015. "The Impact of the Crisis on the Health System and Health in Greece." In *Economic Crisis, Health Systems and Health in Europe: Country Experience*, edited by Anna Maresso, Philipa Mladovsky, Sarah Thomson, Anna Sagan, Marina Karanikolos, Erica Richardson, Jonathan Cylus, Tamás Evetovits, Matthew Jowett, Josep Figueras, and Hans Kluge. Brussels: European Observatory on Health Systems and Policies. https://www.ncbi.nlm.nih.gov/books/NBK447857/.

Edgeworth, Francis Ysidro. 1881. *Mathematical Psychics: An Essay on the Application of Mathematics to the Moral Sciences*. London: Kegan Paul.

Ellerman, David. 1993. *Property and Contract in Economics: The Case for Economic Democracy*. Oxford: Blackwell.

Elster, Jon. 1978. *Logic and Society: Contradictions and Possible Worlds*. Chichester: Wiley.

———. 1982. "Sour Grapes—Utilitarianism and the Genesis of Wants." In *Utilitarianism and Beyond*, edited by Amartya Sen and Bernard Williams, 219–38. Cambridge: Cambridge University Press.

EPA (Environmental Protection Agency). n.d. "Mortality Risk Valuation." https://www.epa.gov/environmental-economics/mortality-risk-valuation.

Espinet, Xavier, Julie Rozenberg, Kulwinder Singh Rao, and Satoshi Ogita. 2018. "Piloting the Use of Network Analysis and Decision-Making under Uncertainty in Transport Operations: Preparation and Appraisal of a Rural Roads Project in Mozambique under Changing Flood Risk and Other Deep Uncertainties." World Bank Policy Research Working Paper 8490. https://elibrary.worldbank.org/doi/abs/10.1596/1813-9450-8490.

Executive Order 12866 of September 30, 1993: Regulatory Planning and Review. 1993. Presidential Documents vol. 58, no. 190. Title 3. https://www.reginfo.gov/public/jsp/Utilities/EO_12866.pdf.

Farrant, Andrew, Edward McPhail, and Sebastian Berger. 2012. "Preventing the 'Abuses' of Democracy: Hayek, the 'Military Usurper' and Transitional Dictatorship in Chile?" *American Journal of Economics and Sociology* 71 (3): 513–38.

Fearon, James. 1996. "Causes and Counterfactuals in Social Science: Exploring an Analogy between Cellular Automata and Historical Processes." In *Counterfactual Analysis in World*

Politics, edited by Philip E. Tetlock and Aaron Belkin, 39–68. Princeton: Princeton University Press.

Feinberg, Joel. 1984. *Harm to Others: The Moral Limits of the Criminal Law*, vol. 1. Oxford: Oxford University Press.

———. 1986. *Harm to Self: The Moral Limits of the Criminal Law*, vol. 3. Oxford: Oxford University Press.

Fischhoff, Baruch. 1982. "For Those Condemned to Study the Past: Heuristics and Biases in Hindsight." In *Judgment under Uncertainty: Heuristics and Biases*, edited by Daniel Kahneman, Paul Slovic, and Amos Tversky, 335–51. Cambridge: Cambridge University Press.

Fischhoff, Baruch, and Ruth Beyth. 1975. "I Knew It Would Happen: Remembered Probabilities of Once-Future Things." *Organizational Behavior and Human Performance* 13 (1): 1–16.

Fisher, Max. 2021. "Indigenous People Advance a Dramatic Goal: Reversing Colonialism." *New York Times*, June 17, 2021. https://www.nytimes.com/2021/06/17/world/canada/indigenous-kamloops-graves.html.

Fogel, Robert. 1964. *Railroads and American Economic Growth: Essays in Econometric History*. Baltimore: Johns Hopkins University Press.

Fremstad, Shawn, Hye Jin Rho, and Hayley Brown. 2020. "Meatpacking Workers Are a Diverse Group Who Need Better Protections." Center for Economic and Policy Research, April 29, 2020. https://cepr.net/meatpacking-workers-are-a-diverse-group-who-need-better-protections/.

Frey, Bruno, Felix Oberholzer-Gee, and Reiner Eichenberger. 1996. "The Old Lady Visits Your Backyard: A Tale of Morals and Markets." *Journal of Political Economy* 104 (6): 1297–1313.

Fried, Barbara. 1998. *The Progressive Assault on Laissez Faire: Robert Hale and the First Law and Economics Movement*. Cambridge, MA: Harvard University Press.

Friedman, Milton. 1962. *Capitalism and Freedom*. Chicago: University of Chicago Press.

Friedman, Milton, and Rose Friedman. 1980. *Free to Choose: A Personal Statement*. New York: Avon Books.

Furner, Mary. 1975. *Advocacy and Objectivity: A Crisis in Professionalization of American Social Sciences, 1865–1905*. Lexington: University of Kentucky Press.

Gabel, Jon R., Cheryl Fahlman, Ray Kang, Gregory Wozniak, Phil Kletke, and Joel W. Hay. 2008. "Where Do I Send Thee? Does Physician-Ownership Affect Referral Patterns to Ambulatory Surgery Centers?" *Health Affairs (Project Hope)* 27 (3): w165–74. https://doi.org/10.1377/hlthaff.27.3.w165.

Gallagher, Kevin, Juan Carlos Moreno-Bird, and Roberto Porzecanaski. 2008. "The Dynamism of Mexican Exports: Lost in (Chinese) Translation?" *World Development* 36 (8): 1365– 80.

Galtung, Johan. 1969. "Violence, Peace, and Peace Research." *Journal of Peace Research* 6 (3): 167–19.

Gasper, Des. 2016. "The Ethics of Economic Development and Human Displacement." In *The Oxford Handbook on Professional Economic Ethics*, edited by George F. DeMartino and Deirdre N. McCloskey, 534–57. Oxford: Oxford University Press.

Geistfeld, Mark. 2008. *Tort Law: The Essentials*. Austin: Wolters Kluwer.

Gibson-Graham, J. K. 1996. *The End of Capitalism (as We Knew It): A Feminist Critique of Political Economy*. Oxford: Blackwell.

———. 2006. *A Postcapitalist Politics*. Minneapolis: University of Minnesota Press.

Giubilini, Alberto, Thomas Douglas, Hannah Maslen, and Julian Savulescu. 2018. "Quarantine, Isolation and the Duty of Easy Rescue in Public Health." *Developing World Bioethics* 18 (2): 182–89.

Goertz, Gary, and Jack S. Levy. 2007. "Causal Explanation, Necessary Conditions, and Case Studies." In *Explaining War and Peace: Case Studies and Necessary Condition Counterfactuals*, edited by Gary Goertz and Jack S. Levy, 9–45. New York: Routledge.

Goldberg, Pinelopi Koujianou, and Nina Pavcnik. 2007. "Distributional Effects of Globalization in Developing Countries." *Journal of Economic Literature* 45 (1): 29–82.

Goldin, Claudia. 1973. "The Economics of Emancipation." *Journal of Economic History* 33 (1): 66–85.

Goodman, Nelson. 1947. "The Problem of Counterfactual Conditionals." *Journal of Philosophy* 44 (5): 113–28.

Gove, Michael. 2017. "Michael Gove Clarifies Stance on Experts." *BBC News*, February 27, 2017. https://www.bbc.com/news/av/uk-39102847.

Grabel, Ilene. 2000. "The Political Economy of Policy Credibility: The New-Classical Macroeconomics and the Remaking of Emerging Economies." *Cambridge Journal of Economics* 24 (1): 1–19.

———. 2004. "Trip Wires and Speed Bumps: Managing Financial Risks and Reducing the Potential for Financial Crises in Developing Economies." Intergovernmental Group of Twenty-Four (G-24), G-24 Discussion Paper Series No. 33, November 2004.

———. 2015. "Finance, Development and Social Economics in View of the Global Crisis." In *The Elgar Companion to Social Economics*, edited by John B. Davis and Wilfred Dolfsma, 566–92. Cheltenham, UK: Edward Elgar.

———. 2017. *When Things Don't Fall Apart: Global Financial Governance and Developmental Finance in an Age of Productive Incoherence*. Cambridge, MA: MIT Press.

Grant, Ruth. 2012. *Strings Attached: Untangling the Ethics of Incentives*. Princeton: Princeton University Press.

Greenspan, Alan. 2008. "The Financial Crisis and the Role of Federal Regulators." Transcript of hearing before the Committee on Oversight and Government Reform, House of Representatives, 110th Cong., 2nd sess., Washington, DC, October 23, 2008. https://www.govinfo.gov/content/pkg/CHRG-110hhrg55764/html/CHRG-110hhrg55764.htm.

Greenstone, Michael, and Visham Nigam. 2020. "Does Social Distancing Matter?" Becker Friedman Institute for Economics, University of Chicago, Working Paper 2020-26, March 31, 2020. https://doi.org/10.2139/ssrn.3561244.

Griffin, James. 1986. *Well-Being: Its Meaning, Measurement, and Moral Importance*. Oxford: Clarendon.

Griffiths, Peter. 2003. *The Economist's Tale: A Consultant Encounters Hunger and the World Bank*. London: Zed.

Grosskopf, Ofer, and Barak Medina. 2009. "Economic Analysis of the Irreparable Harm Concept in Preliminary Injunctions." *Seattle University School of Law Review* 32 (4): 903. https://digitalcommons.law.seattleu.edu/sulr/vol32/iss4/2/.

Groves, David, Jordan R. Fischbach, Evan Bloom, Debra Knopman, and Ryan Keefe. 2013. "Adapting to a Changing Colorado River: Making Future Water Deliveries More Reliable through Robust Management Strategies." RAND Corporation, RR-242-BOR. http://www.rand.org/pubs/research_reports/RR242.html.

Groves, David, Robert J. Lempert, Deborah W. May, James R. Leek, and James Syme. 2016. "Using High-Performance Computing to Support Water Resource Planning: A Workshop Demonstration of Real-Time Analytic Facilitation for the Colorado River Basin." RAND Corporation and Lawrence Livermore National Laboratory. https://www.rand.org/pubs/conf_proceedings/CF339.html.

Groves, David G., Nidhi Kalra, James Syme, Edmundo Molina-Perez, and Chandra Garber. 2021. "Water Planning for the Uncertain Future: An Interactive Guide to the Use of Methods for Decisionmaking Under Deep Uncertainty (DMDU) for U.S. Bureau of Reclamation Water Resources Planning." RAND Corporation. https://www.rand.org/pubs/tools/TL320.html.

Haasnoot, Marjolijn, Jan Kwakkel, Warren Walker, and Judith ter Maat. 2013. "Dynamic Adaptive Policy Pathways: A Method for Crafting Robust Decisions for a Deeply Uncertain World." *Global Environmental Change* 23 (2): 485–98. https://doi.org/10.1016/j.gloenvcha.2012.12.006.

Haasnoot, Marjolijn, Andrew Warren, and Jan H. Kwakkel. 2019. "Dynamic Adaptive Policy Pathways (DAPP)." In *Decision Making under Deep Uncertainty*, edited by Vincent A. W. J. Marchau, Warren E. Walker, Pieter J. T. M. Bloemen, and Steven W. Popper, 71–92. Heidelberg: Springer. https://doi.org/10.1007/978-3-030-05252-2_4.

Haering, Norbert. 2018. "Who is behind the Campaign to Rid the World of Cash?" *Real World Economics Review* 86:2–14. http://www.paecon.net/PAEReview/issue86/Haering86.pdf.

Hale, Robert. 1923. "Coercion and Distribution in a Supposedly Non-coercive State." *Political Science Quarterly* 38 (3): 470–94.

Hallegatte, Stephane, Ankur Shah, Robert Lempert, Casey Brown, and Stuart Gill. 2012. "Investment Decision Making Under Deep Uncertainty: Application to Climate Change." World Bank Policy Research Working Paper No. 6193. https://doi.org/10.1596/1813-9450-6193.

Hamilton, Darrick, Emanuel Nieves, Shira Markoff, and David Newville. 2020. "Birthright to Capital: Equitably Designing Baby Bonds to Promote Racial and Economic Justice." Kirwan Institute for the Study of Race and Ethnicity, The Ohio State University. https://prosperitynow.org/resources/birthright-capital-equitably-designing-baby-bonds-promote-economic-and-racial-justice.

Hansson, Sven Ove. 2013. *Ethics of Risk: Ethical Analysis in an Uncertain World*. London: Palgrave Macmillan.

Hardwig, John. 1994. "Toward an Ethics of Expertise." In *Professional Ethics and Social Responsibility*, edited by Daniel E. Wueste, 83–101. Lanham, MD: Rowman & Littlefield.

Hardy, Alfredo Toro. 2019. *The Crossroads of Globalization: A Latin American View*. Hackensack, NJ: World Scientific.

Harsanyi, John. 1982. "Morality and the Theory of Rational Behavior." In *Utilitarianism and Beyond*, edited by Amartya Sen and Bernard Williams, 39–62. Cambridge: Cambridge University Press.

Hausman, Daniel, and Michael McPherson. 2006. *Economic Analysis, Moral Philosophy, and Public Policy*. Cambridge: Cambridge University Press.

Hawthorn, Geoffrey. 1991. *Plausible Worlds: Possibility and Understanding in History and the Social Sciences*. Cambridge: Cambridge University Press.

Hay, Colin. 2020. "Brexistential Angst and the Paradoxes of Populism: On the Contingency, Predictability and Intelligibility of Seismic Shifts." *Political Studies* 68 (1): 187–206. https://doi.org/10.1177/0032321719836356.

Hayek, Friedrich. 1974. "The Pretence of Knowledge." Nobel Prize Lecture in Economic Sciences, December 11, 1974. https://www.nobelprize.org/prizes/economic-sciences/1974/hayek/lecture/.

———. (1944) 2007. *The Road to Serfdom*. Chicago: University of Chicago Press. Citations refer to the 2007 edition.

Heckman, James. 2001. "Econometrics, Counterfactuals and Causal Models." Keynote address delivered at the International Statistical Institute, Seoul, August 27, 2001. https://www.re

searchgate.net/profile/James-Heckman-3/publication/246006523_Econometrics_Counterfactuals_and_Causal_Models/links/55c249e208aebc967defd97d/Econometrics-Counterfactuals-and-Causal-Models.pdf.

———. 2008. "Econometric Causality." *International Statistical Review* 76 (1): 1–27. https://doi.org/10.1111/j.1751-5823.2007.00024.x.

Herszenhorn, David M., and Steven R. Weisman. 2008. "Republican Leader in U.S. House Confident in Rescue Plan." *New York Times*, July 17, 2008. https://www.nytimes.com/2008/07/17/washington/17fannie.html.

Hicks, John. 1939. "The Foundations of Welfare Economics." *Economic Journal* 49 (196): 696–712.

———. 1941. "The Rehabilitation of Consumers' Surplus." *Review of Economic Studies* 8 (2): 108–16.

———. 1980. *Causality in Economics*. Canberra: Australian National University Press.

Hillman, Bruce J., Catherine A. Joseph, Michael R. Mabry, Jonathan H. Sunshine, Stephen D. Kennedy, and Monica Noether. 1990. "Frequency and Costs of Diagnostic Imaging in Office Practice—A Comparison of Self-Referring and Radiologist-Referring Physicians." *New England Journal of Medicine* 323 (23): 1604–8. https://doi.org/10.1056/NEJM199012063232306.

Hillyard, Paddy, Christina Pantazis, Steve Tombs, and Dave Gordon, eds. 2004. *Beyond Criminology*. Ann Arbor, MI: Pluto Press.

Hillyard, Paddy, and Steve Tombs. 2017. "Social Harm and Zemiology." In *The Oxford Handbook of Criminology*, edited by Alison Liebling, Shadd Maruna, and Lesley McAra, 284–305. Oxford: Oxford University Press. https://doi.org/10.1093/he/9780198719441.003.0013.

Hirschman, Albert. (1970) 2013. "The Search for Paradigms as a Hindrance to Understanding." In *The Essential Hirschman*, edited by Jeremy Adelman, 137–54. Princeton: Princeton University Press.

Holland, Paul W. 1986. "Statistics and Causal Inference." *Journal of the American Statistical Association* 81 (396): 945–60.

Hotelling, Harold. 1938. "The General Welfare in Relation to Problems of Taxation and of Railway and Utility Rates." *Econometrica* 6 (3): 242–69. https://doi.org/10.2307/1907054.

Horgan, John. 1992. "The New Challenges." *Scientific American* 267 (6): 16–23. http://www.jstor.org/stable/24939319.

Howard-Snyder, Frances. 2008. Updated by Fiona Woollard, 2016. "Doing vs. Allowing Harm." *The Stanford Encyclopedia of Philosophy*, edited by Edward N. Zalta. https://plato.stanford.edu/entries/doing-allowing/.

Hume, David. (1741–1777) 1985. *Essays, Moral, Political and Literary*. Edited by E. F. Miller. Reprint, Indianapolis: Liberty Classics.

———. (1748) 2007. *An Enquiry Concerning Human Understanding*. Reprint, Oxford: Oxford University Press.

Hurd, Heidi. 1996. "The Moral Magic of Consent." *Legal Theory* 2 (2): 121–46. https://doi.org/10.1017/S1352325200000434.

Illich, Ivan. 1976. *Medical Nemesis: The Expropriation of Health*. New York: Pantheon Books.

Jackson, James. 2016. "The Trans-Pacific Partnership (TPP): Analysis of Economic Studies." Congressional Research Service Report, June 30, 2016. https://crsreports.congress.gov/product/pdf/R/R44551/4.

Jackson, Wes. 2005. "Toward an Ignorance-Based Worldview." *Land Report* 81 (Spring): 14–16. https://2hyzup3gkq37nm98l33j3iwt-wpengine.netdna-ssl.com/wp-content/uploads/2018/05/101992-LR-81.pdf.

Jevons, William Stanley. (1888) 2010. *Elementary Lessons in Logic: Deductive and Inductive*. London: Macmillan. Reprint, Auburn, AL: Ludwig von Mises Institute. Citations refer to the 1888 edition.

Ji, Minsun. 2018. "The Worker Cooperative Movement in South Korea: From Radical Autonomy to State-Sanctioned Accommodation." *Labor History* 59 (4): 415–36.

Johnson, Simon. 2009. "The Quiet Coup." *Atlantic*, May 2009. https://www.theatlantic.com/magazine/archive/2009/05/the-quiet-coup/307364/.

Kahlenberg, Richard D. 2010. *Affirmative Action for the Rich: Legacy Preferences in College Admissions*. New York: Century Foundation.

Kahneman, Daniel, Paul Slovic, and Amos Tversky, eds. 1982. *Judgment under Uncertainty: Heuristics and Biases*. Cambridge: Cambridge University Press.

Kaldor, Nicholas. 1939. "Welfare Propositions of Economics and Interpersonal Comparisons of Utility." *Economic Journal* 49 (195): 549–52.

Kalra, Nidhi, and David G. Groves. 2017. "The Enemy of Good: Estimating the Cost of Waiting for Nearly Perfect Automated Vehicles." Santa Monica, CA: RAND Corporation. https://www.rand.org/pubs/research_reports/RR2150.html.

Kalra, Nidhi, and Susan M. Paddock. 2016. "Driving to Safety," Santa Monica, CA: RAND Corporation. https://www.rand.org/pubs/research_reports/RR1478.html.

Kanbur, Ravi. 2003. "Development Economics and the Compensation Principle." *International Social Science Journal* 55 (175): 27–35.

Kant, Immanuel. (1785) 1993. *Grounding for the Metaphysics of Morals*. Translated by James W. Ellington. Reprint, Indianapolis: Hackett.

Karanikolos, Marina, and Alexander Kentikelenis. 2016. "Health Inequalities after Austerity in Greece." *International Journal for Equity in Health* 15 (83). https://doi.org/10.1186/s12939-016-0374-0.

Katz, Leo. 2006. "Choice, Consent, and Cycling: The Hidden Limitations of Consent." *Michigan Law Review* 104 (627): 627–70.

Katzenstein, Peter J, and Lucia A. Seybert, eds. 2018. *Protean Power: Exploring the Uncertain and Unexpected in World Politics*. Cambridge: Cambridge University Press.

Kay, John, and Mervyn King. 2020. *Radical Uncertainty: Decision-Making beyond the Numbers*. New York: W. W. Norton.

Keeler, Lucy Elliot. 1913. "My Garden Beasts." *Atlantic Monthly* 112:134–41.

Keynes, John Maynard. 1936. *The General Theory of Employment, Interest, and Money*. London: Palgrave Macmillan.

———. 1937. "The General Theory of Employment." *Quarterly Journal of Economics* 51 (2): 209–23.

Keynes, John Neville. 1891. *The Scope and Method of Political Economy*. London: Macmillan.

King, Gary, Robert O. Keohane, and Sidney Verba. 1994. *Designing Social Inquiry: Scientific Inference in Qualitative Research*. Princeton: Princeton University Press.

Klein, Ezra. 2021. "Four Ways of Looking at the Radicalism of Joe Biden." *New York Times*, April 8, 2021. https://www.nytimes.com/2021/04/08/opinion/biden-jobs-infrastructure-economy.html.

Knight, Frank H. (1921) 2014. *Risk, Uncertainty, and Profit*. Reprint, Chicago: University of Chicago Press.

Kohn, Linda T., Janet M. Corrigan, and Molla S. Donaldson, eds. 2000. *To Err is Human: Building a Safer Health System*. Washington, DC. National Academies Press. http://doi.org/10.17226/9728.

Koppl, Roger. 2018. *Expert Failure*. Cambridge: Cambridge University Press.

Kornhauser, Lewis. 2001. "On Justifying Cost-Benefit Analysis." In *Cost-Benefit Analysis: Legal, Economic, and Philosophical Perspectives*, edited by Matthew D. Adler and Eric A. Posner, 201–21. Chicago: University of Chicago Press.

———. 2015. "Incentives, Compensation, and Irreparable Harm." In *Distribution of Responsibilities in International Law*, edited by André Nollkaemper and Dov Jacobs, 120–52. Cambridge: Cambridge University Press.

Krueger, Anne O. 2017. Book review, "The Oxford Handbook of Professional Economic Ethics." *Journal of Economic Literature* 55 (1): 209–16.

Krugman, Paul. 1997. "In Praise of Cheap Labor." *Slate*, March 21, 1997. https://slate.com/business/1997/03/in-praise-of-cheap-labor.html.

———. 2007. "Divided over Trade." *New York Times*, May 14, 2007. https://www.nytimes.com/2007/05/14/opinion/14krugman.html.

———. 2009a. "How Did Economists Get It So Wrong?" *New York Times Magazine*, September 2, 2009. https://www.nytimes.com/2009/09/06/magazine/06Economic-t.html.

———. 2009b. "School for Scoundrels." *New York Times Magazine*, August 6, 2009. https://www.nytimes.com/2009/08/09/books/review/Krugman-t.html.

———. 2019. "What Economists (Including Me) Got Wrong about Globalization." *Bloomberg*, October 10, 2019. https://www.bloomberg.com/opinion/articles/2019-10-10/inequality-globalization-and-the-missteps-of-1990s-economics.

Larson, Magali Sarfatti. 1977. *The Rise of Professionalism: A Sociological Analysis*. Berkeley: University of California Press.

Lawrence, Robert. 2016. "Studies of TPP: Which Is Credible?" Peterson Institute for International Economics, Trade and Investment Policy Watch, January 29, 2016. https://www.piie.com/blogs/trade-investment-policy-watch/studies-tpp-which-credible.

LDN (Lakota, Dakota, Nakota Spiritual/Traditional Nation). 2020. "Lakota Document of Rejection of Supreme Court 'Award' Offering Funds in Exchange for Portion of Treaty Lands (including the Black Hills)." http://lakotadakotanakotanation.org/LEGAL-1992RejectionofFundsResolution.html.

Leahy, Joe. 2011. "Brazilian Factories Tested by Chinese Imports." *Financial Times*, January 30, 2011. https://www.ft.com/content/5efdeffc-2c99-11e0-83bd-00144feab49a.

Leamer, Edward E. 2009. *Macroeconomic Patterns and Stories*. Heidelberg: Springer.

Lebow, Richard Ned. 2010. *Forbidden Fruit: Counterfactuals and International Relations*. Princeton: Princeton University Press.

LeGro, Tom. 2011. "Why the Sioux Are Refusing $1.3 Billion." *PBS News Hour*, August 24, 2011. https://www.pbs.org/newshour/arts/north_america-july-dec11-blackhills_08-23.

Leibenstein, Harvey. 1965. "Long-Run Welfare Criteria." In *The Public Economy of Urban Communities*, edited by Julius Margolis, 39–51. Baltimore: Johns Hopkins University Press.

Lempert, Robert. 2014. "Embedding (Some) Benefit-Cost Concepts into Decision Support Processes with Deep Uncertainty." *Journal of Benefit-Cost Analysis* 5 (3): 487–514.

———. 2019. "Robust Decision Making (RDM)." In *Decision Making under Deep Uncertainty: From Theory to Practice*, edited by Vincent A. W. J. Marchau, Warren E. Walker, Pieter J. T. M. Bloemen, and Steven W. Popper, 23–51. Heidelberg: Springer. https://link.springer.com/content/pdf/10.1007%2F978-3-030-05252-2.pdf.

Lempert, Robert, and Nidhi Kalra. 2011. "Managing Climate Risks in Developing Countries with Robust Decision Making." World Resources Report. Washington, DC: World Resources Institute.

Lempert, Robert, Steven W. Popper, and S. Bankes. 2003. "Shaping the Next One Hundred Years: New Methods for Quantitative, Long-Term Policy Analysis." RAND Corporation. https://www.rand.org/pubs/monograph_reports/MR1626.html.

Lempert, Robert, Jürgen Scheffran, and Detlef F. Sprinz. 2009. "Methods for Long-Term Environmental Policy Challenges." *Global Environmental Politics* 9 (3): 106–33.

Lempert, Robert, and Shawn McKay. 2011. "Some Thoughts on the Role of Robust Control Theory in Climate-Related Decision Support." *Climatic Change* 107 (3–4): 241–46.

Leopold, Les. 2020. "COVID-19's Class War." *American Prospect*, July 28, 2020. https://prospect.org/coronavirus/covid-19-class-war-death-rates-income/.

Lerner, Abba. 1944. *The Economics of Control*. London: Macmillan.

Levin, Kelly, Benjamin Cashore, Steven Bernstein, and Graeme Auld. 2012. "Overcoming the Tragedy of Super Wicked Problems: Constraining Our Future Selves to Ameliorate Global Climate Change." *Policy Sciences* 45:123–52. https://doi.org/10.1007/s11077-012-9151-0.

Levy, Jack S. 2015. "Counterfactuals, Causal Inference, and Historical Analysis." *Security Studies* 24 (3): 378–402.

Lewis, David. 1973. "Causation." *Journal of Philosophy* 70 (17): 556–67.

Lichtman, Douglas. 2007. "Irreparable Benefits." *Yale Law Journal* 116 (6): 1284–1301.

Lin, Patrick. 2016. "Why Ethics Matters for Autonomous Cars." In *Autonomous Driving*, edited by Markus Maurer, J. Christian Gerdes, Barbara Lenz, and Hermann Winner, 69–85. Berlin: Springer. https://doi.org/10.1007/978-3-662-48847-8_4.

Linklater, Andrew. 2011. *The Problem of Harm in World Politics*. Cambridge: Cambridge University Press.

Lukes, Steven. 1980. "Elster on Counterfactuals." *Inquiry* 23 (2):144–55.

———. 2005. *Power: A Radical View*, 2nd ed. Basingstoke, UK: Palgrave Macmillan.

Lutz, Mark A. 1995. "Centering Social Economics on Human Dignity." *Review of Social Economy* 53 (2): 171–94.

Mackenzie, Donald. 2006. *An Engine, Not a Camera: How Financial Models Shape Markets*. Cambridge, MA: MIT Press.

Macrotrends. n.d. "Latin America & Caribbean Youth Unemployment Rate 1991–2020." https://www.macrotrends.net/countries/LCN/latin-america-caribbean-/youth-unemployment-rate.

Mahoney, James, and Rodrigo Barrenechea. 2017. "The Logic of Counterfactual Analysis in Case-Study Explanation." *British Journal of Sociology* 70 (1): 306–38. https://doi.org/10.1111/1468-446.12340.

Mainelli, Michael, and Ian Harris. 2011. *The Price of Fish: A New Approach to Wicked Economics and Better Decisions*. Boston: Nicholas Brealey.

Mansfield, Carol, George L. Van Houtven, and Joel Huber. 2002. "Compensating for Public Harms: Why Public Goods Are Preferred to Money." *Land Economics* 78 (3): 368–89.

Marchau, Vincent, Warren E. Walker, Pieter J. T. M. Bloemen, and Steven W. Popper, eds. 2019. *Decision Making under Deep Uncertainty: From Theory to Practice*. Heidelberg: Springer. https://doi.org/10.1007/978-3-030-05252-2_4.

Marglin, Stephen A. 2008. *The Dismal Science: How Thinking Like an Economist Undermines Community*. Cambridge, MA: Harvard University Press.

Marshall, Alfred. (1890) 1920. *Principles of Economics*, 8th ed. London: Macmillan. Citations refer to the 1920 edition.

Marx, Karl. (1867) 1977. *Capital*, vol. I. Moscow: Progress Publishers. Reprint, New York: Vintage Books. Citations refer to the 1977 edition.

Mason, Patrick L., Samuel L. Myers Jr., and William A. Darity Jr. 2005. "Is There Racism in Economic Research?" *European Journal of Political Economy* 21 (3): 755–61. https://doi.org/10.1016/j.ejpoleco.2004.07.005.

Maxmen, Amy. 2018. "Self-Driving Car Dilemmas Reveal That Moral Choices Are Not Universal." *Nature* 562:469–70. https://doi.org/10.1038/d41586-018-07135-0.

May, William F. 1980. "Professional Ethics: Setting, Terrain, and Teacher." In *Ethics Teaching in Higher Education*, edited by Daniel Callahan and Sissela Bok, 205–41. New York: Plenum.

McCloskey, Deirdre N. 1990. *If You're So Smart: The Narrative of Economic Expertise*. Chicago: University of Chicago Press.

———. 1998. *The Rhetoric of Economics*. Madison: University of Wisconsin Press.

———. 2005. "The Trouble with Mathematics and Statistics in Economics." *History of Economic Ideas* 13 (3): 85–102.

———. 2006. *The Bourgeois Virtues: Ethics for an Age of Commerce*. Chicago: University of Chicago Press.

———. 2010. *Bourgeois Dignity*. Chicago: University of Chicago Press.

———. 2016a. "The Formula for a Richer World? Equality, Liberty, Justice." *New York Times*, September 2, 2016. https://www.nytimes.com/2016/09/04/upshot/the-formula-for-a-richer-world-equality-liberty-justice.html.

———. 2016b. "Max U versus Humanomics: A Critique of Neo-institutionalism." *Journal of Institutional Economics* 12 (1): 1–27. https://doi.org/10.1017/S1744137415000053.

———. 2016c. *Bourgeois Equality: How Ideas, Not Capital or Institutions, Enriched the World*. Chicago: University of Chicago Press.

McCloskey, Donald N. 1982. *The Applied Theory of Price*. New York: Macmillan.

McConnell, Matt. 2019. "When We Are Dead and Buried, Our Bones Will Keep Hurting: Workers' Rights under Threat in US Meat and Poultry Plants." Human Rights Watch, September 14, 2019. https://www.hrw.org/report/2019/09/04/when-were-dead-and-buried-our-bones-will-keep-hurting/workers-rights-under-threat.

McGowan, David. 2010. "Irreparable Harm." *Lewis & Clark Law Review* 14 (2): 577–96.

McIntosh, Kriston, Emily Moss, Ryan Nunn, and Jay Shambaugh. 2020. "Examining the Black-White Wealth Gap." Brookings, February 27, 2020. https://www.brookings.edu/blog/up-front/2020/02/27/examining-the-black-white-wealth-gap/.

McIntyre, Alison. 2019. "Doctrine of Double Effect." In *The Stanford Encyclopedia of Philosophy*, edited by Edward N. Zalta. https://plato.stanford.edu/entries/double-effect/.

McIntyre, Richard. 2008. *Are Worker Rights Human Rights?* Ann Arbor: University of Michigan Press.

Meessen, Bruno, Zhang Zhenzhong, Wim Van Damme, Narayanan Devadasan, Bart Criel, and Gerald Bloom. 2003. "Iatrogenic Poverty." *Tropical Medicine & International Health* 8 (7): 581–84.

Mian, Atif, and Amir Sufi. 2015. *House of Debt*. Chicago: University of Chicago Press.

Mishan, E. J. 1960. "A Survey of Welfare Economics, 1939–59." *Economic Journal* 7 (278): 197–265. https://doi.org/10.2307/2228726.

———. 1975. *Cost-Benefit Analysis*, 2nd ed. London: Allen & Unwin.

Morgan, Mary S. 2014. "What If? Models, Fact and Fiction in Economics." *Journal of the British Academy* 2:231–68.

Morgan, Stephen L., and Christopher Winship. 2014. *Counterfactuals and Causal Inference: Methods and Principles for Social Research*, 2nd ed. Cambridge: Cambridge University Press.

Murrell, Peter. 1995. "The Transition according to Cambridge, Mass.," *Journal of Economic Literature* 33 (1): 164–78.

Nathan, Marco. 2017. "Counterfactual Reasoning in Molecular Medicine." In *Philosophy of Molecular Medicine*, edited by Giovanni Boniolo and Marco Nathen, 192–214. New York: Routledge.

Nelson, Julie A. 2004. "Clocks, Creation and Clarity: Insights on Ethics and Economics from a Feminist Perspective." *Ethical Theory and Moral Practice* 7 (4): 381–98.

Nelson, Robert H. 1991. *Reaching for Heaven on Earth: The Theological Meaning of Economics*. Lanham, MD: Rowman & Littlefield.

———. 2001. *Economics as Religion: From Samuelson to Chicago and Beyond*. University Park: University of Pennsylvania Press.

———. 2004. "What Is 'Economic Theology?'" *Princeton Seminary Bulletin* [new series] 25 (1): 58–79.

NOAA (National Oceanic and Atmospheric Administration). n.d. "Discounting and Time Preference." http://www.sfu.ca/~heaps/483/discounting.htm.

Nordhaus, William. 2007. "A Review of The Stern Review on the Economics of Climate Change." *Journal of Economic Literature* 45 (3): 686–702. https://doi.org/10.1257/jel.45.3.686.

North, Douglas C. 1999. "Dealing with a Non-ergodic World: Institutional Economics, Property Rights, and the Global Environment." *Duke Environmental Law & Policy Forum* 10 (1): 1–12.

Nozick, Robert. 1974. *Anarchy, State, and Utopia*. New York: Basic Books.

Nussbaum, Martha C. 1992. "Human Functioning and Social Justice: In Defense of Aristotelian Essentialism." *Political Theory* 20 (2): 202–46.

———. 2000. *Women and Human Development: The Capabilities Approach*. Cambridge: Cambridge University Press.

———. 2001. *Upheavals of Thought*. New York: Cambridge University Press.

OECD (Organisation for Economic Co-operation and Development). 2005. *OECD Employment Outlook 2005*. Paris: OECD Publishing. https://doi.org/10.1787/empl_outlook-2005-en.

———. 2020. "Poverty Rate (Indicator)." https://doi.org/10.1787/0fe1315d-en.

OMB (Office of Management and Budget). 2003. "Circular A-4: Regulatory Analysis." 68 *Fed. Reg.* 58,366, October 9. https://obamawhitehouse.archives.gov/omb/circulars_a004_a-4/.

Opotow, Susan. 1990. "Moral Exclusion and Injustice: An Introduction." *Journal of Social Issues* 46 (1): 1–20.

Orrell, D. 2018. *Quantum Economics: The New Science of Money*. London: Icon Books.

Orszag, Peter R., Robert E. Rubin, and Joseph E. Stiglitz. 2021. "Fiscal Resiliency in a Deeply Uncertain World: The Role of Semiautonomous Discretion." Peterson Institute for International Economics Policy Brief No. 2. https://www.piie.com/publications/policy-briefs/fiscal-resiliency-deeply-uncertain-world-role-semiautonomous-discretion.

Ostrom, Vincent, Charles M. Tiebout, and Robert Warren. 1961. "The Organization of Government in Metropolitan Areas: A Theoretical Inquiry." *American Political Science Review* 55 (4): 831–42.

Otero, Gerardo. 2011. "Neoliberal Globalization, NAFTA, and Migration: Mexico's Loss of Food and Labor Sovereignty." *Journal of Poverty* 15 (4): 384–402.

Panda, Ankit. 2018. "Cryptocurrencies and National Security." Council on Foreign Relations. February 28, 2018. https://www.cfr.org/backgrounder/cryptocurrencies-and-national-security.

Parker, Andrew M., Sinduja V. Srinivasan, Robert J. Lempert, and Sandra H. Berry. 2015. "Evaluating Simulation-Derived Scenarios for Effective Decision Support." *Technological Forecasting & Social Change* 91:64–77.

Pavcnik, Nina. 2017. "The Impact of Trade on Inequality in Developing Countries." National Bureau of Economic Research Working Paper No. 23878.

Pearl, Judea, and Dana Mackenzie. 2018. *The Book of Why: The New Science of Cause and Effect*. New York: Basic Books.

Pells, Rachael. 2018. "Understanding the Extent of Gender Gap in Citations." *Inside Higher Ed*, August 16, 2018. https://www.insidehighered.com/news/2018/08/16/new-research-shows-extent-gender-gap-citations.

Pemberton, Simon. 2004. "A Theory of Moral Indifference: Understanding the Production of Harm by Capitalist Society." In *Beyond Criminology*, edited by Paddy Hillyard, Christina Pantazis, Steve Tombs, and Dave Gordon, 67–83. Ann Arbor, MI: Pluto Press.

———. 2015. *Harmful Societies: Understanding Social Harm*. Bristol, UK: Policy Press.

Petri, Peter A., and Michael G. Plummer. 2016. "The Economic Effects of the Trans-Pacific Partnership: New Estimates." Peterson Institute for International Economics Working Paper No. 16-2.

Plott, Charles R. 2010. "Overview." In *Better Living through Economics*, edited by John J. Siegfried, 6–35. Cambridge, MA: Harvard University Press.

Polanyi, Karl. 1944. *The Great Transformation*. New York: Farrar & Rinehart.

Polinsky, Mitchell. 1972. "Probabilistic Compensation Criteria." *Quarterly Journal of Economics* 86 (3): 407–25.

Posner, Richard A. 1973. *Economic Analysis of Law*. Boston: Little, Brown.

———. 1980. "The Ethical and Political Basis of the Efficiency Norm in Common Law Adjudication." *Hofstra Law Review* 8 (3): 487–507.

Postrel, Virginia. 2009. "Macroegonomics." *Atlantic*, April 2009. https://www.theatlantic.com/magazine/archive/2009/04/macroegonomics/307319/.

Rachels, James, and Stuart Rachels. 2015. *The Elements of Moral Philosophy*, 8th ed. New York: McGraw Hill.

Radest, Howard B. 1997. "First, Do No Harm! Medical Ethics and Moral Education." *Humanism Today* 11:105–31. https://americanhumanist.org/humanismtoday/vol11/radest/.

Ramstad, Yngve. 1987. "Free Trade versus Fair Trade: Import Barriers as a Problem of Reasonable Value." *Journal of Economic Issues* 21 (1): 5–32.

Ravallion, M. 2009. "Evaluation in the Practice of Development." *World Bank Observer* 24 (1): 29–53.

Rawls, John. 1971. *A Theory of Justice*. Cambridge, MA: Harvard University Press.

Rendleman, Doug. 2002. "Irreparability Resurrected? Does a Recalibrated Irreparable Injury Rule Threaten the Warren Court's Establishment Clause Legacy?" *Washington and Lee Law Review* 59 (4): 1343–1406.

Resnick, S. A., and R. D Wolff. 1987. *Knowledge and Class*. Chicago: University of Chicago Press.

Rittel, Horst W. J, and Melvin M. Webber. 1973. "Dilemmas in a General Theory of Planning." *Policy Sciences* 4 (2): 155–69.

Robbins, Lionel. 1927. "Mr. Hawtrey on the Scope of Economics." *Economica* 20:172–78.

———. 1932. *An Essay on the Nature and Significance of Economic Science*. London: Macmillan.

———. 1981. "Economics and Political Economy." *American Economic Review* 71 (2): 1–10.

Robinson, Lisa A., Ryan Sullivan, and Jason F. Shogren. 2020. "Do the Benefits of COVID-19 Policies Exceed the Costs? Exploring Uncertainties in the Age–VSL Relationship." *Risk Analysis* 41 (5): 761–70. https://doi.org/10.1111/risa.13561.

Rodrik, Dani. 2001. "The Global Governance of Trade—As If Development Really Mattered." United Nations Development Programme Report. http://www.giszpenc.com/globalciv/rodrik1.pdf.

———. 2017. *Straight Talk on Trade*. Princeton: Princeton University Press.

———. 2018. "Populism and the Economics of Globalization." *Journal of International Business Policy* 1 (1): 12–33. https://drodrik.scholar.harvard.edu/files/dani-rodrik/files/populism_and_the_economics_of_globalization.pdf.

Roese, Neal J., and James M. Olson, eds. 1995. *What Might Have Been: Social Psychology of Counterfactual Thinking*. Mahwah, NJ: Lawrence Erlbaum Associates.

Rogoff, Kenneth. 2018. "Crash Time." *Project Syndicate*, September 7, 2018. https://www.project-syndicate.org/onpoint/crash-time-by-kenneth-rogoff-2018-09.

Romer, Paul M. 2015. "Mathiness in the Theory of Economic Growth." *American Economic Review Papers and Proceedings* 105 (5): 89–93.

Ross, Dorothy. 1991. *The Origins of American Social Science*. Cambridge: Cambridge University Press.

Roubini, Nouriel. 2018. "The Big Blockchain Lie by Nouriel Roubini." *Project Syndicate*, October 15, 2018. https://www.project-syndicate.org/commentary/blockchain-big-lie-by-nouriel-roubini-2018-10.

Ruccio, David F., and Jack Amariglio. 2003. *Postmodern Moments in Modern Economics*. Princeton: Princeton University Press.

Russo, Federica, Guillaume Wunsch, and Michel Mouchart. 2008. "Potential Outcomes, Counterfactuals and Structural Modelling: Causal Approaches in the Social Sciences." Unpublished manuscript, Université Catholique de Louvain. https://sites.uclouvain.be/IAP-Stat-Phase-V-VI/ISBApub/dp2008/DP0826.pdf.

Sachs, Jeffrey. 1991. "Poland and Eastern Europe: What Is to Be Done?" In *Foreign Economic Liberalization: Transformations in Socialist and Market Economies*, edited by András Köves and Paul Marer, 235–46. Boulder, CO: Westview.

———. 2005. *The End of Poverty*. New York: Penguin.

Samuelson, Tracey. 2016. "Modeling the Economic Impact of the TPP." *Marketplace*, January 25, 2016. https://www.marketplace.org/2016/01/25/modeling-economic-impact-tpp/.

Sargent, Thomas. 2019. "The AI Frontier of Economic Theory." *Project Syndicate*, December 2, 2019. https://www.project-syndicate.org/commentary/artificial-intelligence-new-economic-models-by-thomas-j-sargent-2019-11.

Schabas, Margaret. 2008. "Hume's Monetary Thought Experiments." *Studies in History and Philosophy of Science* 39 (2): 161–69.

Scitovsky, Tibor. 1941. "A Note on Welfare Propositions in Economics." *Review of Economic Studies* 9 (1): 77–88.

Shankar, Kunal. 2021. "How India's Tamil Nadu and Kerala States Are Fighting COVID Surge." Al Jazeera. May 11, 2021. https://www.aljazeera.com/news/2021/5/11/how-indias-tamil-nadu-and-kerala-states-are-managing-covid-surge.

Schliesser, Eric. 2017. *Adam Smith: Systematic Philosopher and Public Thinker*. Oxford: Oxford University Press.

Schor, Julie. 1993. *The Overworked American*. New York: Basic Books.

Schumpeter, Joseph A. 1942. *Capitalism, Socialism, and Democracy*. New York: Harper.

Scoones, Ian, and Andy Stirling. 2020. *The Politics of Uncertainty: Challenges of Transformation*. New York: Routledge.

Scott, Robert. 2003. "The High Price of 'Free' Trade: NAFTA's Failure Has Cost the United States Jobs across the Nation." Economic Policy Institute. November 17, 2003. https://www.epi.org/publication/briefingpapers_bp147/.

———. 2013. "No Jobs from Trade Pacts: The Trans-Pacific Partnership Could Be Much Worse Than the Over-Hyped Korea Deal." Economic Policy Institute. July 18, 2013. https://www.epi.org/publication/trade-pacts-korus-trans-pacific-partnership/

Sen, Amartya. 1970. *Collective Choice and Social Welfare.* San Francisco: Holden Day.

———. 1979. "The Welfare Basis of Real Income Comparisons: A Survey." *Journal of Economic Literature* 17 (1): 1–45.

———. 1987. *On Ethics and Economics.* Oxford: Blackwell.

———. 1992. *Inequality Reexamined.* Oxford: Oxford University Press.

———. 1999. *Development as Freedom.* New York: Anchor Books.

———. 2009. *The Idea of Justice.* Cambridge, MA: Belknap.

Sen, Amartya, Angus Deaton, and Tim Besley. 2020. "Economics with a Moral Compass? Welfare Economics: Past, Present, and Future," *Annual Review of Economics* 12:1–21. https://doi.org/10.1146/annurev-economics-020520-020136.

Senate Committee on Finance. 2002. "Trade Adjustment Assistance for Workers, Farmers, Fisherman, Communities, and Firms Act of 2002." Senate Report 107-34. 107th Cong., 2nd sess, Washington, DC, February 4, 2002. https://www.finance.senate.gov/imo/media/doc/Rpt107134.pdf.

Seybert, Lucia A., and Peter J. Katzenstein. 2018. "High-Tech: Power and Unpredictability at the Technological Frontier and in Bitcoin." In *Protean Power: Exploring the Uncertain and Unexpected in World Politics,* edited by Peter J. Katzenstein and Lucia A. Seybert, 124–44. Cambridge: Cambridge University Press.

Shackle, George L. S. (1972) 1992. *Epistemics and Economics: A Critique of Economic Doctrines.* Reprint, New York: Routledge.

Sharpe, Virginia, and Alan Faden. 1998. *Medical Harm.* Cambridge: Cambridge University Press.

Shiffrin, Seana. 2012. "Harm and Its Moral Significance." *Legal Theory* 18 (3): 357–98.

Shiller, Robert. 2008. "Challenging the Crowd in Whispers, Not Shouts." *New York Times,* November 2, 2008. https://www.nytimes.com/2008/11/02/business/02view.html.

———. 2009. "A Failure to Control Animal Spirits." *Financial Times,* May 12, 2009. https://www.ft.com/content/453e55ca-0c0c-11de-b87d-0000779fd2ac.

Siegfried, John. 2010. *Better Living through Economics.* Cambridge, MA: Harvard University Press.

Silverman, Mark. n.d. "The 'Value of a Statistical Life' in Economics, Law, and Policy: Reflections from the Pandemic." Working paper, Franklin & Marshall College, Lancaster, PA. https://marksilverman.academia.edu/research#papers.

Simon, Herbert A. 1952. "On the Definition of the Causal Relation." *Journal of Philosophy* 49 (16): 517–28.

Skyrms, Brian. 1980. *Causal Necessity: A Pragmatic Investigation of the Necessity of Laws.* New Haven: Yale University Press.

Sloman, Steven A., and Philip Fernbach. 2017. *The Knowledge Illusion: Why We Never Think Alone.* New York: Riverhead Books.

Smart, J. J. C. 1973. "An Outline of a System of Utilitarian Ethics." In *Utilitarianism: For and Against,* edited by J. J. C. Smart and Bernard Williams, 3–76. London: Cambridge University Press.

Smith, Adam. (1759) 1976. *The Glasgow Edition of the Works and Correspondence of Adam Smith, Vol. 1: The Theory of Moral Sentiments.* Reprint, Oxford: Oxford University Press.

Sommers, Sam. 2011. *Situations Matter: Understanding How Context Transforms Your World.* New York: Riverhead Books.

Spranca, Mark, Elisa Minsk, and Jonathan Baron. 1991. "Omission and Commission in Judgment and Choice." *Journal of Experimental Social Psychology* 27 (1): 76–105.

Stalnaker, Robert C. 1968. "A Theory of Conditionals." In *Studies in Logical Theory*, edited by Nicholas Rescher, 98–112. Oxford: Blackwell.

Stern, Nicholas. 2007. *The Economics of Climate Change: The Stern Review*. Cambridge: Cambridge University Press.

Stigler, George J. 1943. "The New Welfare Economics." *American Economic Review* 33 (2): 355–59.

———. 1982. *The Economist as Preacher, and Other Essays*. Chicago: University of Chicago Press.

Stiglitz, Joseph. 2009. "Wall Street's Toxic Message." *Vanity Fair*, June 10, 2009. https://www.vanityfair.com/news/2009/07/third-world-debt200907.

Stock, James H., and Mark W. Watson. 2002. "Has the Business Cycle Changed and Why?" *NBER Macroeconomics Annual* 17:159–218.

Streshinsky, Maria. 2011. "Saying No to $1 Billion." *Atlantic*, March 2011. https://www.theatlantic.com/magazine/archive/2011/03/saying-no-to-1-billion/308380/.

Stringham, Edward Peter. 2001. "Kaldor-Hicks Efficiency and the Problem of Central Planning." *Quarterly Journal of Austrian Economics* 4 (2): 41–50.

Stuckler, David, Lawrence King, and Martin McKee. 2009. "Mass Privatisation and the Post-Communist Mortality Crisis: A Cross-National Analysis." *Lancet* 373 (9661): 399–407.

Stuckler, David, and Sanjay Basu. 2013. *The Body Economic: Why Austerity Kills*. New York: Basic Books.

Subin, Dennis, and Vijay Prashad. 2020. "Kerala Is a Model State in the Covid-19 Fight." *New Frame*, April 1, 2020. https://www.newframe.com/kerala-is-a-model-state-in-the-covid-19-fight/.

Sullivan, William M. 2005. *Work and Integrity: The Crisis and Promise of Professionalism in America*, 2nd ed. San Francisco: Jossey-Bass.

Sumner, Leonard W. 1996. *Welfare, Happiness, and Ethics*. Oxford: Oxford University Press.

Szymborska, Wislawa. 1998. "Nothing Twice." In *Poems, New and Collected, 1957–1997*. Boston: Houghton Mifflin Harcourt.

Taleb, Nassim N. 2010. *The Black Swan: The Impact of the Highly Improbable*, 2nd ed. New York: Random House.

———. 2012. *Antifragile: Things That Gain from Disorder*. New York: Random House.

———. 2018. *Skin in the Game: Hidden Asymmetries of Daily Life*. London: Penguin.

Tetlock, Philip E. 2005. *Expert Political Judgment: How Good Is It? How Can We Know?* Princeton: Princeton University Press.

Tetlock, Philip E., and Aaron Belkin, eds. 1996. *Counterfactual Thought Experiments in World Politics: Logical, Methodological, and Psychological Perspectives*. Princeton: Princeton University Press.

Thaler, Richard H., and Cass R. Sunstein. 2008. *Nudge*. New York: Penguin.

Tharoor, Shashi. 2020. "The Kerala Model." *Project Syndicate*, May 11, 2020. https://www.project-syndicate.org/commentary/kerala-model-for-beating-covid-19-by-shashi-tharoor-2020-05.

Thompson, Dennis F. 1987. *Political Ethics and Public Office*. Cambridge, MA: Harvard University Press.

Thunström, Linda, Stephen C. Newbold, David Finnoff, Madison Ashworth, and Jason F. Shogren. 2020. "The Benefits and Costs of Using Social Distancing to Flatten the Curve for COVID-19." *Journal of Benefit-Cost Analysis* 11 (2): 179–95.

Trading Economics. 2020. "European Union Unemployment Rate 2000–2020 Data." Trading Economics. https://tradingeconomics.com/european-union/unemployment-rate.

Truth and Reconciliation Commission of Canada. 2015. "Honouring the Truth, Reconciling for the Future: Summary of the Final Report of the Truth and Reconciliation Commission of Canada." http://www.trc.ca/assets/pdf/Honouring_the_Truth_Reconciling_for_the_Future_July_23_2015.pdf.

United Nations Population Division. 2020. "Life Expectancy of the World Population." Worldometer. Accessed December 16, 2020. https://www.worldometers.info/demographics/life-expectancy/.

USLegal.com. n.d. "Irreparable Harm Law and Legal Definition." https://definitions.uslegal.com/i/irreparable-harm/.

Varian, Hal. 2006. "Recalculating the Costs of Global Climate Change." *New York Times*, December 14, 2006. https://www.nytimes.com/2006/12/14/business/14scene.html.

Viscusi, W. Kip. 2014. "Risks to Life and Health." In *Handbook of Economics of Risk and Uncertainty*, vol. 1, edited by Mark Machina and W. Kip Viscusi, 385–452. Amsterdam: Elsevier.

Viscusi, W. Kip, and Clayton J. Masterman. 2017. "Income Elasticities and Global Values of a Statistical Life." *Journal of Benefit-Cost Analysis* 8 (2): 226–50.

Vitek, Bill, and Wes Jackson, eds. 2008. *The Virtues of Ignorance: Complexity, Sustainability, and the Limits of Knowledge*. Lexington: University Press of Kentucky.

Walker, Warren E., S. Adnan Rahman, and Jonathan Cave. 2001. "Adaptive Policies, Policy Analysis, and Policy-Making." *European Journal of Operational Research* 128 (2): 282–89.

Walzer, Michael. 1983. *Spheres of Justice: A Defense of Pluralism and Equality*. New York: Basic Books.

Weaver, Christopher P., Robert J. Lempert, Casey Brown, John A. Hall, David Revell, and Daniel Sarewitz. 2013. "Improving the Contribution of Climate Model Information to Decision Making: The Value and Demands of Robust Decision Frameworks." *Wiley Interdisciplinary Reviews: Climate Change* 4 (1): 39–60.

Weber, Steven. 1996. "Counterfactuals, Past and Future." In *Counterfactual Thought Experiments in World Politics: Logical, Methodological, and Psychological Perspectives*, edited by Philip E. Tetlock and Aaron Belkin, 268–88. Princeton: Princeton University Press.

Wedel, Janine R. 2001. *Collision and Collusion: The Strange Case of Western Aid to Eastern Europe*. New York: Palgrave Macmillan.

Weidenbaum, Murray L. 2001. *Looking for Common Ground on US Trade Policy*. Washington, DC: Center for Strategic and International Studies.

Welch, Sharon D. 2000. *A Feminist Ethic of Risk*, rev. ed. Minneapolis: Fortress.

Weller, Christian E., and Lily Roberts. 2021. "Eliminating the Black-White Wealth Gap Is a Generational Challenge." Center for American Progress. March 19, 2021. https://www.americanprogress.org/issues/economy/reports/2021/03/19/497377/eliminating-black-white-wealth-gap-generational-challenge/.

Wertheimer, Alan. 1987. *Coercion: Studies in Moral, Political, and Legal Philosophy*. Princeton: Princeton University Press.

Weymark, John A. 2016. "Social Welfare Functions." In *The Oxford Handbook of Well-Being and Public Policy*, edited by Matthew D. Adler and Marc Fleurbaey, 126–59. Oxford: Oxford University Press.

White, Mark D. 2006. "A Kantian Critique of Neoclassical Law and Economics." *Review of Political Economy* 18 (2): 235–52.

———. 2009. "Pareto, Consent, and Respect for Dignity: A Kantian Perspective." *Review of Social Economy* 67 (1): 49–70.

Wiener, Jonathan B. 1998. "Managing the Iatrogenic Risks of Risk Management." *Risk* 9:39–82.

Wilkinson, Richard G., and Kate Pickett. 2010. *The Spirit Level: Why Equality Is Better for Everyone.* London: Penguin.

———. 2019. *The Inner Level.* London: Penguin.

Williams, Bernard. 1973. "A Critique of Utilitarianism." In *Utilitarianism: For and Against*, edited by John J. C. Smart and Bernard Williams, 77–150. Cambridge: Cambridge University Press.

Wilson, Valerie, and Jhacova Williams. 2019. "Racial and Ethnic Income Gaps Persist amid Uneven Growth in Household Incomes." Economic Policy Institute. September 11, 2019. https://www.epi.org/blog/racial-and-ethnic-income-gaps-persist-amid-uneven-growth-in-household-incomes/.

Winfield, Alan F., Katina Michael, Jeremy Pitt, and Vanessa Evers. 2019. "Machine Ethics: The Design and Governance of Ethical AI and Autonomous Systems." *Proceedings of the IEEE* 107 (3): 509–17.

World Bank. 2019. "Countries Ranked by GINI Index (World Bank Estimate)." Development Research Group. https://www.indexmundi.com/facts/indicators/SI.POV.GINI/rankings.

Yeager, Leland B. 1976. "Economics and Principles." *Southern Economic Journal* 42 (4): 559–71.

Ziliak, Stephen T., and Deirdre N. McCloskey. 2008. *The Cult of Statistical Significance: How the Standard Error Costs Us Jobs, Justice, and Lives*. Ann Arbor: University of Michigan Press.

Index

Page numbers in italics reference figures and tables.